7000312825

D1626114

£10.50

Black New Orleans

098321

305.8

Bristol
Polytechnic

19 OCT 1982

Libraries

UWE BRISTOL
WITHDRAWN
LIBRARY SERVICES

0p99.

Bristol
Polytechnic

Author: BLASSINGAME

Title: Black New Orleans 1860 - 1880

This book should be returned by the last
date stamped below.   The period of loan
may be extended if no other reader wishes
to use the book.

-8. NOV 1985	SM 23. OCT. 1989	12. MAY 2003	
-7. MAR. 1986	SM 25. APR. 1990	20. JUN 2006	
18. APR. 1986	SM-BA	6. OCT 2006	
-2. DEC. 1986	BA-1. JUN. 1992		
30. NOV 1987	18 MAY 1994	15. NOV 2006	
18. DEC. 1987	-7. JUN 1994	SM-FR	
SM -3. MAR 1989	13. MAY 1998		
	12. MAY 2003		
SM 20. APR. 1989			

JCA 5/71

7229

UNIV. BRISTOL
PENNSYLVANIA
98331

John W. Blassingame

Black New Orleans

1860-1880

The University of Chicago Press
Chicago and London

The University of Chicago Press, Chicago 60637
The University of Chicago Press, Ltd., London

© 1973 by The University of Chicago
All rights reserved. Published 1973
Printed in the United States of America

International Standard Book Number: 0–226–05707–0
Library of Congress Catalog Card Number: 72-97664

JOHN W. BLASSINGAME, assistant professor of history
at Yale University, is author of *The Slave Community*,
editor of *New Perspectives in Black Studies*, coeditor of
In Search of America, and contributor of numerous
articles to scholarly publications.
[1973]

To Odessa

Contents

Illustrations

Abbreviations

AMA	American Missionary Association Archives
BRFAL	Bureau of Refugees, Freedmen, and Abandoned Land
CA	Civil affairs
DG	Department of the Gulf
FB	Freedmen's Bureau
LC	Library of Congress
LR	Letters received
LS	Letters sent
LSU	Louisiana State University Department of Archives
NA	National Archives
PM	Provost marshal
PMG	Provost marshal general
RG	Record group
SHC	Southern Historical Collection, University of North Carolina

Preface

This book describes and analyzes the economic and social life of the Negro in New Orleans during Reconstruction. It largely ignores the old and often-studied debate over politics. I have taken this new approach because the word *Reconstruction* has been a synonym for narrowly conceived political history for so long that we know very little about the breathtaking changes which occurred in other areas of Southern life during this period. In the hope of developing some new insights about the period, I have chosen to examine those areas of life—education, family, religion, social and economic activities—which were of more immediate concern to blacks than politics.

At the end of the Reconstruction era the balance sheet for the Negro in New Orleans showed a bewildering set of debits and credits. While there was some contrast between the position of the Negro in 1860 and in 1880, the differences were often more apparent than real. The most important similarity of the two periods was the relative political powerlessness of the blacks. In spite of this, the Civil War and Reconstruction brought about significant changes in the Negro community in New Orleans. A few years after the war began, slavery as an institution ceased to exist in Louisiana. Negroes had been enslaved for so long, however, that their efforts to build a meaningful life in freedom were hampered. Given the nature of slavery, blacks could not be expected to

make many advances in the first decades following emancipation.

Although the life of the New Orleans Negro was similar
in some ways to that of blacks in other Southern cities, in
many respects the city's Negro community was sui generis.
It is obvious, for instance, that Negroes in New Orleans were
far more articulate, literate, and cosmopolitan than blacks
in most other Southern cities. Only Charleston, Washington,
and Baltimore were rivals in this regard. In no Southern city
did Negro leaders express their racial, social, and economic
philosophies more clearly or on a more sophisticated level
than in New Orleans. Similarly, the diversity and size of
Negro-owned businesses and the occupational structure of Negroes in New Orleans was not duplicated in other Southern
cities. And, while Washington, Baltimore, and Charleston
Negroes probably had a per capita wealth about equal to that
of Negroes in New Orleans, most other Southern cities lagged
far behind in this area. For instance, while New Orleans
Negroes had a per capita wealth of $40 in 1880, Negroes in
Savannah, Georgia, possessed only $7.31 per capita in 1880.
Furthermore, there was undoubtedly more intimacy between
the races in New Orleans than in most Southern cities, because Louisiana was one of the few Southern states which,
only a decade after the Civil War, permitted interracial marriages, and which outlawed segregation in schools and places
of public accommodations.

The importance of the findings in this study is that they
provide a standard by which scholars can compare Negro life
in other Southern cities. While the truly unique features of
the Negro community in the Crescent City can be explained
largely by its location in the most "non-American" of American cities, the group's uniqueness does not destroy the possibility of studying the features which the Negro population in
New Orleans had in common with blacks in other Southern
communities. This study may help to suggest some of the
general patterns of the economic and social life of Negroes
in Southern cities during Reconstruction.

During the course of my research and writing several scholars gave me invaluable assistance. I am especially grateful to Joseph Logsdon of Louisiana State University in New Orleans for letting me read his notes on the Department of the Gulf and to Louis Harlan of the University of Maryland for giving me access to his voluminous files on school integration. Michael Bagneris of Tulane University, George Ellard, Jr. of Bowdoin College, and Cheryll Ellard of Washington, D.C., helped me compile much of the statistical data. Francis Haber and Mary F. Berry of the University of Maryland, Letitia Brown of George Washington University, Peter Ripley of Florida State University, Clarence Contee of Howard University, and Marcus Christian of Louisiana State University in New Orleans, all unselfishly shared their ideas and the results of their research with me. Dorothy Porter of the Howard University Library, Connie Griffith of the Tulane University Library, and the staffs of the National Archives, Library of Congress, and the libraries of Louisiana State University, Southern University, University of North Carolina, and Yale University were especially helpful in locating material for me. I am deeply grateful for the encouragement I received from my dissertation advisor at Yale, C. Vann Woodward.

Several grants from the Yale University Graduate School and the Esso and Ford Foundations provided financial aid at crucial points in the research and writing of the dissertation upon which this study is based. Mrs. Janet Villastrigo, Miss Fran Drago, Miss Yvonne Winfrey, and Mrs. Shirley Mero cheerfully typed several drafts of the manuscript.

My wife Teasie has been my best critic, hardest-working and lowest-paid research assistant, and biggest booster.

The Negro in Antebellum
New Orleans:
Background for Reconstruction

1

More than one hundred years of slavery and oppression left Negroes in New Orleans with such a heavy burden of sexual immorality, ignorance, broken families, fear, and improvidence that it was difficult for them to build the foundations for a meaningful social and economic life during Reconstruction. As a result of antebellum conditions, the patterns of life in the black community in New Orleans during the Reconstruction period were more varied and more complex than those in any other city in the United States. Composed of a large number of antebellum free Negroes, urbanized former slaves, and freedmen who came directly from Louisiana's plantations, the Negro population contained the highly skilled and the unskilled, the educated and the densely ignorant, the religious and the superstitious, and mulattoes and blacks, all trying to survive in a society which denied their manhood and sometimes their humanity. It was not a static population: the number of Negroes in New Orleans increased from 25,423 in 1860 to 57,617 in 1880 (the white population rose from 144,601 in 1860 to 158,859 in 1880).

The typical black migrant who came to New Orleans between 1860 and 1880 had been counted among the 331,726 slaves in Louisiana in 1860. While most of the plantation slaves had been field hands, many of them had worked as engineers, drivers, overseers, bricklayers, coopers, carpenters, wagon makers, blacksmiths, harnessmakers, nurses, tanners,

1

woodworkers, and sugarmakers. Although these skills would
help the migrants to survive economically, in practically every
other area of life the plantation was a poor school.[1] When
the freedmen arrived in New Orleans they were generally
uneducated, disease-wracked, slovenly, hardened to cruelty
and deprivation, and had little understanding of religion, politics, and family obligations.[2] Had it not been for the pattern
set by the thousands of urbanized former slaves and free
Negroes in New Orleans, the migrants from the plantations
could not have survived urban life.[3]

One of the principal reasons for the successful adjustment
of the New Orleans Negro to freedom was the radical difference between the treatment of slaves on the plantations and
their treatment in New Orleans.[4] The anonymity available
in a large seaport and the sizeable number of free Negroes
made it impossible for New Orleans slaveholders to maintain
the same kind of rigid control over their 14,484 bondsmen
as did planters who had a readily identifiable and largely
immobile labor force. New Orleans slaves were generally
better fed, housed, and clothed than slaves in the countryside.
They also received better medical attention because it was
easier to obtain in New Orleans. Warren Stone's infirmary,
for instance, had 418 Negroes among its 692 patients in
1860.[5]

While most city slaves were domestic servants, there were
also many who were highly skilled. In fact, the return on
skilled labor was so high that many masters paid white artisans to train their slaves and then hired them out; often the
slave had to furnish his own food and give his employer a
portion of his wages. Many of the city slaves worked as
draymen, porters, carpenters, masons, bricklayers, painters,
plasterers, tinners, coopers, wheelwrights, cabinetmakers,
blacksmiths, shoemakers, millers, bakers, and barbers. Most,
however, were unskilled laborers often owned by brickyards,
iron foundries, hospitals, distilleries, railroad companies, and
Catholic convents. Slaves also worked as stevedores on the

city's docks, and as flower girls, seamstresses, nurses, municipal laborers, jockeys, prostitutes, and street vendors.

Because of their mobility and anonymity, the slaves in New Orleans had a richer social life than their counterparts on the plantation; sometimes the slaves were even allowed to hold balls in their masters' homes. Lavishly dressed, the bondsmen frequently ate cakes, fruits, and candies and drank freely of wines and liquors at dances, where they performed the bamboula and the polka to drums and violins played by slave musicians. Their dances also included the "carabine" and the "pile chactas." In the former, the man twirled the woman around while she waved a handkerchief over her head. During the "pile chactas," the woman stood motionless while the male danced around her, kneeling, making faces, and writhing like a serpent. Sunday was a holiday for the slaves; they gambled, got drunk, watched cock fights, gathered in restaurants and barbershops, or congregated in Congo Square to sing and dance.[6]

Drawing on his own reminiscences and old manuscripts, the novelist George Washington Cable described many of the activities which took place in Congo Square. Among the dances performed to a frenzied African beat were the bamboula (New Orleans–born composer Louis Gottschalk used this as the inspiration for one of his pieces), babouille, counjaille, and the calinda.[7] According to Cable, the calinda was "a dance of multitude, a sort of vehement cotillion. The contortions of the encircling crowd were strange and terrible, the din was hideous. One calinda is still familiar to all Creole ears; . . . for generations the man of municipal politics was fortunate who escaped entirely a lampooning set to its air."[8] Among these satirical songs was one about a judge who gave a ball for his slaves:

> *It was in a stable that they had this*
> *gala night*
> *The horses they were greatly astonished.*
> *Préval was captain;*

French Market

> *His coachman, Louis, was master of ceremonies*
> *There were Negresses made prettier than their*
> *mistresses,*
> *By adornments stolen from the ladies'*
> *wardrobes.*
> *But the jailer found it all so funny,*
> *That he proposed to himself to take an unexpected*
> *part.*[9]

Quite frequently the songs accompanying dances in Congo Square were amorous ones. For example, during the counjaille the slaves often sang "Belle Layotte":

> *I done hunt all dis settlement*
> *All de way 'roun fum Pierre Soniat;*
> *Never see yalla gal w'at kin*
> *'Gin to lay 'longside sweet Layotte*
> *I been meet up wid John Bayou,*
> *Say to him. "John Bayou, my son,*
> *Yalla gal nevva meet yo' view*
> *Got a face lak dat chahmin one.*[10]

Many of the instruments seen in Congo Square were similar to those used in Africa. A comparison of drawings of these instruments with those illustrations by African musicologists clearly shows the transfer of forms. As in many African tribes, for example, New Orleans blacks carved figures on their stringed instruments and used hollowed-out pieces of wood with animal skins stretched over them as drums.[11]

There were several other distinctly African features of the slave's culture. In Louisiana many African religious rites were fused into one—voodoo, the worship of Damballa or the snake god. The king and queen of the voodoo sect in New Orleans were "Dr. John" and Marie Laveau, who exacted blind obedience from their followers. Claiming a knowledge of the future and the ability to heal the body and to read the mind, Dr. John and Laveau exercised great control over the blacks. Slaves bought charms and amulets in order to control their masters, obtain money, gain success in love, insure good health, and to harm their enemies. At their annual celebration on the shores of Lake Pontchartrain on St. John's Eve, the devotees of voodoo sacrificed animals and engaged in feverish dances and sexual orgies.[12] At such ceremonies, reported the New Orleans *Delta* on November 3, 1854, the participants often "strip[ped] themselves stark naked and then commence[d] a strange, wild sort of Indian dance."

The sect penetrated into practically every level of society. One scholar reported that Dr. John's "control over the credulous and superstitious element of society was incredible."[13] Many whites, probably influenced by their servants, also believed in voodoo. Henry C. Castellanos, a local historian, wrote that Marie Laveau had great influence over whites as well as blacks: "Ladies of high social position would frequently pay her high prices for amulets supposed to bring good luck."[14] Some of these same ladies even participated in the wild orgies of the sect; on occasion the police found them dancing naked with the black devotees. A New Orleans newspaper described one of these ceremonies in the 1850s which was raided by the police: "Blacks and whites were circling around promiscuously, writhing in muscular contractions, panting, raving and frothing at the mouth. But the most degrading and infamous feature of this scene was the presence of a very large number of ladies (?), moving in the highest walks of society, rich and hitherto supposed respectable, that were caught in the dragnet."[15]

While voodoo held sway over a large part of the black population, many of the slaves received conventional religious instruction from their masters or sat in the galleries of their churches. There were also some churches exclusively for slaves: in 1860 the slaves' Methodist church had a six-hundred-member congregation which worshipped in a building worth $3,000, and the slaves' Baptist church had 500 members and a building worth $2,500. The authorities, however, were suspicious of separate churches for slaves; police frequently broke up meetings of the Baptist church between 1826 and 1844. After the latter date, the slaves were permitted to meet for two hours on Sundays as long as a police officer was present.

In their own churches the slaves could pour out all of their anguish, socialize with their friends, and find some release for their pent-up emotions. The church provided hope of release from earthly bondage and promised satisfaction in the hereafter for the earthly burdens the slave bore.[16] When the European traveler Fredrika Bremer attended the slaves' Methodist church, she was so impressed by the service that she concluded: "The children of Africa may yet give us a form of divine worship in which invocation, supplication, and songs of praise may respond to the inner life of the fervent soul!" During the service, Bremer reported, the audience talked back to the exhorter and then began crying aloud, shouting, having convulsions, groaning, and rolling on the floor. "The whole church seemed transformed into a regular Bedlam, and the noise and the tumult was horrible." One woman, who fainted upon her conversion, began talking quietly to herself when she revived, and, said Bremer, "such

Bamboula

a beautiful, blissful expression was portrayed in her countenance, that I would willingly experience that which she
then experienced, saw, or perceived. It was no ordinary, no
earthly scene. Her countenance was as it were transfigured."
After the shouting subsided and the service ended, people
talked, laughed, and shook hands with each other "with such
cordial warmth and goodwill, that it was a pleasure to behold.
Of the whole raging, exciting scene there remained merely a
feeling of satisfaction and pleasure, as if they had been together at some joyful feast."[17]

In contrast to the pleasure the slave found in religion, he
encountered many problems in his efforts to build a stable
family. The slave family in New Orleans suffered most of the
disabilities of the plantation family, although it also had some
advantages not available in the countryside. The greatest of
these advantages was that a slave could often set up a household with little interference from his master. On January 31,
1859, for example, the New Orleans *Picayune* charged that
there were "hundreds" of places "in which the slave is the

keeper of the house—a slave over whom the master pretends to exercise no control." Since so many of the slaves were house servants, a number of them adopted the mores of their masters in regard to the family. As a result, a higher percentage of urban than of rural slaves were married in churches. In spite of these advantages, however, the city slave family was a fragile institution. In the first place, the number of slave women far exceeded the number of slave men (in 1860 there were only 78 males to every 100 female slaves in Orleans parish). Secondly, a severe strain was put on the slave family by the loose morality frequently characteristic of ports such as New Orleans, and by the fact that the number of white males far exceeded the number of white females.[18]

According to the English traveler Harriet Martineau, few slave women in New Orleans were chaste, because their masters were generally indifferent to promoting slave morality. "None but a virtuous mistress," she wrote, "can fully protect a female slave, and that too seldom."[19] Those slaves who lived with their owners frequently had a difficult time developing normal conjugal or filial relations: they were often prohibited from even using the ordinary names which indicate family relationships.

In spite of restrictions on the development of stable families, and in spite of a few cruel and sadistic slaveholders, prohibitions against slaves mingling with free Negroes, and city regulations requiring slaves to wear badges indicating their status, the New Orleans slaves were so much more sophisticated and enjoyed so much more freedom from the surveillance of their masters than did plantation slaves that they emerged from bondage with relatively few psychological scars. The slave in New Orleans was generally cautious, but he could be insolent. In fact, there are numerous accounts of slaves' having insulted or struck whites; and sometimes slaves stole, drank, and caroused almost at will. The penalties, when they were caught, were usually light.[20]

The white man was the enemy from whom it was justified to steal and with whom one dissembled. The Englishman S.

A. O'Ferrall declared that the slaves in New Orleans "steal, cheat, and hate their masters! They justly consider whatever they take to be but a portion of their own labor."[21] The New Orleans slaves' acceptance of white supremacy was only superficial—too many blacks danced, gambled, drank, and copulated with whites to be cowed by them. The historian Joseph Tregle concluded from his study of antebellum New Orleans that the behavior of the slaves was "singularly free of that deference and circumspection which might have been expected in a slave community."[22] The New Orleans *Picayune* would have agreed emphatically. On January 27, 1859, it complained that the slaves "have become intemperate, disorderly, and have lost the respect which the servant should entertain for the master."

Inevitably, there were hundreds of slaves who refused to give any account to their masters. The English traveler Robert Everest reported that there were 108 fugitive slaves arrested in New Orleans in December 1853, and he estimated that one percent of the slaves were always absent from their owners. A number of slaves must also have thought of rebelling. According to an English visitor named J. E. Alexander, in the 1830s New Orleans whites were startled to find handbills

telling the slaves to rise and massacre the whites; that Hannibal was a negro, and why should not they also get great leaders among their number to lead them on to revenge? that in the eyes of God all men were equal; that they ought instantly to rouse themselves, break their chains and not leave one white slave proprietor alive; and, in short, that they ought to retaliate by murder for the bondage in which they were held.[23]

Although few slaves rose up to break their chains, many of them did obtain their freedom. The first free Negroes appeared in New Orleans in the 1720s; by 1860 the number had increased to 10,939. While a majority of them were probably the manumitted children of white men, many gained their freedom by meritorious or faithful service, by fighting in the colonial French or Spanish militia, or by purchase. Hundreds of other free Negroes came from Maine, Massachusetts, New York, Ohio, and Pennsylvania, or from Haiti during the revolution on that island. In fact, the most distinctive feature of the free Negro population was the large number of foreign-born blacks. For example, in 1850 there were 889 Negroes who had been born in Germany, England, France, Mexico, Spain, the West Indies, or several other countries.[24]

There were several features of the antebellum free Negro community which helped blacks to adjust to their new status during Reconstruction. The role of blacks in New Orleans economy, for instance, while restricted, still enabled them to compete successfully against whites in many areas after the war. Much of the black success in competing with whites for jobs during Reconstruction was a direct result of the large number of highly skilled free Negro men in antebellum New Orleans.

In 1850 an overwhelming majority of the free Negro men in New Orleans worked as carpenters, masons, cigarmakers, shoemakers, clerks, mechanics, coopers, barbers, draymen, painters, blacksmiths, butchers, cabinetmakers, cooks, stewards, and upholsters. The ratio of skilled to unskilled laborers among free Negroes, according to historian Robert Reinders, was "considerably higher than among the Irish and German immigrants."[25] This was apparently true, for the 1,792 free Negro males listed in the 1850 census were engaged in fifty-four different occupations; only 9.9 percent of them were unskilled laborers. Some of them even held jobs as architects, bookbinders, brokers, engineers, doctors, jewelers, merchants, and musicians.

During the antebellum period, a number of free Negroes were successful as money lenders, real estate brokers, grocers, tailors, and general merchandising agents. For example, one of the wealthiest real estate brokers, Drosin B. Macarthy, purchased $56,081 and sold $50,355 in real estate between 1849 and 1859. One of the best-known businesses was the import house operated by Cécée Macarthy, who inherited $12,000, which she increased to $155,000 by the time of her death in 1845. A free Negro undertaker, Pierre Casanave, relying on his predominantly white clientele, built a business valued at $100,000 in 1814.

The free Negroes invested heavily in real estate and slaves. In 1830, for instance, 735 New Orleans Negroes owned a total of 2,351 slaves; 153 Negro masters owned 5 or more slaves; and 23 Negro masters owned from 10 to 20 slaves. Generally, free Negro masters owned only one or two slaves, usually members of their own families whom they often manumitted; such masters entered 501 of the 1,353 manumission petitions in the emancipation court between 1827 and 1851. The strongest economic base of the free Negroes, however, rested on ownership of real property. By 1850 they held $2,214,020 in real estate, with much of it in the center of the city. Aristide Mary, for instance, inherited an entire city block on Canal Street from his white father.[26]

Partially as a result of their wealth, the free Negroes were able to build several relatively stable social institutions and organizations to serve community needs. Benevolent associations, churches, and schools helped to knit the black community together, create a leadership class, foster an awareness of social problems, and promote racial uplift. Among the most important of the institutions serving the community was the school. The significance which blacks placed on education is indicated by the 1,000 free Negroes attending private schools in Orleans parish in 1850 and the 336 of them attending three schools in 1860. In the latter year, 5 teachers taught students who paid a total of $1,244 in tuition annually. About 2,000 free Negroes also attended schools in Paris and in the North and West during the antebellum period.[27]

Many of the free Negroes were highly educated, cultured, and cosmopolitan men. James Derham, the city's first Negro doctor, corresponded with Benjamin Rush of Philadelphia, and two other Negro doctors, Louis Charles Roundanez and Alexandre Chaumette, received their professional training in Paris. A number of the free Negroes were well-known scientists and artists. Norbert Rillieux gained international

Marie Laveau

recognition in 1846 for his invention of the vacuum pan used in sugar refining, and Eugene Warbourg, a marble cutter, became a renowned sculptor in Europe. Since many of the free Negroes were Creole, their culture was decidedly European in flavor; the songs they composed, their concerts, and their literature were practically all in French. The most noted composer of the period was Edmond Dédé, who went to France in 1857 and later served as director of the Alcazar Orchestra in Bordeaux. Free Negroes also organized a Philharmonic Society and two theaters in New Orleans. The greatest literary achievement of the free Negro was the publication in 1845 of *Les Cenelles*, a collection of poems. Written in the French romantic tradition, the poems were compiled by the greatest of New Orleans' poets, Armand Lanusse.[28]

The cultural and social life of the free Negroes was relatively rich. Dancing, gambling, drinking, and singing were their major forms of recreation, though they also attended the theater, opera, the races, cock fights, and circuses. They organized more than thirty social and benevolent societies during the antebellum period, and one orphan asylum. The best-known organizations were La Société Catholique pour l'Instruction des Orphelins dans l'Indigence, the Colored Female Benevolent Society of Louisiana, the Union Band Society, and the Benevolent Association of the Veterans of 1815.

Two of the most important and durable free black institutions, the church and the family, were controlled and manipulated by whites. Still, they played significant roles in the black community and helped to create traditions which would contribute to its stabilization during Reconstruction. Most free Negroes attended the Catholic church and had no control over religious activities, but by 1860 they had four Methodist churches with a total membership of 1,700 and property valued at $22,000. There were also two Baptist churches with a total of 1,000 members and property valued at $10,600. Although many of the first ministers of the Baptist and Methodist churches were illiterate, a number of those who were active in the 1850s were well trained. St. James A.M.E. (African Methodist Episcopal) congregation had the most illustrious ministers during the antebellum period; one of them, John M. Brown, later became a bishop of the A.M.E. church.[29]

In addition to its role in training leaders among the free Negroes, the church upheld the ideal of a stable, monogamous family at a time when instability was the norm. Rampant miscegenation, the imbalances in the sex ratio, and endemic social problems made it practically impossible for the family life of the free Negro to develop along conventional lines. First of all, as in the case of the slaves, the number of free Negro women far exceeded the number of free Negro men. In 1850, for instance, there were only 57 free Negro men for every 100 free Negro women between the ages of fifteen and fifty. Consequently, there were few marriages in the free Negro community: only thirty-three were reported in 1850. The birth rate was also low; there were only 226 births in 1850, a rate of 79 births per thousand among free Negro women aged 15 to 50. In the second place, the number of white men exceeded that of white women in New Orleans. As a result, there were many casual alliances between white men and Negro women. The large transient white population of New Orleans, prostitution, and the general philandering propensities of white males were almost as destructive to family life and sexual morality among free Negroes as among slaves. In spite of all the obstacles they faced, however, the free Negroes did adopt some of the conventional mores regarding the family; many of them were married in the St. Louis Cathedral, entered into marriage contracts, gave dowries, and apparently were as faithful as whites were to their vows.[30]

Although the free Negro made a concerted effort to create a viable community, he was severely handicapped in his struggle. The free Negro's color associated him with the slave, and he suffered many penalties as a result. Although his property rights were protected and he had the right to sue and to be sued, the free Negro had no guarantee of justice in Louisiana's courts. He was barred by law from engaging in a public horse race or owning any establishment where liquor was sold: arson and the rape of white women were capital crimes only when Negroes were involved; and the free Negro might be arrested at any time as a runaway slave. An anomaly in Louisiana, the free Negro was neither bound nor free. He was required to be respectful in the company of whites and to obtain the permission of the mayor when he left the city, held balls, or formed social and benevolent societies.

The free Negro was a quasicitizen—he bore much of the responsibility of citizenship with few of its privileges. The vote was usually denied to him in spite of the equal treatment guaranteed him by the treaty ceding the Louisiana Territory to the United States, and in spite of his wealth and his education. Although the free Negroes were permitted to enjoy few of the privileges of antebellum society, they were required to protect that society: they served as city guardsmen in New Orleans and went on slave patrols in the parishes to keep peace. During the colonial period, both the Spanish and the French utilized the free Negroes in their militias to fight the Indians, crush slave uprisings, or to meet the threat of foreign invasion. Andrew Jackson did the same thing in January 1815 when he called upon the free Negroes to defend a city which denied their manhood.[31]

Frequently accused of being "insolent" to whites, and sometimes engaging in fights with them, the free Negroes were not crushed by the burdens they bore. Charles Gayarré, a famous nineteenth-century Louisiana historian, recalled that the free Negroes neither fawned on whites nor despaired because of discrimination. "They," he wrote, "walked erect."[32]

Race relations in antebellum New Orleans were so complex that one has to be extremely careful in drawing generalizations. Profession and practice varied so much in race relations that they were frequently two radically different things. Most whites argued that Negroes were inferior, ugly, dirty, servile, debased, criminal, and stupid. Such derogatory terms as "Cuffee," "Sambo," "buck," and "woolly heads" were used to characterize them in the newspapers of the period. Practice often belied these stereotypes: the law reflected the white man's fear that the Negro was too intelligent, strong, and industrious for the white man to succeed in free competition with him. One result of these fears was an attempt to segregate the Negro and to insure his subordination to whites.

On practically all public occasions when Negroes interacted with whites, Negroes had to be in a subordinate position; there had to be a visible demonstration of the white man's superiority. As a result of the need of most whites to have constant reminders of their "superiority," practically all jails, theaters, Protestant churches, schools, hospitals, and streetcars were rigidly segregated, and restaurants, hotels, and private clubs generally excluded Negroes.[33] Nevertheless, race relations in Louisiana were not cast in a monolithic Jim Crow mold. The most notable exception to the rule was in the Catholic Church. For example, free Negroes owned half of the pews in St. Augustine's Catholic Church and attended many other Catholic churches in New Orleans without having any distinction made against them. Harriet Martineau reported in 1835 that all men worshipped as brothers at the St. Louis Cathedral: "Within the edifice there is no separation." Thomas L. Nichols was amazed by what he saw in the cathedral: "Never have I seen such a mixture of conditions and colours. . . . White children and black, with every shade between, knelt side by side. In the house of prayer they made no distinction of rank or colour."[34]

While there were few instances of true integration similar to that in the Catholic Church, there were other cracks in the color line. One of the most important determinants of race relations was the absence of residential segregation in New Orleans: whites and free Negroes lived side by side on the same streets or shared rooming houses, and slaves often lived in cabins behind the homes of their masters. Frequently the interracial housing pattern led to "flagrant" disregard of the color line. For example, free Negroes and whites drank, danced, gambled, and caroused together in many bars and restaurants in the city in spite of regulations against such activities, and houses of prostitution often had an integrated clientele and an integrated staff.

Friendly and intimate relations sometimes developed between free Negro and white families.[35] Eliza Potter, a Negro hairdresser who spent much time in New Orleans, declared, "There is a great deal of sociability between the free colored and the rich whites in the slave states." Upper-class whites who had no fear of public disapproval and no need for artificial props for their egos often violated social taboos: they hired free Negro men to teach their daughters music, dined with blacks, and also attended public functions with Negroes. Interracial social functions were so customary among the veterans of the Battle of New Orleans that the New Orleans *Tribune* observed with regret on January 10, 1865, that for the first time in fifty years "white and black veterans of 1815 did not . . . take their seats around a common board, to partake of a cordial and fraternal repast." Wealthy whites crossed the color line almost with impunity. A number of wealthy white males, for example, enrolled their Negro children in the public schools of New Orleans.[36]

The most unique feature of race relations in antebellum New Orleans was the pervasiveness of miscegenation. The desire of white men for sexual relations with Negro women was so great that special institutions grew up to satisfy it. Casual liaisons with Negro women were so common that there was no social stigma attached to them. Negro prostitutes were at a premium; comely slave girls were hired by the month as concubines; the test of a white's manhood, and the height of pleasure for him, was an assignation with a Negro woman. Wealthy white men purchased beautiful Negro women for their concubines, on occasion paying as much as $8,000 for them. The best-known institutional arrangement for miscegenation, however, was the *plaçage*.[37]

A plaçage might begin in many ways. When a white man found a Negro woman whom he desired (often at the almost

Voodoo Ceremony

nightly quadroon balls) he courted her as assiduously as he would any of his white paramours. According to Eliza Potter, the quadroons were "courted by gentlemen the same as other ladies."[38] The wealthiest and most beautiful quadroons frequently chose from among several white suitors. After a period of courtship a wealthy white suitor met with the girl's parents and agreed to purchase her a house and to give a certain amount of money to each of the children which might result from the union. Consensual unions and not recognized by the law, most of these arrangements were of short duration.

Although many historians have described the plaçage arrangements as a system of prostitution, it seems more accurate to describe them as common-law marriages. In this sense they were no better or worse than the numerous arrangements in which white and Negro couples lived together without ever taking marriage vows. Many of the plaçages were permanent unions. For instance, a man named Eugene Macarthy lived with one Negro woman from 1796 until his death in 1845.[39]

In regard to this woman, a state court argued that "she had, in all respects, rendered her condition as reputable . . . as it could be made. . . . The state in which she lived was the nearest approach to marriage which the law recognized, and in the days in which their union commenced it imposed serious moral obligations." A resident of New Orleans declared that plaçage arrangements "often continued for years, and frequently become such that an attachment and even an affection grows up, as strong and enduring as was ever witnessed between man and wife."[40]

Although sexual contacts between black men and white women were not as numerous as those between white men and black women, they did take place. Occasionally slave men engaged in extramarital affairs with their white mistresses or other white women. Morris Helpler, in his study of New Orleans crime, asserted: "Each year during the 1850s police arrested several white women for taking up with slave men."[41] Considering the taboo against the practice, the punishment was relatively light: the white women involved might be sentenced to anywhere from one to six months in jail, and the slave might receive fifteen or twenty-five lashes. In the last years of the 1850s the severity of the punishment for white women involved in these assignations decreased. As a matter of fact, the undermanned police department and the public showed little interest in these affairs as long as upper-class white women were not involved. It was obvious, however, that upper-class women were not immune from seduction by black men. Thomas J. Martin, a free Negro music teacher, for instance, seduced many of his upper-class white students. Unfortunately for Martin a number of them got pregnant, the public became aroused, and in 1860 he was imprisoned.[42]

Not only was interracial sex common in New Orleans, there were also a number of black-white marriages in spite of the antebellum law prohibiting them. The white cashier of a New Orleans bank, for example, married a Negro woman by transferring some of her blood to himself and claiming to be a Negro. Priests were regularly bribed to perform religious marriages and a few white men moved to Cuba or France and married their concubines.[43] On occasion black men also married white women during the antebellum period. Public reaction to such unions was ambivalent; a man who was known to be a mulatto could, if he were wealthy, marry a white woman with no furor developing. For example, Eliza Potter reported that one rich mulatto had married a white belle from Virginia in New Orleans: "He came back [from Paris] highly educated, a wealthy gentleman, and greatly sought after for his millions and his handsome appearance, and he married this great *belle*. Many knew who he was, but on account of his millions and his father, nothing was said. And there are many in the same situation." Alice C. Risley, a Louisiana white woman who had taught in a Negro school in Baton Rouge, reported a similar case. On December 20, 1864, she "met an old acquaintance in Mrs. Corlin, her husband was a light mulatto, but one of the wealthiest men on the Teche, she is purely white." A number of white women claimed they were Negroes and married the black men they loved.[44]

It is obvious that whites had an ambivalent attitude towards Negroes. They loathed and hated the Negro, but they also loved and respected him. Often one man might hold all of these contradictory attitudes. While on an intellectual or conscious level a white man might claim that a Negro was inhuman, his own experience often disproved this. Intimately associated with Negroes for most of his life, recalling his black mammy, his black playmates, the old Negro who regaled him with stories, it was inevitable that the white would consider some Negroes worthy of his respect. Because of their historical intimacy with Negroes, most Louisiana whites manifested far less abhorrence for blacks than did their brothers in the North and far less than their rhetoric often implied. A number of travelers noted this phenomenon. C. G. Parsons claimed, perhaps a bit naïvely, that there was great prejudice against the Negro in the North but that there was "none of this prejudice in the South. If the slaves could be set at liberty today, there would be nothing of this kind to exclude them from genteel society. The whites are accustomed now to associate with them as intimately, though not on the same terms of equality, as with each other." Thomas L. Nichols agreed with Parsons and asserted that "in New Orleans, as in all the South, the negro was certainly treated more like 'a man and a brother' than I had ever seen him in the North." Eliza Potter argued that in spite of the animosity between the races, "they will associate much more so in the slave States than in the free States."[45]

Because most whites believed in white supremacy, their attitudes had a profound effect on the way Negroes viewed themselves. Since white skin was glorified, since whites had all of the power and most of the wealth and education, many Negroes accepted the concept of the goodness, purity, and sanctity of whiteness and the degradation of blackness. Consequently, many of them tried and a number succeeded in passing for white. Mulatto women sometimes spurned unions with blacks and welcomed white males because they were flattered by the attentions they received from the "superior" race. Henry Johns reported that in New Orleans the Negro women "seem proud of their almost white children, holding the fruit of their adultery as an evidence of their charms."[46] Some of the mulattoes also tried to erect a color line against blacks. This separation was encouraged by the whites as a means of dividing the Negroes and making it easier to control them. Social classes grew up around color primarily because a mulatto was generally a free man (77 percent of the free Negroes in 1860 were mulattoes) and a black man was almost always a slave (74 percent of the slaves in 1860 were black). In fact, color was closely correlated with status: 80 percent of all blacks were slaves and 70 percent of all mulattoes were freemen. By law the light-skinned free Negro was barred from mingling with the dark-skinned slave, and he sometimes held slaves. The education, wealth, occupations, and refinement of the mulattoes also acted as a barrier to their intercourse with the poorer, less-skilled, and less-educated blacks.[47]

In spite of class differences and the proscriptions against them, many Negroes during the antebellum period had established the beginnings of cultural and intellectual life, stable family relations, religious, social, and educational institutions, and had obtained occupational, business, and political knowledge and skills which would be invaluable to the black community during Reconstruction. A large number of them had preserved enough of their manhood and desire for liberty to impel them to fight for their freedom during the Civil War. At the same time, however, the dark night of slavery had been so crushing for many of them that they would never regain their sense of manhood, be able to interact on terms of equality with whites, develop strong family ties and morality, or become industrious. Their churches and schools would suffer from their ignorance, superstition, and improvidence. Fortunately, there had also developed a well-educated, skilled class of free Negroes and bold, intelligent slaves who could provide leadership for their more unfortunate fellows.

Fighting for Freedom

2

During the Civil War Negroes pressed their claims to equal treatment in American society and died in large numbers to make that dream a reality. Louisiana slaves demonstrated their desire for freedom by deserting the plantations in droves. To the New Orleans slaves the Civil War was a time of breathtaking changes, boundless dreams, and painful disappointments. The first visible change was a tightening of the patrols and a greater restriction on their freedom of movement. Otherwise, the slave continued his usual labor, and continued to receive his usual stripes and to hear the auctioneer's gavel occasionally.[1] While the traditional relations between masters and slaves continued for some time, they changed radically when Union soldiers entered the city in May 1862. Almost immediately slaves began running away and frequently found sanctuary in the customhouse and other camps of the troops.[2] Thomas J. Durant, a Southern Loyalist, described the situation perfectly for Lincoln on July 15, 1862. He wrote that the sanctuary the slaves found in Union camps "operated as a general enticement to the slaves to abandon their master's service; while the master no longer knew when he could command his servant's labor, who might at any moment leave without the possibility of recovery; thus filling the master's mind with doubt, anxiety, disappointment and resentment."[3]

Although Durant pleaded with Union officials that "the slaves [be] let alone," many Union soldiers did everything they could to entice the bondsmen away from their owners.[4] According to Julia LeGrand, a local observer, the slaves were "promised by the Yankees freedom, riches, free markets, a continual basking in the sun, places in the Legislative Halls, possession of white people's houses and a great deal more."[5] Abolitionist soldiers often told the slaves in Orleans parish that they were free, and sometimes they stood by to make sure that their owners did not prevent them from leaving the plantations.[6] General Benjamin Butler charged that General John W. Phelps frequently ordered his troops to liberate slaves: "If on any of the Plantations here a Negro is punished when he deserves it, the fact becoming known to Genl. Phelps' Camp, a party of soldiers are sent immediately to liberate them and with orders to bring them to Camp."[7] The intransigence of the whites, their inflexibility, and their attempts to continue their normal controls over the slaves encouraged the blacks to run away. By March 1863, 29 percent of the slaves on fifteen plantations in Orleans parish were fugitives. There were, of course, a few slaves who were so fond of their masters that they refused to leave their service; generally they were the most aged ones.

Most slaves gloried in their owners' bitter defeat. They gave vent to their pent-up hatred, regularly insulted whites, and generally refused to stay in "their place." No longer would they stand when whites entered a room, move off the street to let whites pass, allow their owners to control their families, work when they were ordered to do so, cower before a white man's frown, or stand passively while they were slapped, kicked, or flogged. Because of the new attitudes of the slaves, the New Orleans *Picayune* charged on June 29, 1862, that blacks in the city were becoming lazy, saucy, and unmanageable. The slaves eventually became so unmanageable that the whites began to fear that they would rebel. During the early months of the federal occupation this was the agonizing nightmare that made life miserable for most whites.[8] For example, Clara Solomon, a New Orleans schoolgirl, declared on May 8,

1862, "I fear more from the negroes than Yankees and an insurrection is my continual horror."[9]

New Orleans whites were dismayed over the practical freedom the slaves enjoyed. Destitute, starving, savage, dishonest, stupid, immoral, superstitious, and irresponsible, the Negro, whites felt, had no idea of what freedom entailed and would find it difficult to survive without the paternalistic guidance of his owner.[10] The slave's concept of freedom, whites claimed, was to have no responsibility, no work, and plenty of food.[11] Paradoxically, the laboring whites feared that these same "lazy" blacks would take their jobs away from them. The New Orleans *Picayune* reflected this fear on June 10, 1862, when it argued that Negroes only flocked to the Union camps to avoid work and that harboring them would only increase military expenses and exclude many poor white men from employment. One Irishman told the Englishman W. C. Corsan that " 'them d—— niggers will starve a poor white man out of house and home, if they sits them free, and be d——d to them.' " Thomas Durant recognized these fears and urged Union officials on July 15, 1862, to employ neither free Negroes nor slaves while there were so many poor whites unemployed. He contended that officials should forbid bondsmen from entering the Union lines and "take no slave from the service of his master for military purposes or needs when a white person can be hired to perform the work." Lincoln gave a characteristic reply to the complaints of New Orleans whites on July 29, 1862: "What is done and omitted about slaves is done and omitted on . . . military necessity. It is a military necessity to have men and money; and we cannot get neither [sic], in sufficient numbers or amounts, if we keep from or drive from our lines slaves coming to them."[12]

At the same time that Union officials were trying to decide what was to be done with the slaves in New Orleans, the army was liberating thousands of blacks in the interior and bringing them to the city. When Union troops began marching into the parishes, the slaves greeted them with open

arms and flocked to the army camps and began singing, dancing, and praying.[13] Finally able to leave the plantations, the
slaves took their masters' horses and mules and lightheartedly
followed the Union armies back to New Orleans.[14] Some plantation owners near New Orleans contributed to the hegira by
ordering their slaves off the plantations when they became
unmanageable. In June 1862, for example, an enraged plantation owner ordered his slaves off the plantation "and bade
them go to the devil."[15] They all went to New Orleans instead.[16]

Not all slaves waited passively for their owners or for
Union troops to liberate them. Some were treated so cruelly
or were so desperate for freedom that they eluded their overseers, crept through Confederate lines, and then dodged the
city police in order to reach Union camps. In July, August,
and September of 1862 large groups of slaves armed themselves with cane knives, clubs, and old guns, stole horses
and mules, eluded rebel pickets, marched to the city, and
then fought pitched battles with city policemen who tried to
capture them.[17]

Some of these slaves found refuge in the army camps;
others, less fortunate, were beaten or killed; and a number
were sentenced to three months at hard labor. In spite of the
dangers involved, about two hundred slaves were entering
Union lines daily by December 1862. No longer would they
live in hovels, starve, be flogged or be degraded by white
men. They had had enough; they would risk all for freedom.
The New Orleans *Black Republican* characterized them perfectly on May 13, 1865:

Our people came naked, starving, sick, frightened, hunted,
and filled with doubt and fear. Thoughtful men were not
wanting, who trembled at what seemed inevitable, namely:
That these freedmen could hardly avoid extermination. On
every hand they came. They came poor—they came with
hardly a pillow on which the aching head might rest—they
came with sad and sorrowing faces—they came cut, scarred,
mangled. . . . History furnishes no such intensity of deter-

Pickets of First Louisiana Native Guards

mination, on the part of any race, as that exhibited by these people to be free. . . . nobly did many thousands die in the swamps, or give their bodies to the black waters of the bayou, rather than go back to their worse than Egyptian bondage.

At first the escape of the blacks from their masters did not improve their situation, because Union officials did not know what to do with them. Although General Butler had become famous by designating fugitive slaves as "contraband" and welcoming them to Fort Monroe, Virginia, during the early months of the war, he decided on May 23, 1862, in

New Orleans that since he was unable to feed the resident population, slaves should be prohibited from entering his lines and that those who did so should be returned to their owners. Anti-Negro officers responded with alacrity to his orders. One soldier, Homer Sprague, reported that in May 1862 "repeatedly slaves were seized in the Custom House, sometimes by the connivance of United States officers; repeatedly they were knocked down, and brutally dragged away from under the folds of the 'Flag of the Free'."[18] Many of Butler's troops, however, flatly refused to obey his order. They justified their action by quoting from Deuteronomy: "thou shalt not deliver unto his master the servant which is escaped from his master unto thee." Eventually it became too much of a burden to imprison fugitive slaves; in November 1862 Butler ordered all of the slaves in jail freed unless their owners paid their jail fees. Although military officials claimed that they would not return fugitive slaves, they did allow loyal owners to enter camps and try to "persuade" their bondsmen to return, and they "recommended" to the Negroes that they return to loyal planters. Loyal city slaveholders were permitted to recover their slaves in army camps until the spring of 1863.[19]

The plantation slaves who escaped or who were brought to New Orleans created a problem of massive proportions for army officials. By midsummer of 1862 there were more than 10,000 refugee slaves in the city. Many of them were put to work building fortifications on the levees, cutting wood, policing army camps, and loading and unloading quartermaster supplies. The army also established several contraband camps or refugee colonies which were so unsanitary and overcrowded that blacks died in droves.[20]

Union officials, worried about conditions in the camps and about charges that they were promoting vagrancy and feeding lazy Negroes, decided in the fall of 1862 to find more systematic labor for the slaves and to relieve overcrowded conditions in New Orleans. In October 1862 Butler began the first work in this direction by seizing abandoned plantations and placing the refugees on them. General Nathaniel

Banks continued this policy on a more systematic basis. First, he revived the pass system and ordered the provost marshals to arrest all Negroes without passes and place them on the abandoned plantations. Secondly, in January 1863 he issued an order that all Negroes must work and encouraged them to sign contracts with loyal planters. In a further effort to end vagrancy, on June 1, 1863, the army gave the police jury of Orleans parish the authority "to have arrested any idle, destitute, or vagrant negroes who may be found in the parish, and employ such negroes on any public work." As a result of these orders, Union officers refused to allow fugitives to enter the city and often rounded up black residents. On occasion free Negroes and slaves who had spent all their lives in New Orleans were caught in these dragnets. Once on the plantations, they could not return to New Orleans. For instance, in January 1863 Harris H. Beecher, a Union surgeon, saw a squad on their way "to keep a gang of refractory blacks upon a sugar plantation from strolling about the city, and from going outside the lines."[21]

Although the army officers made some efforts to ameliorate the condition of the blacks, they retained and expanded many features of the antebellum black codes to control free Negroes and slaves.[22] The police, for example, were permitted to enforce the slave code long after the Union army occupied the city. Homer Sprague wrote that in May 1862 "the police as of old were allowed to seize and deliver up fugitive slaves. The punishment of whipping them in jail was still inflicted with the full sanction of the military authorities." As late as April 1863 recalcitrant slaves were still being imprisoned in the city and flogged.[23]

In the fall of 1862 the Army strengthened the pass system; all Negroes who did not have passes from their employers or the provost marshal were arrested as vagrants. Early in 1864 military officials imposed a 7:30 P.M. curfew on all Negroes in New Orleans and required them to obtain permits from the provost marshal in order to hold meetings, none of which could be held at night. Chagrined because they were

Slaves Coming into Camp

classed with slaves, the free Negroes complained that the
army pass system was worse than the antebellum black code
because it required all Negroes, bond and free, to obtain a
pass. On August 17, 1864, Paul Trévigne, J. B. Roudanez,
and other free Negroes asserted that although they were loyal,
decent, and industrious taxpayers, they were arrested as crim-
inals when they did not have passes. Often they had to bribe
provost marshals in order to get out of jail.[24]

Since the free Negroes were being penalized partially because Lincoln had exempted some Louisiana parishes (including Orleans) from the Emancipation Proclamation, they
began a concerted drive to bring about universal emancipation. The most important event in this campaign was the
publication of *L'Union*, a French-language newspaper. Basing
its platform on the Declaration of Independence, the rights
of man, liberty, and republican principles, *L'Union* saw no

possibility for saving the Union with slavery intact. A hindrance to progress, a degradation to the bondsman, and a shackle on the white man, slavery was too much of a burden for the nation to bear. On December 10, 1862, *L'Union* asserted: "The institution of slavery in modern societies is one of the most formidable obstacles which hinders the development of nations." The complaints of the free Negroes and the logic of events slowly crumbled the legal props to slavery. In October 1863 a Louisiana state court ruled that Negroes could no longer be held in slavery. On December 26, 1863, General Banks ordered the removal of all signs in New Orleans regarding the sale and imprisonment of bondsmen. Then, on January 11, 1864, he suspended all of the state's constitutional provisions regarding slavery.

The campaign to emancipate the slaves raises interesting questions about the sympathies of the free Negroes. It is obvious that at the beginning of the war many of them were pro-Confederate. The slaveholders among them were just as committed to preserving the "peculiar institution" as white men. In Pointe Coupée and Natchitoches parishes, for instance, the free Negro planters formed Home Guards companies soon after the war commenced to prevent slave uprisings. Similarly, when the Committee on Public Safety asked wealthy citizens to subscribe to a defense fund for New Orleans, some of the free Negroes contributed. Their support was not, however, unanimous; often there were furious and sometimes violent debates over the matter. For example, in September 1861 two free Negroes argued about the war and then fought a duel in which one man was killed.[25]

In April 1861 the free Negroes in New Orleans, led by Jordan Noble, the drummer boy at the Battle of New Orleans in 1815, held several meetings and offered their services to the Confederacy. According to the New Orleans *Delta* of April 23, 1861, "these men who distinguished themselves at the Battle of New Orleans are determined to give new evidence of their bravery." At about the same time, the free Negroes in Plaquemines parish organized a militia company.

Gratified by such demonstrations of loyalty, Governor Thomas
O. Moore on May 12, 1861, authorized the formation of a
free Negro regiment to guard New Orleans. Early in 1862
more than 3,000 free Negroes enlisted in three regiments with
Negro officers and with uniforms and arms they purchased
themselves. Apparently, however, the Confederates did not
trust the free Negroes, for they rarely used them and refused
to issue them arms and supplies.[26]

Confederate distrust of the free Negroes was probably
well founded. Their apparent enthusiasm for Confederate
service was a result of several factors. The free Negroes
had traditionally fought to defend the de facto government,
whether Spanish, French, or American, and generally had
received some personal reward and some measure of recognition for their services; consequently, they may have felt
that they would improve their civil and political status by
serving the Confederacy. Threats of confiscation and bodily
harm caused many of the free Negroes to enlist in the rebel
army.[27] The officers of the free Negro regiments, for instance,
told General Butler that they had been ordered out and "had
not dared to refuse." A private citizen agreed. He declared
in 1864 that Negroes had contributed financially to the rebel
cause and enlisted in the Confederate army, "but it is known
to all under what pressure of public opinion, under what
threats uttered by the promoters of secession this was done."
If the free Negroes were loyal to the Confederacy in 1861,
they certainly were not in 1862; when rebel troops evacuated
the city, the free Negro soldiers refused to accompany them.[28]

Whatever the reasons for the apparent support of the rebel
cause among free Negroes at the beginning of the war, almost
all of them expressed unionist sentiment after Butler's troops
occupied the city. Julia LeGrand observed early in 1863, for
example, that the Negroes were "constantly singing 'Hang
Jeff Davis on the sour-apple tree.'" On February 21, 1863,
she reported that when a crowd of whites was almost run
down by a Union artillery battery, "the negroes laughed and
clapped their hands to see us run over, and one screamed

out, 'Here, let me get out of this d——d secesh.' " Negroes
cheered Union troops as they marched through the city, and
presented flags to some of the regiments.[29]

One way the Negro demonstrated his support for the federal government was by enlisting in the army and fighting
to preserve the Union. At first this was impossible because
Union officers refused to accept Negro troops. The first test
of this policy came when General John W. Phelps, an old
Vermont abolitionist who had a virulent hatred of slaveholders, formed the fugitive slaves in his camp into regiments
and asked Butler in July 1862 for arms and equipment for
them. Butler refused and Phelps resigned. A month later,
however, Butler was so desperate for troops that he decided
to enlist the free Negroes, since they had been used by the
Confederates. Recruitment for the regiments, designated as
Louisiana Native Guards, began in August 1862.[30]

The Negroes responded with alacrity to the opportunity
to enlist; the first three regiments, composed largely of free
Negroes, were filled by November 24, 1862. These men were
highly skilled, and according to Negro officer Robert H. Isabelle, in spite of their wealth, their jobs, and their businesses,
they volunteered "to defend the flag of their country and keep
Louisiana in the Union." Thomas W. Conway, superintendent
of the Bureau of Free Labor, asserted that the free Negroes
were wealthy men but that "as a general thing they were glad
to go into the army." On March 11, 1863, John B. Bernabe
and other free Negroes declared, "Our great desire is to strike
a Blow for the Union therefore we are both willing and Ready
to forsake our wives and children and Risk the fortunes of
War [.] [A]lthough something new to us we are in hopes that
the task will prove no harder to us than it was for our fathers
in 1812 and 1815." P. B. S. Pinchback, who raised several
companies and served as an officer in one of the regiments,
expressed the sentiments of most of the Negroes in a recruiting
speech he made in 1862. Free Negro men, he said, were being
called upon to help free the oppressed, and although they
had not received martial honors in the past, they could look

BRISTOL POLYTECHNIC
ST. MATTHIAS LIBRARY
FISHPONDS

to the future to enroll their names on the scroll of honor. The occasion for considering such prospects was, he said, "the only time in my life I have felt anything like Patriotism, my Heart is full, my Soul Seams [sic] indeed in arms."[31]

From the outset, Union officials were not particularly interested in the former status of the volunteers as long as they were able-bodied. As the supply of free Negroes was quickly exhausted, Butler declared the slaves of foreign nationals, rebel sympathizers, and of masters who could not pay their slaves' jail fees to be free men and enlisted them. By 1863 all bondsmen who entered the city could volunteer for military service. Recruiting parties also raided rebel-held parishes to find volunteers, and slaves escaped from plantations as far away as Assumption parish in order to enlist in the regiments being formed in New Orleans.[32] A majority of the slaves were eager to enlist. John W. Phelps asserted that the slaves in his camp were anxious to fight: "They are willing to submit to anything rather than slavery." One Negro planter, Francis E. Dumas, allegedly called all of his slaves together, asked them if they were willing to fight to "break the bonds of their fellow men" and then enlisted one whole company of them in the Native Guards. On one foray into the parishes, recruiter Lawrence Van Alstyne found that the Negroes "were more anxious to enlist than we were to have them. Even the women and children wanted to go. . . . the blacks are wild with joy, and eager to become 'Lin'kum Sogers.' "[33] Given an opportunity to fight for their freedom, and promised large bounties, many slaves enthusiastically joined the army. The provost marshal of Iberville parish reported that the "presence of Recruiting Officers, has caused the negroes to become excited and unmanageable, whole plantations become deserted in one night."[34]

General Butler's initial success in recruiting Negro troops in Louisiana cheered those officials in Washington who had been moving slowly toward the general enlistment of blacks. Early in 1863 Lincoln was so impressed by the possibilities of obtaining Negro troops in Louisiana that he gave Daniel

Contrabands Arrested in New Orleans

Ullmann, a New York politician, the authority to raise in
the state a Negro brigade, eventually designated the Corps
d'Afrique. The number of white volunteers was decreasing
so rapidly, and there was so much resistance to the draft, that
Union officials were relying heavily on the Negro to fill the
decimated ranks of the Union army. Brigadier General W. H.
Emory wrote to one of his fellow officers in Louisiana that
administration officials were "placing too much reliance upon
the number and efficiency of the black troops which are raised
and to be raised in our Department."[35] His fears were soon
realized; the number of Negro volunteers began to decline
in mid-1863.

Since the Union war machine could not wait for volunteers, recruiters began a general policy of conscripting Ne-

groes. They marched onto plantations, took laborers away at gunpoint, and dared the planters to intervene.[36] Similar scenes occurred in New Orleans. Early in August 1863 Banks ordered all Negro males without visible means of support in the city to be arrested and conscripted. The recruiting squads went about their work with a vengeance; they pulled blacks out of their homes, arrested them on the street, and threatened them with bodily harm if they did not "volunteer." For example, on August 4, 1863, a raiding party entered the home of a free Negro in order to conscript his son. The son, however, "refused to go and was immediately set upon and cruelly beaten by the squad, one of them using a knife upon him and wounding him in three different places. They then carried him off by force despite the remonstrances of his aged Father." In many cases the former slaves were too ignorant to know what was happening to them. Charles Bosson described what must have been the typical experience for many "volunteers" when he wrote that two companies of Negro engineers were mustered into the service in the following manner: "The men were drawn up in line, when a German officer, who spoke poor English, said something to them . . . and then declared the two companies mustered into service. These negroes afterwards asked what had been going on, and appeared ignorant of the nature of the ceremony."[37]

After the planters complained that the recruiters were interfering with their laborers, on September 28, 1863, General Banks halted conscriptions and ordered that all Negroes in Union-held parishes were to be enrolled and subjected to the draft, but that the draft could be suspended during the harvest season. Even so, the recruitment of Negro troops was a successful venture; there were 10,772 of them serving in Louisiana in February 1865.

The first three regiments recruited in New Orleans began their training at Camp Strong Station about four miles from the city. Generally literate mulattoes, the men of the First Louisiana Native Guards were relatively easy to train in the arts of warfare. Twenty percent of them had been bricklayers,

15 percent carpenters, 12 percent cigarmakers, and only 45 percent laborers. An overwhelming percentage of the men in the Second and Third Native Guards and other regiments, however, were illiterate laborers. The task of training these illiterate recruits was an unenviable one for their officers.[38]

Hundreds of free Negroes served as line officers in the three Native Guards regiments and as field officers in the Third Louisiana Native Guards. Averaging thirty years of age, these free Negroes were wealthy and sophisticated, had been educated in Europe, the West Indies, and in common schools in the United States, and were generally bilingual. Having heard stories of the Negro veterans of the Battle of New Orleans all of their lives, many of them had early begun the study of military tactics. Others had served as officers in the Mexican army.[39] Many observers were impressed by the intelligence, deportment, military aptitude, and courage of the Negro officers. The most glowing description of these officers came from a New York newspaper correspondent who talked to those of the First Louisiana Native Guards and discovered that they "were well posted up in history and general literature, and during the long range of subjects—civil, literary, political or moral . . . I found on one or two occasions that I was conversing with men of no ordinary knowledge and mental capacity."[40]

Among the best trained of the officers were H. Louis Rey, James Lewis, Robert H. Isabelle, James H. Ingraham, William Barrett, C. C. Antoine, P. B. S. Pinchback, and Andre Cailloux, Francis E. Dumas, one of the largest slaveholders and wealthiest Negroes in the state, was offered a colonelcy in one of the Native Guards regiments but declined and was appointed major. Benjamin Butler wrote that Dumas was "a man who would be worth a quarter of a million dollars in reasonably good times. He speaks three languages besides his own, reckoning French and English as his own. . . . He had more capability as a Major, than I had as Major General, I am quite sure, if knowledge of affairs and everything that goes to make a man is any test."[41]

The free Negroes of New Orleans, traditionally proud of their military heroes, were excited by the enlistment of fellow blacks. Hundreds of them visited the training camps daily to view the drill and dress parades. The ladies of the Negro churches presented silk flags to the regiments, and several ministers organized relief committees for the soldiers and their families. *L'Union*, the *Tribune*, and the *Black Republican* all followed the progress of the regiments when they entered the field, and large crowds in New Orleans cheered the troops loudly as they marched to battle.[42]

The reaction of New Orleans whites to the recruitment of Negro troops was mixed. While a few radicals applauded, most whites were dismayed, angered, humiliated, and appalled by this step. It was, they felt, the last of a long line of insults they had suffered at the hands of an unfeeling enemy. Few whites believed that blacks would fight, and greeted the Negro regiments with derision; any three white men, they contended, could scatter a whole regiment with a whip and a few yells.[43]

Whatever the opinion of whites, most Negro soldiers were anxious to fight to prove their bravery and their right to freedom. They had suffered so much at the hands of whites, and so many people felt that they were cowards, that it is difficult to tell whether they were motivated more by a desire for revenge or to prove their manhood. For most of the free Negroes it was undoubtedly the latter. James H. Ingraham probably spoke for most of them when he wrote in the autumn of 1862 that, although the men in the First Louisiana Native Guards had not met the enemy, "we are still anxious, as we have ever been, to show the world that the latent courage of the African is aroused, and that, while fighting under the American flag, we can and will be a wall of fire and death to the enemies of this country, our birthplace."[44]

Many of the slaves were motivated by hatred and a desire for revenge for the wrongs they had suffered at the hands of their masters. While the First Louisiana Native Guards regiment was marching down Canal Street, for example, "one negro, as the regiment passed the store of his former master, who was then in the Confederate Army, shook his rifle at the name over the door and shouted, 'Dat's de man I wants to meet on de field of battle!' at which of course his company grinned." No quarter, such men felt, should be given to whites who had scarred their backs and raped their wives and daughters. To a white officer who counseled magnanimity toward the rebels, one Negro soldier explained:

O lieutenant! its very well for you to talk; you can afford to: you haven't got anything partic'lar against them folks. Your back ain't cut up as mine is. You ain't heard screamin' wimmin, and seen the blood run out at every lick, just 'cause a woman would't leave her husband and sleep with the overseer. They never done you such things; but I could kill 'em easy,—children, wimmin, and all.[45]

The Louisiana Native Guards received few opportunities to obtain revenge or to prove their valor on the battlefield. They spent most of their time marching and counter marching, guarding and repairing railroads and bridges, clearing sugar cane fields, scouting, foraging, guarding prisoners, doing garrison, picket, recruiting, and engineer duty, and unloading commissary stores. The grumbling of the Negro troops and the persistence of their officers, however, forced white officers on occasion to relieve them of fatigue details and to utilize them in combat. The first real test of Louisiana's Negro troops came on May 27, 1863, at the well-fortified and almost impregnable rebel fort at Port Hudson. The First and Third Native Guards advanced on the left of the fort through rough terrain and tangled abatis into a forty-foot-wide creek which was about eight feet deep. They charged six times but were halted each time by the creek and a murderous fusillade of rebel artillery and musket fire. The Third Native Guards had 154 men wounded or killed in the battle.[46]

The charge of the Negro troops at Port Hudson was one of the most important factors in changing sentiment in the army and in the country toward the Negro's ability to fight. General Banks, who had shown little confidence in the ability

Officers of First Louisiana Native Guards

of the Native Guards, wrote Lincoln after the battle that "we could never have accomplished the conquest of Port Hudson *but for the presence* of the negro regiment." On May 30, 1863, he wrote to his wife that the Negro troops "fought ... splendidly! Everybody is delighted that they did so well! Their charges ... exhibited the greatest bravery, and caused them to suffer great losses." A Massachusetts soldier, Frank Flinn, was one of the white troops who expressed his admiration for the Native Guards. He wrote "[they] fought with the desperation of tigers. After firing one volley they did not deign to load again, but went in with bayonets, and wherever they had a chance it was all up with the rebels." The *New York Times* published a panegyric on the bravery of the Native

Guards on June 13, 1863, and predicted that no one would
ever scoff at the courage of Negro troops again. The greatest
demonstration of this new respect came from the rebel governor of Louisiana, Henry W. Allen. He urged the Confederate Secretary of War in September 1864 to recruit Negro
troops because "we have learned from dear-bought experience
that negroes can be taught to fight, and that all who leave us
are made to fight against us."[47]

Paradoxically, the rebels had a greater appreciation of
the black troops than had the Union officials. At first blacks
received less pay than white troops, and on occasion quarter-
masters refused to issue them supplies and would only give
them worn-out muskets and old uniforms. Many white soldiers were opposed to campaigning with Negroes and refused
to respect Negro sentries. When brigaded with white troops,
Negro soldiers were frequently forced to do all of the fatigue
duty while the white soldiers "lay in the shade and watched
them work." The Negro soldiers were also subjected to un-
usually severe punishment for slight offenses.[48]

The Negro officers of the Native Guards bore the brunt
of the hatred against blacks in the Union army. The epaulets
they wore on their shoulders smacked too much of equality,
with all of the dire consequences such a condition entailed
in the eyes of white soldiers and officers. One white Union
soldier declared in February 1863 that he opposed slavery
but that he could not stomach the black officers of the "nigger
regiment" who were "like dogs in full dress, ready to dance
in the menagerie—would you like to obey such a fool?" The
Negro officers of the Third Louisiana Native Guards stated
that they were treated with contempt by their fellow white
officers who considered it "an insult" to be addressed by a
Negro officer. If they requested information from a white
officer, they received "abrupt and ungentlemanly" answers.
It was because of such actions as these that eventually some
of the Negro officers began to resign. Captain Joseph Follin
asserted that he resigned because "daily events demonstrate
that prejudices are so strong against colored officers that no

matter what be their patriotism and their ability to fight . . . they cannot [serve] with honor to themselves."[49]

As soon as he took command of the Department of the Gulf, Banks began a concerted drive to rid himself of the Negro officers. According to the New Orleans *Tribune*, in 1863 Banks had the Negro officers "brought before him, in New Orleans, and told them that the Government policy was to have no colored commissioned officers in the army." One of the officers who was present at this meeting, P. B. S. Pinchback, asserted that Banks said "white men alone are fit to command." On February 14, 1863, Banks declared that he was going to replace the Negro officers with white ones because he was "entirely satisfied that the appointment of colored officers is detrimental to the service. It converts what, with judicious management, and good officers, is capable of much usefulness, into a source of constant embarrassment and annoyance. It demoralizes both the white troops and the negroes."[50]

When the officers refused to resign, Banks placed some of them on detached service and ordered the others to appear before a Board of Examiners. There was no intention of passing them. For example, Captain James Lewis resigned on March 8, 1864, after he had been ordered before such a board, and, he declared, he "was told by a member of the board . . . that it was not the intention . . . to pass any colored officer." When Banks ordered the Negro officers of the Second Louisiana Native Guards before an Examining Board, all but two were declared incompetent, yet Banks dismissed all of them and appointed whites to their posts. Banks claimed that the officers were dismissed for the good of the service. On August 17, 1863, he wrote to Lincoln that the Native Guards were demoralized by "discreditable" officers whose "arrogance and self-assertion" goaded the white soldiers and officers into violence.[51]

Officers such as Banks did much not only to influence the treatment of Negro officers, but also to affect the lives of all blacks in New Orleans in a variety of ways. Although the

slaves were freed, mercurial changes in the Union emancipation policies constantly raised and dashed their hopes before
the dream was realized. Freedom itself was almost an empty
boon because Negroes had few rights and little protection
before the law. In some ways the war created obstacles to
the wholesome development of institutions in the black community. The institution affected most profoundly by the war
was one of the weakest—the family. Some of this, of course,
was a result of the dislocation attendant to war. Most of it,
however, was due to Confederate and Union policies. Negroes
were moved around so much that many family units were
disrupted. First of all, rebel planters often moved able-bodied
males to Texas and never reunited them with their mates.
Secondly, the Union Army transferred slaves from the outlying parishes to New Orleans, then moved them to plantations, and finally conscripted the men from these plantations.
Both slaves and free Negroes were often rounded up so ruth-
lessly in New Orleans and then shipped to the plantations so
quickly that they did not have time to contact members of
their families. Many families separated in this way were never
reunited.[52] Closely allied with the official policies which disrupted Negro families were individual actions of Union soldiers which had the same disrupting effect. With the numerous
unattached women who flocked to the army camps and whose
sense of morality had been blunted by slavery, it was inevitable that sexual promiscuity would be rife.[53] These casual
affairs contributed substantially to the burden of sexual promiscuity which the Negro community bore.

However, the Negro did gain certain advantages from the
war, the greatest of which was education. This was especially
true of the Negro troops. Initially many of the troops were
so overwhelmingly illiterate that their military effectiveness
was seriously hampered; having spent so much of their lives
without receiving any instruction, they could now hardly learn
the rudiments of warfare. One observer reported that only 50
of 400 soldiers in the hospital for Negro troops in New Orleans in April 1864 knew the names of the units to which

they belonged. Most officers of such men realized that their minds had to be unshackled before they would become good soldiers. The enlisted man, barred from promotion to the position of noncommissioned officer because of his illiteracy, and believing that his inferior status was a result of his ignorance, eagerly sought education.

Many officers felt that they had a moral duty to lift the heavy veil of ignorance which hung over their troops. Brigadier General Daniel Ullmann obtained teachers for his brigade of Louisiana Negro troops when he discovered that they had a "great desire" to learn to read and write. More than five hundred of them learned to do so in less than six months. Banks tried to eradicate the widespread illiteracy in his Negro regiments, at first by appointing members of the American Missionary Association as lieutenants in the regiments for the sole purpose of teaching the soldiers. When Banks realized that he could not obtain enough teachers in this manner, however, he ordered the chaplain in each Negro regiment in his department to teach the troops. Thousands of men learned to read and write as a result of these efforts.[54]

Almost equally as important as education for the New Orleans Negro was the sense of manhood which blacks developed during the war. These men were not only fighting to save the Union and to destroy slavery, they were also proving their bravery and their right to freedom, to an honored place in the republic, and to equal treatment after the war ended. The battlefield exploits of the troops increased the self-respect of all Negroes in the city; they constantly stressed the importance of the Negro's contribution to the war effort. On September 15, 1864, for example, the following comment by Abraham Lincoln was proudly quoted by the New Orleans *Tribune*: "Abandon all the posts now garrisoned by black men; take 200,000 men from our side and put them in the battle-field or corn-field against us, and we would be compelled to abandon the war in three weeks." Clearly, since Negroes were contributing so heavily to Union victories, their right to equality of treatment with whites could not be ig-

nored after the war. This claim was one of the major principles in the New Orleans Negro's campaign for justice, and
the main reason for his dreams of the future.

At the end of the Civil War the New Orleans Negro had
the heady feeling of having contributed to the Union victory,
and of saving the nation from dismemberment. Many Negroes
had learned to command men and to gain respect for the first
time; many white men applauded them for their valor. The
visible sign of this valor was the thousands of dollars that
Negro soldiers received in bounties, which gave many of them
the economic foundation to preserve their liberty.

Land, Labor, and Capital

3

The Negro in New Orleans quickly learned the responsibilities of free labor and managed to compete successfully against whites in many areas of economic life. This was especially true in certain occupations in which black workers initially garnered a disproportionate share of the jobs and managed to hold on to them until they were frozen out by white unions in the twentieth century. Although they did not compete as successfully against whites in the professions and industry, blacks obtained a significant share of the brokerage houses, retail groceries, cigar factories, and tailoring shops in the city. Negroes also began to learn more about the complexities of business organization and management and the nature and functions of labor unions; a number of the unions and businesses formed during this period were so strong that they lasted well into the twentieth century. Most of the economic failures of the Negro were due to forces outside the black community: racial discrimination, national and local depressions, and the indifference and criminal negligence of federal officials.

Often prohibited from obtaining loans and barred from jobs in even the most prosperous of times, the Negro began his economic venture into freedom in an unpropitious period. During Reconstruction New Orleans was still suffering from the long general depression in its economy which began in the early 1850s after the railroads began to tap the Mississippi Valley, upon which the commercial life of the city depended.

49

The disruptions caused by the Civil War, the national depression of 1873, periodic yellow fever epidemics, riots, political crises, and by the blockage of the mouth of the Mississippi all exacerbated the situation. The rapid increase in the Negro population in the city between 1862 and 1880 simply added to the number of persons who were competing for the limited number of jobs which were available. Then, too, the initial attempts of Union officials to systematize labor in Louisiana were in many ways worse than the evils they sought to correct.[1]

The thousands of unemployed, ragged, penniless, and starving whites and Negroes in New Orleans in May 1862 posed a problem of massive proportions for Union officials. Even before the Union army occupied the city, thousands of hungry people were regularly receiving rations from the Confederate relief organization, the New Orleans Free Market. The situation was so serious that Benjamin Butler declared on September 1, 1862, that "the condition of the people here is a very alarming one. They have literally come down to starvation."[2] By the end of September 1862, Butler was issuing $50,000 worth of food per month to whites in New Orleans. Between January 1863 and March 1865 the number of white families receiving rations from the Union army varied from four to nine thousand.[3]

The ubiquitous refugee Negro added greatly to the relief problems Union officials faced. Often barefoot, half naked, and lame, sometimes old, feeble, and wracked with disease, the fugitives posed an immediate health problem and strained the ability of authorities to maintain law and order.[4] One officer reported in June 1862 that there arrived at his camp daily hundreds of fugitives who were "quite destitute of provisions, many having eaten nothing for days." On January 27, 1863, W. H. Emory asserted that there were continually arriving in the city Negroes who were "in a wretched and destitute condition, mostly unfit for labor or self support." As the number of fugitives escaping to New Orleans increased and Union officials brought thousands of blacks from the interior to the city, relief supplies were taxed to their utmost and life inside the refugee camps deteriorated rapidly. F. S. Nickerson, an army officer, described a typical camp:

The Negro Quarters are wretchedly poor. But very few of any suitable materials have been provided of which to construct them. A few individuals might occupy them with some degree of comfort, but to crowd so many together in so small a compass is simply brutish. Nearly all of the huts are open and leaky—incapable of protecting either from rain or cold. Many of them are much more suitable for hog-pens than for human beings to inhabit.[5]

Union officials made several moves to alleviate the dangerous situation confronting them. First, they built more temporary shelters and issued rations to the fugitives; by September 1862 Butler was feeding about 10,000 black refugees. Secondly, in order to relieve overcrowding in the camps, army officers seized several abandoned buildings to house the blacks. The refugees' ignorance of sanitation defeated many of the efforts to protect their health. On March 17, 1864, for instance, the military mayor reported that "the colored population of this city are in many cases generating disease, by living in unsuitable tenements, habits of idleness and total disregard for the laws of health."[6]

With little work available for them, many blacks either lived in idleness or engaged in petty pilfering; others simply walked the streets aimlessly. In an effort to end vagrancy and to teach the fugitives that they had to support themselves, hundreds were put to work in the Quartermaster Corps, on the levees, and in constructing fortifications for which they received wages, clothes, and food. The army could not, of course, employ all of the black refugees. When Banks arrived in New Orleans he "found many thousand Negroes in idleness."[7] Banks tried to end this by strictly enforcing vagrancy laws against Negroes and increasing the number of plantations to which they could be sent. He insisted that the blacks were not forced onto these plantations, but that they were

Receiving Rations

"encouraged" to go to them. The primary "encouragement" was undoubtedly Banks's coupling his January 1863 order that all able-bodied Negroes must work with his flat refusal to give rations to them. In January and March 1863 only 9 Negro families received rations; only 1,000 of the 10,286 families receiving rations in December 1863 were black. While Negroes constituted about 25 percent of the city's population during this period, they did not constitute as much as 20 percent of the total number of families on relief (1,284 out of 5,313) until March 1865.[8]

Realizing the importance of working the plantations in order to revive the commercial life of New Orleans and to add money to Union coffers, Banks met with several white planters and prominent Orleanians shortly after his arrival in the Crescent City. In January 1863 he inaugurated one of the earliest and most thorough systems to reconstruct labor and agriculture in the South. Asserting that able-bodied blacks had to work for their living, Banks had all those without visible means of support in New Orleans arrested and placed on plantations where they signed annual contracts with planters who agreed to pay them from three to ten dollars per month.[9] The integrity of the laborer's family, his right to cultivate garden plots, to choose his employer, and to educate his children were guaranteed. While no corporal punishment was permitted, army officials were to promote the "subordination" of laborers and could punish them by fines, imprisonment in stocks, and expulsion from the plantation. Each laborer had to have a pass to leave the plantation and was liable for any damage to his employer's property.[10]

The linchpin of the labor system was the parish provost marshal. Ostensibly detailed to act as a referee between planters and freedmen and to make sure that both abided by the terms of the contract they had signed, the provost marshal soon replaced the slave patroller as a means of keeping laborers in subjection. The provost marshals, often young and inexperienced army officers, usually began their work conscientiously and fairly. They were soon seduced, however, by the hospitality, the wine, the dinners, and the flattery of the planters, and some of them caught blacks who ran away from the plantations, permitted floggings, and placed soldiers on the plantations to make sure the laborers worked. Frequently the provost marshals were unscrupulous and actively worked with the planters to keep the freedmen in thralldom.[11] Playing on the blacks' trust in Yankee blue, these men often disregarded Banks's regulations with impunity.[12]

Banks insisted that his system had "been established upon the basis of absolute emancipation, recognizing the entire freedom of the laborer, and securing to him a compensation at least equal to that paid labor of a like character in any part of the country." Three of Banks's officers, Chaplain T. W. Conway, B. Rush Plumly (Chairman of the Department of the Gulf's Board of Education for Freedmen), and Chaplain George H. Hepworth, along with philanthropist Gerritt Smith, agreed with these views. On June 15, 1863, Hepworth, who had visited several of the plantations, claimed that "the Labor System as a whole is a decided success." In

1865 Conway wrote to Banks of "the wonderful benefits of
your Louisiana policy."[13] A number of blacks also applauded
the system because it gave the freedmen an opportunity to
earn wages, protected their families, and provided education
for them. Banks wrote his wife in February 1863 that "the
better class of colored people are doing all they can to aid
me as they think it is the first chance the Negro slave has had
to try his hand."[14] Some proof of this appeared in March
1865 when the Cailloux Equal Rights League number 9
passed resolutions thanking Banks for all he had done for
blacks in Louisiana. When Banks returned to New Orleans
after a brief absence in April 1865, hundreds of the city's
Negroes greeted his boat, and the *Black Republican* published
an original poem in his honor.[15]

The *Black Republican*, organized with the assistance of
one of Banks's cohorts, Thomas W. Conway, was the general's most enthusiastic supporter. It insisted that only the old
free Negroes opposed the labor system; the freedmen, its chief
beneficiaries, realized that it was the best system in the country, that it had protected and nursed them in the first days of
freedom. The freedmen, the *Black Republican* argued, lauded
Banks because it was he "who gave them homes when they
were homeless; wages and employment when they were in
want; schools and teachers, books and Bibles, when they never
had them before."[16] Banks's humane policy had saved the
poor, defenseless blacks from starvation and ruin. The *Black
Republican* summarized its views on May 18, 1865, when it
asserted that

the poor, who are nine-tenths of the whole colored population,
are rising rapidly each day under the beneficent and humane
policy instituted by him for their good. . . .

There is no Department in the South where our poor
brethren are so well cared for, or where they are so far
advanced as they are in this. By another year we believe Gen.
Banks will bring all labor systems to an end, because by his
practical good sense, the freedmen will have risen to a point
where they can take care of themselves, claiming and
defending their own rights as other people do.

However, free Negroes, contrary to the claims made by Banks and the *Black Republican*, bitterly assailed his policy. Try as they could, they could see little difference between the system and antebellum slavery; laborers were restricted to the plantations, were bound by contract to work for a year, and had to retire at night at a certain hour. Forced to purchase provisions from their employers at ruinously high prices, the laborers obtained little benefit from the wages they received.[17] The wages were so low, according to the *Tribune*, that "the condition of the slave is not materially altered." Describing Banks's system as a "bastard regime" and semi-slavery which was "not complete liberty, but mitigated bondage," the *Tribune* compared the labor regulations with antebellum plantation rules published in *DeBow's Review*. The *Tribune* author was "unable to perceive any material difference [, with the exception of the lash,] between the two sets of regulations. All the important prohibitions imposed upon the slave, are also enforced against the freedman."[18]

Furthermore, the former slaveholder was one of the chief guardians of the Negro in Banks's labor system—another reason why most New Orleans Negroes rejected it. The planters were too interested in maintaining slavery under another name; they established wages without any reference to the laborer or market conditions and unilaterally determined the amount of clothing and provisions each family received. The lessees of abandoned plantations were even worse; they were so bent on making money that they took little interest in feeding and clothing the freedmen.[19] Henry Warner, a free Negro, begged Banks to revise his system in February 1863 because the "selfish and mean" planters were "only after to catch Negroes back which by Law and God they have no right to do." In 1864 George Hanks, the superintendent of the Bureau of Free Labor, asserted that the spirit of slavery was still alive among many planters who were "even more rampant to enslave the negro than ever before. They make great endeavors to recover *what they call their own negroes*. One planter offered me $5,000 to return his negroes.

They have even hired men to steal them from my own camp."[20]

The *Tribune* opposed the idea of apprenticeship precisely because such attitudes were so pervasive in the white community in Louisiana. It cited the central problem of Banks's system on January 12, 1865, when it charged, "there is no white man in a slaveholding country fit to be a negro's guardian. The reason apprenticeship has failed is not because the blacks were not submissive, but because the whites were tyrants, as they always have been."

Despairing of modifying the labor system, the wealthy free Negroes, professing a deep sense of noblesse oblige and racial commitment, began in 1864 to organize to protect the freedmen. They argued that unless the wealthy and educated Negroes tried to educate, aid, and counsel the freedmen they would continue to be oppressed. At a meeting in December 1864 New Orleans Negroes organized the Louisiana Equal Rights League to promote the moral, educational, and industrial development of the black community. The league sent agents to the parishes to check on the condition of the freedmen, appealed to military officials for the redress of grievances, called for the establishment of more schools and asylums, and organized the Bureau of Industry to aid Negroes in New Orleans. In his first monthly report in March 1865, James H. Ingraham, superintendent of the Bureau of Industry, declared that during February the bureau had received and spent $251 in obtaining rations for 190 of the 192 persons who applied for them, had written letters for 36 persons, had obtained employment for 32 of the 37 persons who applied for it, had obtained passes for 22 and been instrumental in getting 11 people out of jail, had obtained wood and coal for several people, and had given general assistance to 586 people.[21]

Members of the Equal Rights League, the *Tribune*, and several whites urged the wealthy free Negroes to help the freedmen to rent plantations. In 1864 the *Tribune* called upon the free Negroes to form a Farmer's Association to buy the

abandoned plantations and lease them to the freedmen to be
worked on shares. Not only would this be a good investment
for the free Negroes, it would also bind their interest to those
of the freedmen, give free Negroes an opportunity to break
the power of the old planters, and help the freedmen learn
to be self-reliant. Under the *Tribune*'s plan the laborers would
feed and clothe themselves, be free to move about, and receive
monthly or weekly wages and a share of the crop.[22] The free
Negroes had a golden opportunity: "We can give the freedmen under the influence of liberty, moral benefits and social
enjoyment all he estimates and contend[s] for. Let us go to
work, organize labor-colonies, and elevate our emancipated
brethren, at the same time that we take our legitimate share
in the cultivation of the country."[23]

The several groups trying to lease abandoned plantations
for the freedmen formed the New Orleans Freedmen's Aid
Association on February 27, 1865. The objectives of the
association were to rent and lease plantations, to give loans,
and to furnish supplies, education, and useful information
to the freedmen. The members of the association also pro-
posed the establishment of a bank, but they did not have
enough capital to do so. In order to help finance its activities,
each member of the association had to pay $20 in dues an-
nually. Some of the wealthiest Negroes in New Orleans were
among the sixty members of the association; they included
J. B. Roudanez, coproprietor of the *Tribune*, grocer Victor
Pessou, brokers Sidney Thezan, John Clay, and Aristide
Mary, poet Camille Thierry, and Oscar J. Dunn, along with
several others. Benjamin F. Flanders and Thomas J. Durant
were the best-known white men who were members of the
association.

The association appealed to Northerners and other freedmen's organizations for money, agricultural implements, and
supplies, and sent agents into the parishes to investigate conditions. By August 1865 the association had rented several
plantations, made loans to freedmen with a lien on their crops,
furnished horses, seeds, and provisions to many laborers, and

Arrest of Vagrants

established prizes "to incite the industry and heighten the zeal of the Freedmen." Unfortunately, the rapid return of the plantations to their owners after the war effectively ended the work of the association.[24]

The Negroes in New Orleans clearly realized that their own economic position could not be secured without some fundamental changes in Louisiana's economy. It was obvious, for example, that too many Negroes were landless and that as such they were subject to every whim of the white planters. For instance, immediately after the war Louisiana planters combined to bar Negroes from renting or buying land. The New Orleans *Tribune* repeatedly called upon the legislature to break up these combinations because they were designed "to keep the colored people in subjection, so that their wages, their votes, their movements may be controlled by the whites. This is a kind of slavery to which our people will not submit."[25] In order to end such practices, the *Tribune* urged the Union to confiscate rebel property, and Negroes to settle on the public lands in Louisiana.

The economic philosophy of the Negroes in New Orleans centered on racial uplift, cooperation, and resistance to white exploitation of blacks. Blacks had to prove that they would work in freedom, support their families, churches, and schools, and end dependency and vagrancy in their community. The road to success, to respect from whites, to political and civil equality, and to self-respect, blacks felt, was through diligence, industry, frugality, self-denial, sobriety, and faithful and honest toil. In speeches and editorials Negro leaders in New Orleans tried to inculcate these virtues in the black community. It was only through consistent labor that Negroes could gain some measure of independence and obtain and maintain their rights.[26]

Although their efforts to find employment were often hampered by the periodic economic depressions in New Orleans, most blacks took advantage of the opportunities available to them. A few observers, however, complained that they were addicted to idleness. Friedrick Gerstäcker, a German traveler, found, he declared, thousands of "black idlers" drifting around the city in 1867. White-owned newspapers in New Orleans frequently repeated these charges, but the comments of disinterested observers disprove them. When Hilary Skinner arrived in New Orleans and saw the many Negro workers, he asked, "If the blacks will not work for wages, and work hard too, then are we gazing on sable phantoms of prodigious strength?" Maria Waterbury observed in 1869 that Negroes were "doing most of the work" in New Orleans.[27]

For the most part, statistical indices support the contentions of Skinner and Waterbury. Not only did blacks constitute a significant element in the New Orleans laboring population, they worked at several different kinds of skilled jobs during the Reconstruction period. A large percentage of the black artisans had learned their trades during the antebellum period, and most, undoubtedly, came from the free Negro class.[28] Discounting mortality, mobility, and other factors, if all the free Negro artisans listed in the 1860 census were still in New Orleans in 1870, they would have accounted for 60 percent of the Negro shoemakers, 52 percent of the printers, 51 percent of the tinners, 48 percent of the masons, 35 percent of the carpenters and joiners, and 100 percent of the tailors, while constituting only 13 percent of all black laborers.[29]

As a result of the training he received during the antebellum period, the New Orleans Negro was probably more highly skilled than black laborers in any other city in the United States. The black occupational structure was very complex. Negro males were engaged in 75 different occupations in 1860; 153 in 1870; and 156 in 1880. Many of them were skilled artisans: in 1880, 48 percent of them were engaged in skilled occupations. While most skilled blacks were heavily concentrated in the building trades, a few blacks also worked as cabinetmakers, jewelers, engineers, bookkeepers, pilots, florists, photographers, and druggists.[30]

The Negro laborer had to fight against great obstacles in order to obtain and to hold his job. First of all, he was illiterate. In 1870 the illiteracy rate of Negro males over ten years of age in New Orleans was 57 percent. Secondly, the Negro laborer suffered more from periodic economic depressions than any other group: white employers were reluctant to hire him during boom periods, and fired him first during hard times. Because of this, he was often engaged in an unequal struggle against white workers. Negroes were excluded from some labor unions and sometimes were attacked when it appeared they were taking jobs from whites. For example, in 1880 white stevedores "forcibly drove the colored men away, by clubbing some, cutting others, and many had to take refuge in stores along the Levee."[31] Because of the violence and discrimination, the Negro male, while he represented only 25

and 23 percent of the labor force in 1870 and 1880, constituted 52 and 44 percent of the unskilled laborers, and 57 and
60 percent of the servants in those years.

In spite of discrimination, blacks were able to garner a
disproportionate share of certain skilled jobs. While Negroes
constituted only 25 percent of the total labor force, they held
from 30 to 65 percent of all jobs as steamboatmen, draymen,
masons, bakers, carpenters, cigarmakers, plasterers, barbers,
and gardeners in 1870. By 1880, though the percentages had
changed, Negroes were still overrepresented in many of these
occupations: constituting only 23 percent of the total labor
force, Negroes held from 25 to 52 percent of the skilled jobs
mentioned above.

Since foreign-born workers constituted 49 and 33 percent
of the total number of laborers in New Orleans in 1870 and
1880, they represented the Negroes' chief competitors for
jobs. The foreign-born workers were much more highly skilled
than the Negro: in 1870, 86 percent of them were skilled.
The differences in the occupational patterns of the two groups,
however, enabled the Negro to hold on to some jobs. Negro
workers tended to concentrate on a limited number of jobs,
while foreign-born workers were spread almost evenly through
the occupational ladder. For example, while 83 percent of all
Negro workers were concentrated in thirteen occupations,
only 31 percent of the foreign-born workers were represented
in the eight occupations in which they were most heavily
concentrated. Because of the differences in occupational patterns, Negroes held a larger percentage of the total number
of jobs in 1870 and 1880 than did foreign-born workers in
such occupations as steamboatmen, masons, cigarmakers,
plasterers, coopers, and bakers.

As the number of foreign-born workers declined in the
1870s, the nature of the economic competition between them
and Negroes changed. By 1880 both groups were being chal-
lenged in a number of occupations by native-born whites. The
foreign-born were hardest hit by competition from native
whites. Although there were seven occupations in 1870 and

1880 in which the percentage of the foreign-born workers exceeded their percentage of the total labor force, their representation in most occupations fell drastically. The percentage of all foreign-born workers had declined in 1880 by 12 to 50 percentage points from their share in 1870 in such occupations as butchers, shoemakers, fishermen, tinners, blacksmiths, barbers, wheelwrights, coopers, cabinetmakers, draymen, carpenters, and painters. In such occupations as steamboatmen, gardeners, printers, cigarmakers, and masons their share declined by from 0.8 to 8 percentage points from 1870. In most of these occupations the Negro's percentage of the total number of workers declined from 1870 to 1880 by from 1 to 11 percentage points.

While the percentage point decline of the Negro was smaller than that of the foreign-born worker in most occupations, the Negro's situation was frequently more serious. Negroes, for example, lost almost half of their share of the jobs as butchers, wheelwrights, and printers. They were already seriously underrepresented in these occupations in 1870. Only in one occupation, fishing, did Negroes threaten foreign-born workers in the 1870s; they took over almost all of the fishing jobs lost by the foreign-born workers. While the foreign-born workers' share of fishing jobs declined by 22 percentage points, the Negro's share increased by 22 percentage points between 1870 and 1880. Negroes also gained a larger share of the shoemaker, cabinetmaker, cooper, machinist, and blacksmith jobs, but the native-born white workers garnered the largest proportion of those jobs lost by the foreign-born. Even so, Negro artisans were able to maintain their supremacy in many jobs until the twentieth century. This was facilitated largely by the relative absence of white-union–controlled apprenticeship programs. Instead of having to struggle against the monolithic wall raised by omnipresent whites-only unions which existed in other cities, young Negroes in New Orleans could learn trades on an informal basis from their relatives or by becoming the apprentices of black artisans.[32]

The occupational base which blacks established during Reconstruction served them well in the twentieth century. Because blacks held on to many jobs, for instance, they had to be included in some fashion in labor unions. Although there were relatively few blacks who served a formal apprenticeship, enough young men learned trades from their fathers, relatives, and friends during Reconstruction and afterwards for blacks to continue their strong representation in these trades. The connection between the Reconstruction patterns and the occupations of blacks in New Orleans in the twentieth century is obvious. In 1910, as in 1880, Negroes held a disproportionately high percentage of all jobs as boatmen, draymen, shoemakers, carpenters, coopers, masons, plasterers, and tobacco workers. The picture was generally the same in 1930. By that year a higher percentage of Negro men were engaged in a number of other occupations than their representation in the total labor force. These occupations included longshoremen, firemen (manufacturing), sawmill operatives, roofers and slaters, and mailmen. The economic successes of Negroes during Reconstruction were the most important factors in their ability to avoid complete strangulation by white unions, corrupt city officials, and anti-Negro employers in New Orleans in the twentieth century.[33]

In spite of the opportunities he had to learn a skilled trade, the black worker faced many problems during Reconstruction. The cost of living was so high and unemployment so endemic in New Orleans that many blacks found it difficult to rise above the subsistence level. The economic security of the Negro worker varied with the differential in wages between different occupations. For instance, while 15 percent of all Negro carpenters, 14 percent of the Negro plasterers, painters, and bricklayers, 11 percent of all Negro shoemakers, and 10 percent of all Negro coopers held $200 or more in property, only 4 percent of all Negro unskilled laborers in 1870 held as much as $200 in property. The most serious problem the Negro worker faced, however, was chronic unemployment. In 1880, for example, 18 percent of all Negro male workers were unemployed for at least one month. The highest rates of unemployment were among Negro laborers, painters, masons, carpenters, steamboatmen, plasterers, coopers, and cigar-makers. The average number of months Negro males were unemployed varied from 3.5 months for barbers to 5.7 months for cigarmakers.[34]

Unemployment, discrimination, and a desire for racial and economic uplift led Negro workers to form several rather weak quasiunions soon after the Civil War ended. The effort to unionize the blacks was seriously hampered, however, by the depressed economic conditions in the city, the lack of organizational skills among the workers, and the physical and political oppression of the blacks.[35] In spite of these problems, during 1865–80 blacks formed at least fifteen workingmen's clubs, benevolent associations, and unions among the long-shoremen, steamboatmen, draymen, waiters, letter carriers, screwmen, cigarmakers, teamsters, and porters. A number of Negro workers also belonged to such integrated unions as the Cotton Yardmen's Beneficial Association and Teamster's Association. By 1880 there were four Negro longshoremen unions, the largest of which was the Longshoremen's Protec-tive Union, organized in 1873, with 450 members. The Teamsters and Loaders Association, organized in 1880, was one of the largest of the Negro unions, with 800 members. In their associations Negro workers set up funds to aid the sick and bury the dead, and provided social outlets for mem-bers and their families. Some of them were more ambitious. In 1875 one union established the short-lived Workingmen's Bank and another organization, the United Brotherhood Protective Association, established a grocery store.[36]

Although the black unions were more social than mil-itant labor organizations, they often played prominent roles in the several strikes which occurred in New Orleans. For instance, one of the most serious strikes in the city began in May 1867 when about 500 Negro longshoremen struck be-cause the contractors who hired them to unload the ships refused to pay them the wages they had agreed upon. On May

16, 1867, the longshoremen attacked one of these contractors
and were about to lynch him when the police rescued him.
The longshoremen then chased all of the other contractors off
the docks, shouted down Mayor Heath when he tried to quiet
them, and marched in a body to the Freedmen's Bureau office.
General Joseph A. Mower, state commissioner of the Freedmen's Bureau, addressed the men, counseled them to be law
abiding and to stop their "rioting," and asserted that if they
did not, "by the eternal God I will throw grape and canister
into you." After a company of army troops was deployed on
the docks, the longshoremen dispersed. They refused, however, to go back to work. When the contractors hired scabs
at $13.00 per day, the longshoremen chased them away from
the ships. Mower ended the impasse by issuing an order that
all captains and agents of vessels in New Orleans would be
"held responsible for wages due freedmen."[37] On June 15
another dangerous situation arose on the docks. When a white
engineer struck a Negro at the levee, the longshoremen chased
him into a store and would not allow him to leave until the
police arrived and dispersed the crowd.

The Negro longshoremen struck again in October 1872.
During the strike they boarded a ship being loaded by scabs,
and when the captain fired on them, they murdered him.[38]

There was an epidemic of strikes in New Orleans among
both white and black workers in 1880. The first of these
occurred in March when Negro longshoremen struck in
Algiers. In July the 500 white and black members of the
Cotton Yardmen's Association demanded higher wages. When
the employers rejected the demand, the yardmen unilaterally
set a wage scale to go into effect on September 1, 1880. This,
too, was rejected by the owners. The yardmen then went on
strike and won acceptance of their demands. The integrated
Teamsters Association went on strike on September 6, for a
raise in wages to $3.00 per day. At about the same time black
and white roustabouts, steamboatmen, and longshoremen
struck for higher pay. This strike was broken with scabs from
Mobile and Louisville. On October 15, the Negro waiters at

the St. Charles Hotel struck for an increase from $15.00 (plus food and lodging) to $25.00 per month. The proprietors promptly fired all of the waiters and replaced them with white girls hired for $12.00 per month.[39]

The long and aggressive campaign of black workingmen to improve their lot in life was part of a multipronged drive to insure economic survival. The most consistent fight of blacks in New Orleans was their effort to promote thrift in the community. Negroes, their leaders asserted, spent far too much of their money for new fashions, whiskey, and pleasure, when they should have been saving to educate their children or to buy homes. Considering the ignorance and poverty in the community, the *Louisianian* was distressed by the Negroes' extravagance and pleaded with its readers to seek less pleasure and more wealth:

Until we learn to become economical, we must ever be the dependent, helpless creatures that we are. Poverty is always to be deplored, and yet we as a people, don't seem to think it an inconvenience. We plead earnestly for more economy and less pleasure, much as we know we are thereby treading on the weakness of our people.[40]

Money, community leaders contended, was second only to education as a means of uplifting blacks and winning the respect of whites; it was the road to security, confidence, social standing, and self-reliance.[41] In an 1875 speech militia colonel James Lewis struck a refrain repeated by black leaders throughout the period when he insisted that the question of civil rights would be resolved by the Negro's industry and acquisition of wealth: "It is only interest which will drive out prejudice from the minds of whites. . . . Remember that the roads to prosperity are to be reached only through intelligence, and wealth and industry."[42]

Perhaps the most important impetus to the accumulation of wealth in the black community came from the Freedman's Savings and Trust Company chartered by Congress in 1865. Drawing on the pronouncements of Benjamin Franklin about the advantages of savings, bank officials convinced many blacks that this was the road to true freedom. Negro soldiers deposited their bounties (the bounty office was in the bank building), holders of the lucky lottery tickets their winnings, benevolent organizations and churches their dues, and hard-working laborers the few dollars left from their wages after providing for the necessities of life. By June 1867 more than $1,994,340 had been deposited. During the bank's seven-year existence, more than 10,000 individual deposits were made.[43]

After emancipation itself, the event which had the most far-reaching economic influence on the black community was the collapse of the Freedman's Savings and Trust Company in 1874. Many Negro businessmen, already operating on a small margin, saw their small reserves disappear overnight. The simple laborers who had trusted in the United States government and had started saving money to buy homes or to gain some security were probably the hardest hit by the disaster. Having little understanding of bankruptcy proceedings, many of them quickly sold their deposit books to speculators for ten cents on the dollar. The treasuries of churches and philan-thropic and benevolent societies either disappeared or were so sadly depleted by the crash that the organizations had to curtail activities. This was undoubtedly one of the reasons for the death of many clubs.

The baneful effects of the crash reverberated throughout the black community. Depositors bitterly assailed the Northern missionaries, philanthropists, and abolitionists who had, they felt, tricked them into putting their hard-earned money in the bank and then defrauded them. The most crippling and long-lasting effect of the crash was psychological: many Negroes would never again trust a bank. After all, if one could not safely deposit money in an institution chartered by the federal government, then no bank was sound. It was better, many blacks felt, to spend their money for immediate pleasure rather than to try to save for the future and be cheated out of it. The New Orleans *Louisianian*, which had been in the fore-front of those urging Negroes to put their money in the Freed-

Roustabouts

man's Savings and Trust Company, almost despaired of ever convincing them to be frugal after the bank's crash.[44] The failure of the bank, it declared, "has caused on the part of our people, not only a feeling of distrust for other moneyed corporations, but has created a feeling of apathy in regard to saving and intensified the desire to spend in a round of pleasure, the earnings of a week, after the expenses of the household have been met."[45] Major responsibility for the lack of frugality among blacks in New Orleans in the 1870s rested squarely on the shoulders of the criminally incompetent officials of the bank and an indifferent United States Congress.

The failure of the bank and the general depreciation of property values in New Orleans in the 1860s and 1870s prevented the growth of a large black property-holding class. The total amount of personal property held by Negroes actually declined from $655,820 in 1860 to $560,143 in 1870. The overwhelming majority of the personal property holders held from only $20 to $500 worth of property; only 44

Negroes held more than $3000 worth of personal property in 1860, and only 9 in 1870. One Negro possessed $50,000 worth of personal property in 1860, while no one in the black community held more than $20,000 worth of personal property in 1870. However, Negroes made much more impressive gains in real estate between 1860 and 1870.

The number of Negroes who possessed real estate in New Orleans increased from 486 in 1860 to 933 in 1870, and the total value of real estate possessed by blacks increased from $1,488,500 in 1860 to $2,104,865 in 1870. While a majority of the Negro real estate owners in 1860 held property valued at $3,000 or less, in 1870 a majority of the Negro landowners possessed property valued at $1,500 or less. There were, however, more Negroes who were large landowners in 1870 than in 1860. While only 17 Negro landowners held property worth more than $10,000 in 1860, there were 25 of them in 1870. Six Negroes in 1870 owned land worth more than $40,000; there had been none in 1860. The total value of property possessed by Negroes increased from $2,144,230 in 1860 to $2,664,828 in 1870.[46]

Since the 1880 census does not list property and the Orleans parish tax assessment rolls do not indicate race, it is practically impossible to do any more than estimate the total value of property Negroes possessed in 1880. This can be done by taking a sample of black property holders listed in the 1870 census and ascertaining how much taxable property they had in 1880. Forty-five of the Negro property holders listed in the 1870 census were also listed on the Orleans parish tax assessment rolls. In 1870 these blacks possessed $350,025 in property, 13 percent of all of the property held by blacks in that year. Ten years later these same people held $241,830 worth of property. If their share of the total amount of property held by Negroes in 1880 was the same as it was in 1870, then blacks possessed at least $1,820,230 worth of property in 1880. They probably held considerably more than this, since the bias of the sample is toward an underestimate of property, for it does not in any way measure the new property holders. From 1860 to 1870 new property holders and the increase in wealth of the old ones led to an increase of $520,598 in the property held by Negroes. If there was the same total increase from 1870 to 1880, Negroes would have held $2,340,828 worth of property in 1880. Accepting this estimate as sound, the per capita wealth of Negroes in New Orleans was $40.58 in 1880.[47]

The largest black property holders in New Orleans during Reconstruction were the businessmen. While they were few in number, they exercised great influence in the black community: they were models to be emulated and were proof that the Negro could succeed in freedom. Successes in business, Negroes felt, represented the growth of the power they needed in order to obtain and to maintain their rights. Negro leaders urged their followers to enter all lines of business in order to keep the wealth they created in the black community.[48] Colonel James Lewis spoke for many of them in 1875 when he said, "Our labor and our crops bring us money; we need banks wherein we have an interest in which to deposit. We like to insure our houses and our furniture, we then need insurance companies. The fact is we need to enter all the branches of trade." As Negroes were increasingly and violently driven out of politics in the mid-1870s, economic enterprise became the new panacea, and a number of prominent Negro politicians began to devote their full attention to business. The *Louisianian* expressed both the despair and the hope in the Negro community during this period when it declared, "Politics as a paying investment has had its days, and we must now look for other avenues and pursuits to build up our fortunes, and to recover in a measure the ground lost in its avocation."[49]

Generally barred from intimate contact with white businessmen and, before the war, from buying stock or engaging in some enterprises, rarely able to borrow money from white-owned banks, and largely ignorant of business organization and practices, most Negro businessmen were concentrated in small, one-owner, service-oriented concerns. Of 169 Negro businesses listed in the 1870 city directory, all but three were one-owner concerns, and 42 percent of them were located in the home of the owner. These businesses included coffee-houses, restaurants, barbershops, rooming houses, cigarstores, ice houses, wood and coal shops, saloons, bakeries, shoe shops, and others. By 1880 many of these businesses had disap-peared and more Negroes were concentrated in those requiring the smallest capital investment.[50]

The paucity of black-owned manufacturing concerns is indicative of many of the problems they faced. For instance, in 1875, after the New Orleans *Republican* called on the old wealthy abolitionists and blacks to organize cotton mills, several New Orleans Negroes met with the president of the New Orleans Chamber of Commerce to discuss the idea. Unfortunately, lack of capital and know-how, coupled with the hostile attitudes of the business community, prevented the establishment of this and any other large manufacturing con-cern by Negroes. There were, however, some manufacturing establishments run by Negroes; most of them were one-owner businesses employing a few workers and producing a small number of articles.[51]

The most important Negro establishments were those of cigarmakers and clothiers. Many of the plants were small; in 1870 three of the four Negro cigar manufacturers listed in the city directory had their plants located at their place of resi-dence, and of the twenty-five property-holding cigarmakers listed in the 1870 census, fourteen owned $1,500 or less in property. Only three possessed more than $5,000 worth of property. The four Negroes listed among the cigarmakers in the 1880 census of manufacturing had an average of only $518 capital invested in their plants, employed an average of four workers, each of whom they paid an average of $503 annually in wages, and produced cigars valued at $1,699 annually.[52]

There were three Negro clothiers and tailors listed in the 1880 census of manufacturing in New Orleans. Etienne Du-bois had the smallest business, with only $200 in capital invested and one worker whom he paid $2.00 for a ten-hour day and $625 annually. He operated his business all year, purchased $500 in raw material, and produced clothes valued at a total of $2,500 annually. Paul Bonseigneur had the largest business, with $1,000 in capital invested in his tailoring shop in 1880 and with five workers, each of whom he paid $1.00 to $2.50 for a ten-hour day and a total of $2,000 annually. He operated his shop only six months out of the year, purchased $900 worth of raw material, and produced clothing valued at $5,000 annually.[53]

While largely unsuccessful in manufacturing pursuits, blacks did organize a number of family partnerships and joint-stock companies. The New Orleans *Louisianian*, for example, was started in 1870 as a joint-stock company by Pinchback, Antoine, and several other Negro politicians. In December 1870, Antoine, Pinchback, Alexander E. Barber, P. G. Deslonde, George F. Kelso, J. J. Monette, and others incorporated the unsuccessful Mississippi River Packet Company, to be capitalized at $500,000 with shares to sell for $100.00. Several wealthy Negroes also organized the Metropolitan Loan, Savings and Pledge Bank Association in 1870. Although the wealthiest Negroes in the state, F. E. Dumas and L. T. Delassize, were on the board of directors, there is no indication that the bank did much business. Probably the most durable joint-stock company Negroes organized was the Economy Hotel Joint-Stock Company founded by the Economy Society, a benevolent organization. Another business which had some limited success was the Cosmopolitan Insurance Association, organized in 1882 with a capital stock of $25,000 and with C. C. Antoine as president, J. B. Gaudet as vice-president, William G. Brown as treasurer, and Aristide Dejoie as secretary.[54]

The existence of a relatively large number of wealthy planters in Louisiana encouraged a few Negroes in New Orleans to establish commission houses. Pinchback and Antoine opened one in New Orleans in 1869 with a branch in Shreveport; and J. F. Winston, a Negro bookseller, had established a similar business by 1870. C. C. Antoine and William G. Brown organized a commission house in 1877, and T. B. Stamps established one in 1878. Engaged in a highly competitive and risky business, the Negro commission merchants had to struggle against great odds. First of all, they had to win customers away from the houses with which they had been doing business for years. Secondly, they had to compete with rural merchants who obtained first liens on crops. While many of these same problems bedeviled white merchants, the Negro often fought a losing battle to win the confidence of his customers. Most of the Negro merchants conceded white planters to white merchants and appealed to Negro planters to support black business. The Negro merchants saw that they could build large businesses if they could only gain the patronage of the Negro planters—the Negro planters in Iberville, Natchitoches, and Plaquemines parishes alone could have supported several commission houses. T. T. Allain of Iberville parish, for instance, owned a 790-acre sugar plantation worth $15,000, employed 35 laborers on it, produced 7,000 hogsheads of sugar, 4,000 gallons of molasses, and other farm produce valued at $14,400 in 1870.[55]

Utilizing their prestige in the black community, appealing to racial pride and their political acquaintances, some of the Negro commission merchants built up sizable businesses.[56] The most successful and imaginative commission merchant during this period was the former legislator T. B. Stamps. When Stamps opened his house, he sent a circular to all of the Negro ministers to be read to their congregations urging Negro planters to support black merchants. He then took out a large ad in the *Louisianian* guaranteeing "prompt" sales, to purchase goods at the "lowest rates," and to give "liberal advances" to his customers. Stamps followed this up by sending an agent through the parishes in Louisiana and then by touring the state and parts of Mississippi and Arkansas himself to drum up business. The New Orleans *Louisianian*, praising Stamps for his "energy, determination and pluck," predicted in September 1879 that he would "receive nearly

6,000 bales of cotton this year, besides sugar and other produce. . . . In two years he estimates he will have employ-ment for twenty men."[57] In November the *Louisianian* revised its estimate upward and predicted Stamps would handle 20,000 bales of cotton during the year. Apparently Stamps was successful in his endeavors: on March 6, 1880, the *Louisianian* reported that he was "rapidly building up a large business."

One of the largest groups of Negro businessmen was the grocers. Most of them ran small neighborhood concerns. Seven of the eight Negro-owned grocery stores listed in the 1870 city directory were located at the owner's residence. Twenty-two of the thirty-five Negro grocers listed in the 1870 census owned $3,000 or less in property, and only six owned more than $5,000 worth of property. The inventory of the small grocer was, of course, limited. The merchandise in a typical small Negro grocery store appeared in the inventory of the estate of thirty-year-old Murville Cheval; when he died in 1865 he had merchandise worth only $274.[58]

Several Negro grocers, however, owned sizable businesses. The contents of J. A. Lacroix's "well assorted" grocery store, for instance, were auctioned off for $4,500 after his death in 1868. Jean Baptiste Deterville Bonseigneur, a native of Haiti and veteran of the Battle of New Orleans, was one of the wealthiest of the Negro grocers. When he died in 1871 he had $2,111 in currency and an estate worth $19,669. Another large grocer was J. J. Montford who owned $17,500 worth of property in 1860. The largest Negro grocer in New Orleans during the Reconstruction period was Victor Pessou, a whole-saler. He sold his products to small retail grocers, coffee houses, restaurants, plantations, and several prominent Or-leanians. He had a thriving business; in 1871 there was a total of $60,678 due him from his customers, and the contents of his grocery store were valued at $15,818.[59]

The wealthiest Negro businessmen in New Orleans during Reconstruction were the brokers. By purchasing real estate, renting houses, managing the property of wealthy Negroes,

making loans, and serving as executors of estates, a number
of Negro brokers amassed a considerable amount of property.
One of them, Myrtille Courcelle, made sizable loans to Negro
businessmen and whites in New Orleans and charged them
8 percent annual interest. He loaned Dr. L. C. Roudanez
$1,200 for his unsuccessful bid to save the New Orleans
Tribune, Peter Caulfield $800 for his jewelry business, Gadane
Casanave $300 for his funeral parlor, and J. J. Montford
$2,350 to operate his grocery store. Between 1860 and 1872
Courcelle purchased $16,000 and sold $12,460 worth of real
estate. When he died in 1872, he owned $15,000 in real
estate and held 26 promissory notes worth $21,968.[60]

Another wealthy broker was Sidney Thezan. His "finely
furnished" house on Esplanade Street was worth $5,000 and
was run by his cook, gardener, and servant. In his brokerage
business Thezan employed one clerk full-time and his son,
Joseph, part-time. Between 1860 and 1875 Thezan purchased
$7,670 and sold $15,900 in real estate, but he actually made
much of his money from the 6 percent annual interest he
received on the short- and long-term loans he made, primarily
to whites. At the time of his death in 1875, six people owed
him a total of $4,205, and he owned $13,650 in real estate.

By 1870 Thezan had begun to manage the property of
several wealthy Negroes in New Orleans, charging them from
2 to 5 percent interest on the income earned on their property.
The largest of these accounts was that of Camille Thierry, a
Negro poet who resided in France. Thierry's property, consisting of 55 shares of stock in the New Orleans Gas Light
Company, 18 shares of the Citizens Bank of New Orleans, one
U.S. Bond, and 6 houses, was worth $43,195. In his numerous
letters to Thierry, Thezan kept him posted on commercial
affairs in the city and advised him of the best times for buying
and selling property. Thezan received a commission of 5 percent on the rent he collected for Thierry from 1872 to 1874
($187 out of $3,735) and a commission of 2 percent on the
stock and monies he managed for him ($226 out of
$12,790).[61]

Probably the only successful Negro father-son brokerage team in the city was that of John Francis and John Racquet Clay. Beginning in 1860 John Francis Clay began to purchase several shares of stock. By 1864 he held 19 shares of the New Orleans Gas Light Company stock, 10 shares of stock in the Bank of Louisiana, and $270 worth of the New Orleans Mutual Insurance Company scrip. The total value of the stock at the time of his death was $3,248. Clay made most of his loans to whites, including Christian Roselius, C. Toledano, and James P. Freret. Most of these were relatively large loans at 8 percent annual interest; of the 23 promissory notes in Clay's possession at his death, only 4 were for less than $500, and one was for $3,187. The total amount of money due to John Francis Clay's estate from promissory notes, debts, and stock was $21,376. After his father's death, John Racquet Clay took over the business. Between 1871 and 1880 John R. Clay purchased $29,298 and sold $21,690 in real estate, and was more successful than his father in obtaining business as an executor of the estates of wealthy Negroes. For instance, when Myrtille Courcelle died, John R. Clay received a 2½ percent commission as executor of his estate ($912 out of $36,482). In 1870 Clay possessed property valued at $21,500.[62]

The wealthiest Negro brokers in New Orleans were Aristide Mary, Drosin B. Macarthy, and Thomy Lafon; between them in 1870 they owned $253,800 in property. Aristide Mary, described as "wealthy, educated and refined," had inherited his money from his white father along with valuable real estate, including a whole block of Canal Street, the main thoroughfare in New Orleans. The most impressive of the trio was Thomy Lafon, who began life in relative poverty and died in 1893 with an estate worth almost half a million dollars. Although Drosin B. Macarthy already came from one of the wealthiest families in the state, he utilized his skill to increase his legacy from $35,000 in 1860 to $77,300 in 1870.[63]

For most of the period under review, Macarthy was the most successful of the Negro brokers. Between 1860 and 1870 he purchased more than $64,000 in real estate and sold more than $27,000 in property. After 1870 Macarthy retired from active trading and lived on the rent he collected. Thomy Lafon, the second leading broker until the 1870s, purchased more than $61,000 and sold more than $26,000 in real estate between 1860 and 1870. From 1871 to 1880, Lafon bought $41,000 and sold $22,000 in real estate. Unlike Lafon and Macarthy, Aristide Mary had inherited so many buildings on Canal Street that he rarely bought or sold land. Instead, he leased his buildings for $6,000 each every four years.[64]

The acquisition of sizable fortunes by a few blacks does not obscure the fact that most blacks were severely handicapped by the general depression in New Orleans' economy. Unemployment was endemic and ensured that the labor unions formed among Negro workers would be weak. At the same time, the general decline in property values (50 percent between 1870 and 1880) caused Negroes to hold property which was valued at only a little more in 1880 than in 1860. Apparently, however, there was an increase in the total amount of real estate that Negroes possessed in the city. Even so, in 1870 Negroes held only 1.4 percent of the total amount of property in Orleans parish and only 2.5 percent in 1880. For the most part, although there were some large Negro-owned businesses, the majority of them were small, one-owner concerns. In spite of the fact that there were few Negro apprentices during this period, Negro workers held on tenaciously to many of the jobs in the city. This was their most important economic victory. And although the criminal mismanagement of the Freedman's Savings and Trust Company deprived the Negro of thousands of dollars and encouraged extravagance in the black community, Negro workers maintained their dominant position in certain trades and gained a near monopoly of others.

Family Life

4

The history of the Negro family is a largely uncharted field. The signposts, where they exist, frequently lead the researcher down false trails.[1] Regardless of the false trails, however, it is obvious that the Negro community in New Orleans was remarkably successful in stabilizing families during Reconstruction. In spite of slavery's legacy of immorality and instability, Negroes responded enthusiastically to the urgings of white missionaries, Negro ministers, and newspaper editors to adopt new family mores. Denied an opportunity for legal marriage or preserving family unity during slavery, Negroes adopted most of the missionaries' Victorian values regarding the family. The nineteenth-century ideals of romantic love, the place of women in society, and the dominant position of males in the family were espoused almost as consistently by Negro as by white males in the Crescent City. Consequently, by 1880 the Negro family had evolved into a patriarchal institution almost as stable as the white family. Most of the weaknesses of the black family were a result of the unhealthy condition of the black population and social problems endemic to New Orleans.

The Negro family during Reconstruction was a product of both the general social milieu and the peculiar historical circumstances surrounding it. The crippling effects of slavery, with its tendency toward family disorganization, continued for several years in the Negro community after the war. Many blacks, for instance, began their first year of freedom searching for mates who had been torn away from them as slaves or by the exigencies of war. Even as late as 1880 Negroes published notices in the newspapers trying to find members of their families.[2]

The family ties in the slave quarters had been tenuous at best. The slave's family was an institution subject to the whims of his master; it was weak at almost every point: slave marriages were illegal, and laws prohibiting rape were rarely applied by white juries to protect black women. Slave families were, by their very nature, impermanent. Even so, there were perhaps more planters in Louisiana who encouraged monogamous mating arrangements among their slaves than in any other Southern state. Not only did monogamous mating arrangements reduce dissension in the quarters, they also helped in disciplining the slave: many slaves were obedient because they feared separation from their families. While the need for discipline was probably the most important reason for the planters' support of monogamous mating arrangements, many of the planters were religious and did so because the church stressed the sanctity of the family. Whatever the reasons, many slaves adopted white mores regarding courtship, marriage, and weddings.

Although most slaves simply moved into a cabin and consummated their union after their master approved it, a large number of them went through the same marriage ceremony as their owners. Some of these weddings (especially of house servants) were elaborate affairs. The bride and bridegroom often dressed in the traditional fashion and repeated their vows before regularly ordained white ministers.[3] Rarely, however, did any but the most highly favored house servants have the kind of wedding which Priscilla Bond witnessed in Terrebonne parish on January 4, 1862:

The bride looked quite nice dressed in white. I made her turban of white swiss—pink tarlton and orange blossoms. They were married at the galey [sic]. The moon shown [sic] beautifully. The[y] afterwards adjourned to the "hospital" [where they had a ball]. . . . how happy they were, dressed in their ball *dresses*. The groom had on a suit of black, white gloves, and a tall beaver. The bride dressed in white swiss, pink trimmings and white gloves. The bride's-maid and groom's man wore dress to correspond.[4]

Regardless of the kind of "wedding" he had, it was impossible for a slave to exercise much authority over his family. His master provided the cabin, the food, and the clothes for his mate and children, and determined when they ate, slept, and rose and the hours and extent of their labor. Some planters also punished both the man and his mate when they had loud arguments in their cabin, and prevented them from exercising parental control over their children. Whatever control the slave exercised over his family, he did so only because of the sufferance of his master. His master granted the slave this right, and he could always take it away; his master consented to his taking a mate, but he could always separate him from her.[5] The most painful reminder of the slave's lack of control over his family was his inability to maintain his family unit intact. Although most planters wanted to maintain the bondsman's family unit, if for no other reason than to make it easier to control him, the exigencies of slavery militated against this objective. The French had recognized this and had tried to protect the slave by prohibiting the separation of families. Louisiana state law, however, was more in keeping with the logic of slavery. Casting aside sentiment, Louisiana lawmakers only forbade the separation of a slave mother and any of her children under ten years of age; the slave father was not even recognized as a part of the family. Meager as it was, this provision was added only because slaveholders realized that it would be easier for a mother to care for small children than it would be for the planter himself. Generally speaking, the planter's self-interest led him to respect this provision of the law. Still, it provided little protection to the slave.

The slave family was the most unstable institution imaginable. The evidence of this appeared clearly in the marriage certificates of the freedmen which have been preserved for one Union army post in Concordia parish for 1864 and 1865. Among the 540 Negroes who reported that they had been "married" while they were enslaved, only 90 of the families were unbroken.

Regardless of the professed opposition of planters to the separation of families, death reaped too frequently in the master's household, the planters were too extravagant, and banks foreclosed on mortgages too regularly for most slaves to escape the auction block. Since Louisiana was a receiving state in the interstate slave trade, many of the slaves had already been separated from their families when they reached the sugar plantations. Many would hear the auctioneer's gavel again in New Orleans and outside parish courthouses.[6] According to one Louisianian, the planters made no effort to maintain family units or to develop parental or filial feelings among their slaves. Instead, he wrote,

kindred ties, and parental affection, and the attachment between man and wife, are among the first things to be broken-up. . . . A connection among them as "man and wife," in which the planter sometimes officiates in a mock ceremony of marriage, is allowed under certain rules, yet care is taken that such alliances do not continue for a long time. When they are broken up they are allowed to seek other companions for a short time. Thus they succeed in preventing anything like affection, or attachment, or respect for an alliance in the character of "man and wife."[7]

Although the callousness of the planters was not the primary cause for the dissolution of most of the slave families (the statistics from Concordia parish for 1864 and 1865 show that 292 of the unions were dissolved as a result of death, personal choice, or war), it was responsible for breaking up a good many of them. For example, statistics for Concordia also show that 158 (29.2 percent) of the slave unions were broken up by the planters. Many of these unions were not allowed to continue for very long but were disrupted after an average of only 5.6 years. Thus, although some couples were able to cohabit for 20 and even 40 years, the dread of separation from loved ones made all of the slave's days miserable. When the blow fell, many of them went insane, became morose and indifferent to their work, developed suicidal tendencies, or ran away in search of their loved ones.[8]

An equally painful (and more frequent) demonstration of the bondsman's powerlessness was his inability to protect his mate and his daughters from the sexual advances of white men who considered every slave cabin a bordello. Helpless slave women were bribed, cajoled, and beaten into satisfying the white man's sexual desires.[9] The legal and practical helplessness of slave women was recognized by a Louisiana court in 1851 when it declared, "It is true, the female slave is peculiarly exposed to the seductions of an unprincipled master."[10] The large number of mulattoes and various court records attest to the large percentage of planters who were "unprincipled masters." One long-time resident of Louisiana asserted:

wanton intercourse with slave women is general on plantations, and in small towns and villages, among planters, overseers and drivers. . . . It is also a uniform practice with the planters in the lower slave states, when called upon by those to whom they extend their hospitalities, to offer them a bed companion from among their slaves. And in doing this they only treat their friends with the common civilities of the day.[11]

Having no one to turn to for protection or a moral code upon which to rely, bondswomen lost all feelings of sexual morality or of chastity. J. B. Roundanez, a free Negro mechanic who had worked on many sugar plantations, asserted:

As to chastity, . . . no such thing was known on the plantations. In the first place, the overseers had the run of all the field women, and if one of them refused, an occasion was very soon found for subjecting her to a severe punishment. . . . The practice of indiscriminate sexual intercourse . . . was so universal that a chaste colored girl at the age of seventeen was almost unknown.[12]

The unbridled licentiousness of the planters was one of the primary reasons for the sexual immorality in the quarters and for strains on the slave family. Since so many of the bondswomen had adopted the licentious habits of their masters, "adultery" was rife, and "divorce" casual and all too frequent. Such practices prompted Henry Bibb to declare that "a poor slave's wife . . . can not be true to her husband contrary to the will of her master. She can neither be pure nor virtuous contrary to the will of her master. She dare not refuse to be reduced to a state of adultery at the will of her master."[13]

Slavery left a heavy burden in the form of casual mating arrangements on the Negro community. One observer charged that, since slavery had only permitted cohabitation, it caused "chaos" in the black family immediately after the war.[14] In the first few postwar years casual mating arrangements were common. When the Reverend A. H. Newton, a Negro clergyman from Connecticut, visited New Orleans in 1865, he found that marriage among the Negroes "was rather an uncommon thing and that a man could establish almost any relationship that pleased him and enter into Creole life and be received and welcomed as one of them."[15] In a sense the Louisiana legislature gave its stamp of approval to such unions when, in the first few years after the war, it refused to enact any law regarding marital relations among the freedmen.[16] Since there was no law requiring a ceremony, certificate, or any positive public act to legitimitize slave unions, it took many of the freedmen years to learn that marriage was a permanent union and that a man did not lightly unite with the first woman who met his fancy and then casually desert her when he found other attractions. It would have been far better for the freedmen if the legislature had required them to be married by a minister or justice of the peace and had requested that ministers read the law to their congregations. Given the faith of the freedmen in their ministers and their literal interpretation of the Bible, such a procedure would have contributed greatly to the growth of family stability in the black community.

Wedding

Marching to Wedding Reception

Negro leaders, ministers, and teachers, and Freedmen's Bureau agents and army officers, began a massive campaign to strengthen the black family during and after the war. In 1865 the Freedmen's Bureau distributed a pamphlet, *Address to Masters and Freedmen*, in which it urged the former slaves to contract legal marriages, support their families, and cast off slavery's licentiousness and adultery. Bureau officials were

empowered to perform the marriage ceremony for any freedmen who wanted it, and they reprimanded white justices of
the peace who refused to do the same. Correspondents in the
Negro newspapers urged the freedmen to get married in order
to make their children legitimate.[17]

This campaign succeeded largely because of its association
with emancipation. Since Negroes had been denied the opportunity to contract a legal marriage in slavery, a marriage license became one of the most important badges of freedom.
It symbolized the end of the debauchery of Negro women by
white masters and overseers, of loved ones being sold, of white
men controlling a black man's family. The marriage license
meant so much because it guaranteed the freedman what he
had never had and redeemed him from the most hellish practices of slavery. Now he could love a woman and his children
free of the nightmare, the dread of their being flogged, starved,
or separated from him. For these reasons freedmen flocked
to provost courts, army camps, churches, and Freedmen's
Bureau offices to get married.

The freedmen's enthusiasm for marriage was not a testa-
ment to the Christianity of their former owners. On the contrary, it indicated how much family life had been denied to
the Louisiana slave. Violating Negro women, encouraging
immorality, and separating families with impunity, the planters
had created in the freedmen a deep hunger for stable family
relations. Slavery contributed to the freedman's enthusiasm
for marriage in the same way that a long sojourn in the desert
creates a desire for water. Emancipation brought the freedman
to a new oasis, where he had an opportunity to satisfy his
thirst for regularized family relations. One former Louisiana
slave, Henry Bibb, summed up this phenomenon perfectly
when he observed that "there are no class of people in the
United States who so highly appreciate the legality of marriage as those persons who have been held and treated as
property."[18]

While reactions to the restrictions of slavery gave the
initial impetus to marriage in the black community, the move-

ment was sustained by the Negro churches and newspapers. Through poems and editorials, the newspapers (even when edited by bachelors) sang the praises of love and delineated the blessings of marriage.[19] Powerful arguments were brought to bear on those who paused on the threshold. Marriage, its proponents contended, was the foundation of social order; through marriage a man obtained a friend and children to cheer him in his old age. Marriage bells, one poet wrote, brought heavenly delight:

> *Oh, happy peals within whose music dwells*
> *The magic rune*
> *That sets to sweet accords and joyous swells*
> *Two lives in perfect tune!*[20]

With all of the delights it portended, the marriage relation was not to be entered into lightly. Love, with its ennobling power, had to be a major consideration. One should not marry for wealth or social position: "With love, the marriage rite is truly a sacrament. Without it the ceremony is a base fraud, and the act a human desecration."[21] However, love was not the only consideration in choosing a mate. One's prospective partner should be industrious, religious, attentive, ambitious, and modest. A prospective bride should be even-tempered, frugal, and a good housekeeper.[22]

The Negro male had a typical nineteenth-century view of woman. Her gentle nature and ennobling spirit, he argued, were the major forces for good in society. Essays on the role of women in civilizing man, in uplifting the race, appeared frequently in the Negro newspapers. It was woman's destiny, Negroes felt, to calm man's savage nature and to inculcate morality in his children. These views were apparently widely held in the black community.[23] For instance, when James D. Kennedy, a journalist, gave the following toast to woman before an all-male Negro social club, there was loud applause:

At every period of the world's progress, her influence has been felt, and felt for good, . . . every advance of the world . . . owes something at least to the generous impulse of her spirit, to the purifying and refining influences of her example. She has ever been the safeguard of our childhood, the comfort and support of our manhood.[24]

The Negro male contended that a woman's sphere of action was the home. Timid and affectionate by nature, she owed blind obedience to man. Her intellect was such that she had little understanding of the complexities of society, and shunned books.[25] Woman, Negro men felt, was destined to occupy an inferior position in society. Unfitted by nature for the kinds of jobs men held, it was natural that she received lower wages. Made for love, how could she take part in ward club squabbles? She made her impact on society through the influence she had over her husband and children; according to the Bible and the rules of society, she could play no other role.[26] Within the family circle, the woman was expected to manage the household, care for children, wash, iron, and sew clothes. Through her love and efficient management of the household a wife could prepare a haven to which her husband could retire from the day's toil. The wife was supreme in the affairs of the household and should be proud of the duties she performed.[27]

Although a woman was supreme in regard to the management of the household, she had to bow to the will of her husband. Soft words and submission to her husband was what was expected of her. One anonymous Negro poet felt that a woman should be

> *In person decent, and in dress,*
> *Her manners and her words express,*
> *The decency of mind.*
> *Submission to her husband's will,*
> *Her study is to please him still*
> *His fond and faithful friend.*[28]

Negro women in New Orleans, however, did not passively accept the inferior status men accorded them. They joined with their white sisters in demanding equality with men in education, jobs, property rights, and politics.[29] The black woman was in a better position to demand equality from her man than was her white sister. She had, after all, suffered as much as he had in slavery. Generally the Negro woman began her plea for equal rights by demanding equal treatment of Negroes by whites. Then she talked about the role of education, self-reliance, and frugality in uplifting the race. But the only way immorality could be stamped out in the community, the only way the race could rise, she continued, was to elevate the Negro woman.

The New Orleans Negro woman's campaign for equal rights began in 1871. In April Frances E. W. Harper, the Negro poet, delivered a series of speeches in which she called for the elevation of the race through education and wise use of the franchise. She also gave "a spirited defence of woman's rights." To the Negro woman she declared, "on the foundation of peace, justice, integrity, education and virtue, must we build and elevate ourselves and our race to a higher and better life."[30]

In subsequent years, Negro women in New Orleans continued the campaign. If an oppressed race could rise, they argued, so could women. God had created no distinctions among his children; woman had taken her place beside man in life's labors, had an intelligence equal to his, and had inculcated her children with ennobling virtues. Man had no God-given right to oppress women. "C. R." probably represented the views of most Negro women in New Orleans in her plea for equal rights in 1875:

If men have ruled the world for many centuries is it just that they should rule it for ever? or does it mean that woman's mind is weak and incapable of reasoning? . . . ah, selfish lords, the day has past [sic] when subjection shall content the minds of women! Ere long you shall feel the *want* [wail?] *of every woman's voice* to enforce and strengthen that of which you are now laboring to deprive them.[31]

While few black males were willing to admit that their wives had a right to share authority in the family, they did recognize that they had some responsibilities to them. The husband's role in the family was to be a companion to his wife and a breadwinner for his children. He had to be loving, faithful, and attentive to his wife, and he had to work industriously to support his family and to educate his children.[32] In this regard, the *Louisianian* declared, "let it never be forgotten, the husband must . . . be everywhere the breadwinner. Children must always look to their father for most of the arms with which they face the world."[33] The family hearth, Negroes argued, was to be valued above all other things. Philandering and drink were so destructive to domestic tranquility that they were to be avoided at all costs.

The campaigns of Negro newspapers and ministers, combined with the effects of freedom, probably led to an increase in stability in the Negro family by the 1870s. Since the 1860 and 1870 manuscript censuses do not indicate family relationships, it is impossible to document this change statistically, though there were some observers who contended that the Negro family was growing stronger during this period. However, there are several problems involved in any attempt to verify this view. First of all, the Negro population in New Orleans was so large (57,617 in 1880) that it is difficult to analyze. Secondly, scholars have done so little sophisticated research on the family (and practically none on the Negro family) that a reliable set of answerable questions can be formulated only after much work.

The following conclusions about the nature of the Negro family are based on a statistical analysis of the 1880 census. For some questions an analysis was made of all Negro families in New Orleans. These included questions on the sex of heads of families, mixed marriages, size of family, employment, divorces, adopted children, unemployment, working wives, unwed mothers, illiteracy, property holdings, and age at marriage. In order to provide answers to questions which were ignored in the census, the annual reports of the Louisiana Board of Health and the state census of 1875 were also analyzed by sanitary or health districts. The statistics in many cases are not conclusive. There are too many limitations of the raw data.[34]

The data on heads of families is a case in point. It is impossible to tell, for instance, how many couples who told the census taker they were married were, in fact, legally married. In all censuses people tend to lie about this because of the stigma attached to illegal unions. Women lie about it much more frequently than men do; consequently, there are usually more women than men listed as married in any census. There is also a bias in the census toward listing males as heads of families. Because American society "naturally" accords males authority in the family, census takers often listed any male present in the family as the head regardless of his physical or mental condition. The most serious limitation of the data, however, is that changes in the family during this period cannot be documented. Because of differences in census-taking procedures in 1860, 1870, and 1880, the questions raised above cannot be answered for these different time periods.[35]

Since there were frequent complaints during the antebellum period about the large number of common-law marriages among whites in New Orleans, and since slave families were broken up so frequently that many blacks viewed serial monogamy as a social norm, any statistics on male-headed households may contain so many casual unions that they may be misleading. In other words, the presence of males in households in June 1880 reveals little about the durability of such unions. In a sense, of course, practically all statistics taken from the census are limited in accuracy to the time at which the count was made. Even so, an analysis of the 1880 manuscript census reveals a great deal about the nature of the Negro family during Reconstruction.

The underlying assumption of this analysis is that a male-headed family is a "stable" one and that if a majority of the families are headed by males, the institution is "patriarchal" in nature. Although this implies that male presence is being translated into male dominance, the concepts of "patriarchy" and "stability" in this study have been defined as "the presence of males" because this is easier to document than most other indices. And, given the norms of American culture, it is probably the most reliable index. Of course, in a strict sociological sense, the presence of an adult male is simply the first prerequisite in patriarchal families. Proof of patriarchy lies in who actually controls and makes decisions in the family.

The average family in the black community, then, was patriarchal, or male-dominated. Of the 12,452 Negro families listed in the census, 9,776 (78.5 percent) were headed by males in 1880. Negro families were generally very small; in 1880 the average size of the Negro family was 3.79 members. Because of poverty and lack of prenatal care, the birth rate of Negroes generally lagged behind that of whites. In 1870 there were 1,259 Negro births, or a rate of 73.51 per thousand Negro women aged 15 to 49. By 1880 the birth rate had fallen to 72.37 per thousand Negro women of child-bearing age. In contrast, the birth rate among white women of child-bearing age in 1870 was 98.33 per thousand; in 1880 it was 85.56 per thousand. In spite of the low birth rate and small size of the families, normal family relationships were severely strained by overcrowding. In 1880 the average number of people living in each of the 9,451 dwellings inhabited by Negro families was 6.0, or an average of 2.2 nonfamily members per family dwelling.

Poverty and unemployment placed a severe strain on the Negro family and probably tended to undermine the authority of the Negro male. In 1880 at least 1,760 (18 percent) of all married men were unemployed. Partly as a result of this, 2,187 of the 7,168 married Negro women (30.5 percent) were employed outside the home. Even with two breadwinners, few Negro families rose above the subsistence level. Whether poverty-stricken or not, however, most Negroes in New Orleans lived in families headed by males. Only 8,690 Negroes lived in the 2,666 female-headed families (only 18.3 percent of all Negroes living in families). Although unemployment was a serious problem, in most Negro families wives were dependent on their husbands for support; at least 69.5

Christmas Eve

percent of all married Negro women in New Orleans did not
go outside their homes to work. The economic dominance
of the Negro male is also revealed in statistics on the sex of
Negro property holders: male heads of Negro households
held 77.7 percent of all property possessed by Negro households in 1870.[36]

Statistical data are not infallible indices of patriarchy and
matriarchy. In spite of their economic dependence on their
husbands, Negro women may have had a strong voice in their
families. Dominance in interpersonal relations is rarely determined solely by economic or cultural factors. Inevitably, because of their mental or physical superiority, many wives,
black or white, are able to dominate their husbands. Several
factors, however, limited the ability of black women to do
this. The most important of these was the shortage of men
and the restriction of matrimonial opportunities for women.

Although the *Louisianian* declared in 1880 that "the
marriage business has become epidemic among us," the mar-

riage rate was apparently low in the Negro community.[37]
Among those Negroes fifteen to forty-five years of age, only
8.3 per thousand married in 1880, a rate of 4.21 per thousand persons. (In Massachusetts there were 17.42 marriages
per thousand persons in 1880.) Since statistics on marriages
were so haphazardly compiled, it is practically impossible to
make any definitive statements on the Negro marriage patterns. In 1877, the first year that the Board of Health collected
statistics on marriage, it reported that only 105 Negro and
363 white couples were married in that year. Two years later
there were 368 Negro and 1,151 white marriages reported;
in 1880, the figures were 243 for Negroes and 1,049 for
whites. The average age of the seventy-one Negro men listed
in the 1880 census as having married during the census year
was 28.3 years; that of the sixty-eight Negro women was 23.4
years (the average age of white males married in Michigan
in 1880 was 28 years and of white females, 23.2 years). Although the evidence is limited, the apparent cause of the low
marriage rate in the Negro community was the imbalance in
the sex ratio among blacks.[38]

Matrimonial opportunities for the New Orleans woman
were severely limited during Reconstruction. For the Negro
woman, the war simply exacerbated a situation which had
been intolerable before 1860. There were so many more Negro females than males in postwar New Orleans that for many
women there was no chance of marriage. In 1870 there were
only 65 Negro males to every 100 Negro females in the age
group 15 to 45. Even if Negro females aged 15 to 45 were
willing to marry Negro males aged 15 to 65, there still were
only 87 Negro males to every 100 females. The situation had
improved little by 1880; in that year the ratio was 69 Negro
males aged 15 to 45 to every 100 females aged 15 to 45; the
ratio of Negro males aged 15 to 65 to Negro females aged 15
to 45 was 92 to 100. Such disparities in the sex ratio often
prevented Negro women from dominating their husbands.[39]

There were so many more women than men in New Orleans that Negro women had to fight (almost literally) to
obtain husbands. It was unlikely that many of them would
risk alienating the males they had "captured" when they
realized that the chance of getting another one was minimal.
Even so, many of the Negro women were shrewd enough to
dominate their husbands without alienating them. Undoubtedly, many males had more of the illusion than the substance
of power in the family. Still, all of the measurable indices
point to a stable patriarchal family structure in the Negro
community.

There were several important general indications of Negro
family stability during this period. For example, there were
only a few divorcees and unwed mothers listed in the 1880
census. The low divorce rate can be explained partially by
the Negro's poverty and ignorance of the law. In all probability, however, the low divorce and illegitimacy rates reflected the high percentage of New Orleans Negroes who were
members of the Catholic church, which historically has always
tried to encourage family stability. At any rate, there were
only 110 Negro divorcees listed in the 1880 census. The rate
of illegitimacy was also apparently low; only 138 unwed Negro mothers appeared in the 1880 census. This could be
explained, of course, by the reluctance of women to report
their children as illegitimate. On the other hand, it may also
have reflected the actual rate of illegitimacy. For example,
in Michigan only 3.52 percent of all Negro children born in
1880 were illegitimate. Most of the unwed mothers in New
Orleans were relatively mature women; their average age at
the birth of their first child was 20.1 years.[40]

The most striking thing about the Negro family in New
Orleans was the variation in the percentage of males heading
the institution in different sections of the city. For example,
while males headed 70.3 percent of the Negro families in the
second health district, they headed 89.8 percent of the fami-

lies in the fifth district, a difference of 19.5 percentage points. These differences must be explained in order to understand the roots of Negro family stability.

Many variables associated with stability and instability in the family are inexplicable without a description of the districts. Districts one, two, and four were located in the most densely settled and oldest areas of New Orleans. According to the state census of 1875, these districts contained 798 (95.9 percent) of all boarding houses and hotels in New Orleans. In 1880 these districts had $102 million worth (75.5 percent) of the property and 6,303 (89.4 percent) of all stores and factories, and still contained a large proportion of all the tenements, boarding houses, and hotels in the city. Encompassing the central business section, these districts also had the highest population density of any section of the city: 127,665 people (62 percent of the total population), 30,764 of whom were Negroes (53 percent of the Negro population), lived in the first, second, and fourth districts, which had only about one sixth of the total amount of land in the city.

Although the third and sixth districts lay within the city proper, they differed strikingly from the others. Larger in area than the first, second, and fourth districts combined, they contained only 61,615 people (28 percent of the total population), 15,934 of whom were Negroes (27 percent of the total Negro population). Primarily residential in nature, much of the third and sixth districts was sparsely settled, and they contained within their boundaries a number of small truck farms and dairies.

Two districts, five and seven, were actually rural areas lying within the city limits. The fifth district, lying directly across the Mississippi River from the central business district, contained the old city of Algiers, many small farms, and a few plantations. Most of the Negroes in the fifth district, according to the New Orleans Board of Health, were "laborers on the small farms and plantations skirting the river; they occupy the small cabins of these places."[41] The seventh district, containing the old city of Carrollton, was similar in makeup to the fifth. These districts were large and sparsely settled. They had the lowest percentage of foreign-born inhabitants; the highest percentage of Negroes in their total population; only thirty-nine stores, factories, boarding houses, and hotels; and the lowest crime rate in the city.

Several factors usually associated with Negro family stability seem not to have been important in New Orleans when they are analyzed by districts. Factors such as illiteracy, unemployment, and the percentage of skilled Negro workers were more closely related to location in the city than to family stability. At first glance there appears to be an almost perfect correlation between these factors and the percentage of male-headed households in a district, but in all probability the correlations are spurious. High rates of literacy, employment, and skilled occupations are features of city life, whereas there are usually higher rates of illiteracy, seasonal unemployment (or underemployment), and fewer skilled jobs in the countryside. While the figures on unemployment and skilled occupations seem to challenge some traditional views on the relationship between economic conditions and family stability, they can be explained by looking at the districts. The fifth district had the highest rate of unemployment (55 percent) and yet had the highest percentage of male heads of families. Since this was an agricultural district, where few families had to pay rent and most had garden plots, seasonal unemployment of the males did not represent as much of a burden on the family as it did in the central city.[42]

There are only a few factors which seem to have been closely related to family stability. For instance, the statistics on the sex ratios of Negroes over twenty-one years of age in the 1877 Board of Health report for three districts suggest that there was a correlation between the sex ratio and the percentage of black male-headed families if the three-year interval and the changes in population between 1877 and 1880 are discounted. Both the percentage of male-headed families and the number of Negro males to every 100 females varied widely from one district to another. While in the second and

A Father's Guidance

fourth districts the number of males to every 100 females
was low (72 and 60, respectively), the number in the seventh
(84) was high. The correlation between the sex ratio and
male-headed families appears to be high, for the districts with
the lowest male-to-female ratio also had the lowest percentage
of male-headed families: the second district (70.3), and the
fourth (76.4).

On the other hand, there was no correlation between
Negro family stability and the number of mixed marriages
per thousand of the total population. The districts with the
highest mixed-marriage rates were district two (2 mixed marriages per thousand), three (1 per thousand), five (1 per
thousand), and seven (1 per thousand). There was, however,
considerable variation in the percentage of male-headed families in these districts, with the second, third, fifth, and seventh
districts having 70.3, 82.2, 81.4, and 87.9 percent male-
headed families respectively. The districts with the lowest
rates of mixed marriages per thousand persons, the first (0.5),
fourth (0.2), and sixth (0.4), had 77.0, 76.4, and 81.4 percent of their Negro families headed by males.

There was also little relationship between stability in the
white families and stability in Negro families. In four of the

Entertaining the Family

districts the percentage of male-headed white and Negro families was about equal; there was only 0.7 to 3.7 percentage points difference between the frequency of Negro and white male-headed families in the first, third, fourth, and fifth districts. In the other districts, however, the correlation was not high; there was a difference of 8.4 to 13.1 points in the percentage of Negro and white male-headed families in the second, sixth, and seventh districts.[43]

The relationship between the sex ratio among whites and family stability among Negroes was apparently close, according to statistics for three districts in the Board of Health report for 1877. As the number of white males to every 100 white females over the age of twenty-one decreased, the percentage of male-headed Negro families also declined. The correlation between these two factors is almost perfect. While the seventh, fourth, and second districts had 94, 80, and 50 white males to every 100 white females over twenty-one, they had 87.9, 76.4, and 70.3 percent male-headed Negro families respectively. Two conclusions can be drawn from these statistics. First, since white women had so few white males to marry, many of the women may have established common-law unions or irregular alliances with Negro men, thus undermining Negro family stability (there is considerable evidence in the census that this was true, especially for the second district). Second, this pattern may have emerged as a result of the imbalance in the sex ratio in the total population: the number of males to every 100 females over twenty-one were 88, 75, and 57 in the seventh, fourth, and second districts respectively. In other words, the most important factor in the lack of Negro family stability was probably the scarcity of black males in these districts (the sex ratio of Negroes followed the same pattern as that of whites).

Slavery also apparently affected the development of stability in the Negro family. The districts with the lowest percentage of male heads of families in 1880 (districts one, two, and four) had had the highest percentage of slaves in the Negro population in 1860, with 79, 49, and 81 percent respectively. By contrast, the third district, with only 28 percent of the Negro population as slaves in 1860, had from 5.2 to 11.9 percentage points more male-headed families than the other districts. The sexual immorality and broken families which had been the slave's lot in the antebellum period apparently had left too heavy a burden to overcome in just twenty years. The traditions of the free Negro, on the other hand, apparently encouraged the growth of Negro family stability.[44]

Geographical propinquity to the center of the city was one of the most important causal factors in the stability or instability of the Negro family. The three districts in the center of the city, the first, second, and fourth, ranked higher on almost every index of Negro family instability. The high population density in these districts contributed to this. For example, although the average size of the Negro family in the first, second, and fourth districts was 3.3, 3.9, and 3.7 respectively, there were actually 6.9, 7.0, and 5.4 persons in the average Negro family dwelling in these districts. The only other district where the average number of people living in the Negro family dwelling was close to that in these three districts was the third district (5.6). In this district, however, there were only 1.4 nonfamily inhabitants per family dwelling, while there were 3.0, 3.1, and 1.7 in the first, second, and fourth districts respectively.[45]

The generally disorganized state of social life in the central city further affected the stability of the Negro family. A large percentage of the population in these districts consisted of "floaters": sailors, fishermen, immigrants, and steamboatmen. In 1875 the sailors, fishermen, and immigrants in these districts constituted 89.4, 92.6, and 68.4 percent, respectively, of their total population in the city. To complicate matters even more, most of the ruralites who came to New Orleans between 1860 and 1880 settled in the districts in the inner city. Frequently crowded into tenements near the river, they were forced to move whenever the Mississippi overflowed. As a result of a series of disastrous overflows in the first and second districts between 1870 and 1875, more than 7,525 of the people residing in these districts in 1870 had moved by 1875. Five years later all of these people had either returned or been replaced by new migrants: there were 2,761 more people in the first and second districts in 1880 than there had been in 1870. This rapid turnover in the population must have loosened the bonds of social control and further hampered the development of family unity.

Without roots in New Orleans, many transient males often entered into casual, fleeting unions with native women and then deserted them. The population in this area was so unstable, had such loose morals, and was so dense that the Negro families located in it were deeply affected by sexual immorality, casual matings, and desertions. The state of morals in this area was indicated clearly in the police records. For instance, most of the 3,606 prostitutes incarcerated in 1872 were arrested in the first, second, and fourth districts. In fact, 6,690 of the 8,703 women imprisoned in 1872 were arrested in these districts. This area also accounted for the largest proportion of all criminal acts committed in the city. Most of the houses of prostitution, gambling dens, saloons, and dance halls were located in districts one, two, and four. The impact of this social disorganization on the Negro family was apparent in several statistical indices. The first, second, and fourth districts had 86.2 percent of all unwed Negro mothers, 58.5 percent of all orphans, and 60.9 percent of all Negro divorcees in the city in 1880.[46]

Other reports further indicate how the Negro family in these districts was caught up in the matrix of crime. The 1872 report of the metropolitan police shows that 66.8 percent of all arrests in the city occurred in the first, third, and fourth precincts, which covered the first and second districts. The superintendent of police reported that the residents of the third and fourth precincts were "composed of all nationalities, and much of the turbulent law-defying portion of the community is to be found within . . . [their] limits." His description of the fourth precinct was applicable to much of the first, second, and fourth districts:

A large number of lewd and abandoned women, of every grade of depravity, from the occupants of palatial residents to the totally abandoned creatures, who, clothed in rags, find shelter in some vile hovel unfitted for a human habitation, and who prey upon the equally depraved of the opposite sex, with whom they come in contact. Women of this class necessarily draw around them vicious and disreputable men, who are equally with them, lost to all sense of shame and self-respect, who make night hideous with their drunken orgies, and annoy the respectable residents of the neighborhood with their indecent behavior.[47]

Unfortunately, more than half of the Negro families in New Orleans resided in the three districts in the center of the city. In 1880 there were 7,388 Negro families, 59.3 percent of the total number, living in districts one, two, and four. The conditions in these districts had a depressing effect on the percentage of male-headed families in the Negro community. While males headed 84.3 percent of the Negro families in the outlying districts, they headed only 74.5 percent of those families residing in the center of the city. Generally this same pattern prevailed among whites, but apparently the central city was not as destructive to their family life as it was to that of Negroes. In 1880 there was only a difference of 2.9 points in the percentage of males heading white families in the center of the city and those heading families in the outlying districts. Among Negroes, however, there was a difference of 9.8 percentage points. This difference can be explained by several factors. First of all, most of the whites in New Orleans were accustomed to city living or at least to the style of life in New Orleans, while more than half of the blacks were not. In the second place, there was a large difference in the percentage of blacks and whites who migrated to the districts in the inner city after the war. While there was a 3 percent decrease in the white population in these districts between 1860 and 1880, there was a phenomenal 91 percent increase in the Negro population during that period. Since most of the black newcomers were apparently former slaves from the outlying parishes, they had to try to adjust to urban life at the same time that they attempted to learn how to survive in freedom. None of the whites had this double burden.

The most important cause of Negro family disorganization during Reconstruction, however, was the high rate of mortality among Negro males. In the age group 15 to 44, the death rate of Negro females was 15.93 per thousand in 1880; of Negro males, 26.66, or an excess of 10.73 deaths per thousand. Moreover, the excess of deaths of Negro males over females increased at almost every age stratum. Between the ages of 15 and 54, there were 16.48 Negro female deaths per thousand and 30.10 Negro male deaths, an excess of 13.62 deaths per thousand Negro males. The death rates between the ages of 15 and 64 were 18.21 for Negro females and 29.98 for Negro males, an excess of 11.77 deaths per thousand Negro males. Between the ages of 20 and 54, there was an excess of 14.87 deaths per thousand Negro males, and between the ages of 20 and 64 there was an excess of 14.23 deaths per thousand Negro males. Although the same pattern of increasing sex differentials in death rates at each age stratum prevailed among whites in New Orleans, it was not as serious as among blacks. While the excess of deaths per thousand of black males over black females varied from 10.73 to 14.87, the excess of deaths per thousand of white males over white females varied from only 5.48 to 8.90 in different age strata.

The impact which the sex differential in the mortality rate made on the Negro family is revealed clearly in the percentage of widows among the female heads of families: 81.5 percent of these family heads were widows. In the fifth district 92.5 percent of the female heads of families were widows. If the Negro family is analyzed without counting the families headed by widows, the percentage of male-headed families rises from 78.5 to 95.1 percent. Even in the first, second, and fourth districts, the percentage of male-headed families rises dramatically from 77, 70.3, and 76.4 to 93.5, 91.7, and 95.3 percent respectively. In the third, fifth, sixth, and seventh districts the percentage of male-headed families increases to 97.8, 99.1, 96.2, and 97.6 percent respectively. In short, if 95.1 percent of the Negro families were headed by males when widows were excluded, then poverty, unemployment, desertion, divorce, and illegitimacy could only have caused 4.9 percent of the families to be headed by females.[48]

In spite of the fact that there was a much greater sex differential in the Negro than in the white death rate, and despite the social problems encountered in the inner city, by 1880 the Negro family was apparently as stable as the white family in New Orleans. A comparison of Negro families with a sample of 5,819 white families revealed little difference between them. While 78.5 percent of the Negro families were headed by males, 79.8 percent of the white families were headed by males, a difference of only 1.3 percentage points. And in three of the seven health districts in New Orleans (third, fifth, and seventh) the percentage of Negro males heading families was larger than that of white males by 0.7 to 13.1 percentage points.[49]

All the evidence suggests that the Negro family, only fifteen years removed from slavery, was remarkably strong by 1880. The only threat (and a serious one) to family stability was the unhealthy condition of the Negro population, espe-

cially the Negro male. The Negro community had so completely adopted nineteenth-century attitudes toward the family
that it was able to overcome much of slavery's legacy of immorality and family disorganization. Apparently the campaign
of Negro ministers, newspaper editors, politicians, and white
missionaries impressed upon the minds of most Negroes the
importance of marriage and family life. The fact that Negroes
could enter a number of trades and earn enough to support
their families must have helped to maintain family unity.
Considering the Negro male's conception of the family and of
women in conjunction with the statistics on male-headed
households, the almost inescapable conclusion is that the
Negro family in New Orleans during Reconstruction was
patriarchal in nature. This was true in spite of the excess of
females over males, a high unemployment rate among Negro
males, and the fact that a majority of Negroes lived in the
most densely populated, crime-ridden, and socially disorganized section of the city. Even though most Negroes lived in
the center of the city, the absence of residential segregation
prevented them from being permanently trapped in it and
subjected to all of the liabilities this entailed. Relatively open
housing, memories of the denial of opportunities for stable
family life during slavery, concerted drives to promote family
stability, and the economic opportunities resulting from weak
labor unions led to a relatively stable patriarchal Negro
family in New Orleans during Reconstruction.

Schools, Colleges, and Intellectual Life

5

Largely debarred from the schoolhouse as slaves, and perceiving that all of their efforts at political, economic, social, and racial progress were crippled by widespread illiteracy, New Orleans Negroes invested education with an almost magical quality. Although a few of them had learned to read before the Civil War, the overwhelming majority of the Negroes in New Orleans during this period were illiterate. For example, 24,884 of the 40,242 blacks over ten years of age in the city in 1870 could not read or write, an illiteracy rate of 61.8 percent; only 6.5 percent of the whites were illiterate. According to the 1875 state census, 37,708 of the 57,647 Negroes in the city could not read or write, an illiteracy rate of roughly 65 percent. The rate of illiteracy among Negroes, while high, was lower than the rates in Russia (91 percent), Poland (91 percent), Greece (83 percent), Spain (80 percent), and Italy (73 percent) in 1880. The Negro's problem was compounded, however, by his living among a population which was highly literate.[1]

By establishing private schools, fighting successfully first for admission to the public schools and then for integrated education, and by supporting the establishment of three colleges, Negroes in New Orleans inaugurated their long campaign to eradicate illiteracy from the black community. However, slavery had left them with such a heavy burden of ignorance, there was so much opposition among whites to educating Negroes, and there was so much corruption in the state government, that they had relatively little success in this area.

Most blacks realized that ignorance was the greatest threat to their freedom. They felt they had no chance of competing successfully against whites so long as Negroes had a disproportionately small share of the education in the community.[2] Because of such views, asserted journalist Charles Nordhoff, New Orleans Negroes were "almost universally . . . anxious to send their children to school."[3]

As a result of their anxiety, Negroes began establishing small private schools in 1862. At first most of the new private schools were inadequately financed and haphazardly run. Later, New Orleans Negroes made several attempts to organize their private schools on a systematic basis. Their most ambitious effort was the Louisiana Educational Relief Association, formed in July 1866 by the Reverend John Turner, James Lewis, and J. Willis Menard. Charging monthly dues of $.25, the association established or supported a number of church schools in 1866 and 1867. One of these, in the St. James A. M. E. Church, had 125 indigent pupils in 1867.[4] The most famous Negro private school was the Institution des Orphelins built in 1846 from money left by Madame Bernard Couvent. The instructors in the school were among the best in the city and included Armand Lanusse, a famous Negro poet; Joanni Questy, Negro linguist, poet, novelist and contributor to *Album Littéraire* and the New Orleans *Tribune*; and Adolphe Duhart, a Negro dramatist. Catering to the upper-class free Negroes, the school offered courses in French and Spanish and concentrated on the works of Fontaine, Boileau, Fénelon, Racine, and Corneille. A few other small private schools offered education for Negroes, and by 1867 there were 793 pupils studying in four schools. After this date private schools decreased in importance, and the only other permanent schools were the three founded in the 1870s by the Third Order of Mount Carmel and the Sisters of the Holy Family.[5]

Generally speaking, only the wealthy free Negroes could afford to send their children to private schools. If the majority of the freedmen had been forced to pay for the education of their children, an overwhelming majority of them would have remained in ignorance. Fortunately, a number of white abolitionists were anxious to educate the recently freed slaves. Feeling that Louisiana blacks were "more intelligent" than those they had seen in South Carolina, men of this stripe contended that Northerners could thoroughly change Louisiana society by educating them.[6] Lieutenant Edwin M. Wheelock declared that the education of the Negro would lead to "a general resurrection of buried mind through the wasted South. Our military expeditions do the pioneer work of blasting the rock and felling the forest. Education follows to sow the grain and raise the golden harvest. . . . Behind the advancing lines of our forces follows the small pacific army of teachers and civilizers, and the schoolhouse takes the place of the whipping post and scourge."[7]

The "pacific army" began marching into New Orleans in June of 1863 when Thomas Conway and the Reverend George Hepworth began urging Nathaniel Banks to establish the Board of Education for the Freedmen to complement his labor system. In September 1863, Union officials, acting upon the request of Negroes in the city, appropriated $3,000 for the education of about 250 indigent children. After Banks authorized the establishment of Negro schools in October 1863, officials began systematically to educate Negroes in New Orleans. By December 1864 there were 54 teachers and 3,220 Negro students in school in the city.[8] To insure a high level of performance by the teachers, the board of education inspected the schools every week and also established a normal school.[9]

At first the teachers faced a severe problem in trying to instruct students who had never seen the inside of a schoolroom before. The problem was also compounded by overcrowding; the teachers simply had too many students to maintain discipline. In March 1864, for example, there was an average of 84.6 pupils per teacher. Ranging in age from six to eighteen and often including a few adults, the students were frequently disorderly. A number of teachers resorted to the traditional nineteenth-century disciplinary device, the rod, to maintain order in their classrooms. Generally, however, the pupils were so interested in obtaining an education that the threat of exclusion was more effective than the rod in maintaining discipline.[10] Edwin Wheelock, chairman of the Board of Education for the Freedmen, declared on March 19, 1864, that in the Negro schools "no severity of discipline is used or required; the threat of exclusion from the privileges of instruction being sufficient to tame the most mounting spirit."[11]

After their initial restlessness, the Negroes became "eager pupils, all alive to the importance of education."[12] While at first they were deficient in memory and reflective powers, they were very perceptive and, according to Wheelock, displayed "great eagerness for knowledge and facility of acquisition."[13] Mortimer A. Warren, Yale graduate and superintendent of Freedmen's Bureau schools in New Orleans, concurred. He asserted in 1865, "I have never witnessed such progress among white children, or those of any other color, as I daily see in the schools under my charge. . . . A thirst for knowledge has been kindled in young and old which will not soon die out. It is talked of at home, it is preached from the pulpit, it is advocated at the rostrum."[14]

Because of the New Orleans climate and the board of education was organized long before most freedmen aid societies, few Northern teachers came to New Orleans.[15] Those who came received transportation and rations from the Army and their salaries from Northern freedmen's aid associations. One of the most important of the Northern agencies was the American Missionary Association, which worked closely with the board of education. By December 1864 the A. M. A. had distributed more than 7,500 Bibles to the freedmen and was supporting seven teachers in schools with 600 students and a Sunday school with 950 students. The National Freedmen's Relief Association supported six teachers and spent thousands of dollars for books, supplies, clothing, Sabbath schools, and orphanages in Louisiana from 1865 to 1866. By May 1866 the New York branch of the American Freedmen's and Union

Commission had opened two schools in New Orleans with a total of 61 pupils and 2 teachers. Association schools, never very strong in Louisiana, declined rapidly after the war. By May 1867 there were only 8 association schools in New Orleans containing 340 students.[16]

After its organization in 1865, the Freedmen's Bureau took control of the Negro schools. The schools were expensive: between April 1864 and September 1865 officials received $249,588 from the Quartermaster Corps and the Corps D'Afrique fund to support the schools. The bureau itself spent $83,577 to operate Negro schools in Louisiana from August to November 1865. In an effort to reduce expenses, the bureau closed all the free schools in New Orleans and inaugurated a tuition system in February 1866. The effect of this change was catastrophic: the number of schools in Orleans parish declined from nineteen in October 1865 to ten in February 1866; the number of students enrolled declined from 5,330 in December 1865 to 1,359 in February 1866. Private schools obviously represented a heavy financial burden for most Negro parents: between July 1866 and July 1867 they paid $8,369 in tuition, or an average of $597 per month.[17] Negroes received little sympathy from whites over their financial plight.

Initially there was great opposition from most whites to the "education of 'niggers'" and especially to being taxed for the support of the Negro schools in New Orleans; a few school houses were apparently destroyed by incendiaries, and white women who taught blacks bore a heavy "load of calumny, sneers, and social proscription." Virulent opposition soon gave way, however, to studied indifference or moderate enthusiasm. Even so, most whites felt that Negroes themselves should pay for their education; consequently, from 1862 to 1867 the city officials refused to appropriate any money for Negro schools in New Orleans.[18]

By 1867 the Negro schools were in desperate shape. Of 23,183 Negroes between the ages of six and eighteen in New Orleans, only 2,713 were in school in May 1867. Responding to pressure from blacks and military officers, the city council appropriated $60,000 for Negro schools in July 1867, but Mayor Edward Heath vetoed the bill because the appropriation was too small and because there were no blacks on the school board. The council then passed the bill over the Mayor's veto. In August a new city council (with Negroes on it) dismissed the school board and postponed the opening of schools until the new board of education began organizing separate Negro schools. By December 1867 there were about 5,000 Negro students in school.[19]

Almost from the beginning of Reconstruction, Negroes complained about segregated schools. As property holders they contended that a dual school system would be too expensive to maintain. The most important reason for their opposition to segregated schools, however, was the feeling that such schools were degrading to blacks, that they fastened a badge of inferiority on Negro children.[20] Complaining that separate schools made an "odious discrimination" against Negroes, the *Tribune* asserted, "Separation is not equality. The very assignment of schools to certain children on the ground of color, is a distinction violative of the first principles of equality."[21] Closely allied with the idea that separate schools were degrading was the fear that they would perpetuate caste feelings in the community and postpone the day when equal rights would be granted to Negroes.[22]

The best mechanism, many blacks argued, for ending prejudice among whites was integrated schools. If blacks and whites were educated together, they would learn to respect each other. Robert H. Isabelle, representative from New Orleans, told his colleagues in the state legislature, "I want the children of the State educated together. I want to see them play together; to be amalgamated [Laughter]. I want them to play together, to study together; and when they grow up to be men they will love each other, and be ready, if any force comes against the flag of the United States, to take up arms and defend it together."[23]

Most whites were violently opposed to integrated schools. The public schools were established by whites and belonged, by right, they said, to them exclusively. It was enough that whites were magnanimous enough to pay for the education of blacks, without having all their principles of justice violated by mixing black and white students. When Negroes demanded mixed schools, they were stepping beyond guarantees of political equality to demands for social equality.

Integrated schools, whites felt, would humiliate them because such schools represented an admission of the Negro's equality. Social equality could not be enforced by legislation; God had made the two races different, and they were destined to remain separate in all institutions and walks of life. Equality was a utopian dream; there had never been social equality in human societies. Consequently, integrated schools violated divine, human, and natural laws.[24] A mass meeting of New Orleans whites declared in September 1875 that "the compulsory admixture of children of all races, color and condition in the schools, in the same rooms and on the same benches, is opposed to the principles of humanity, repugnant to the instincts of both races, and is not required by any provision of the laws or constitution of this State."[25] Segregated schools were a recognition of the superiority of the white race; mixed schools might undermine this superiority. One of the most prominent defendants of white supremacy during this period was Robert Mills Lusher, state superintendent of schools. In his diaries, public pronouncements, and annual reports, Lusher continuously argued that all-white schools should be preserved as a bastion of white supremacy. Writing about his feelings during Reconstruction in 1899, Lusher recalled that he had contended that white pupils should be "properly prepared to maintain the Supremacy of the white race."[26]

It was better, whites contended, for Negroes to recognize the implacable prejudice of the "ruling white race of the world." No law could change this prejudice. Any attempt to integrate the schools would end in the exclusion of blacks from all schools: there would either be separate schools or no schools at all, for if the public schools were integrated, whites would reject public education and send their children to private schools.[27]

Many whites alleged that black children, degraded, semi-barbaric, and immoral, would have an injurious effect on their children and would teach them vicious habits if schools were integrated. A "Mechanic" wrote that he objected to integrated schools, saying, "especially do I object that my daughters be exposed to the contaminating influence of girls and women of that race, who are notorious as being in great part destitute of chastity. . . . I do most earnestly protest against placing my sons and my girls in daily contact with such associates. . . . you know that it is notorious that there is no public sentiment among negroes attaching disgrace and obloquy to theft or immorality."[28]

Often disclaiming any racial prejudice, many whites argued that their children should not be "sacrificed" to improve Negro children. If this were attempted in integrated schools with ignorant and filthy black children, white children would suffer. One citizen, who signed his letter "Fair Play," spoke for many whites when he opposed integrated schools and asserted that if the Negro's "children have bad habits—have been brought up in filth and ignorance—if they are accustomed to do and speak what is wrong—I do not wish that my children should be compelled to sit by their side and to call them equals. It may be good for them but it is not good for my children."[29]

Many whites opposed integrated schools because they feared that they would increase racial animosities and inter-racial clashes between black and white youths. Besides, the Negro child would be degraded by the white child conscious of and determined to assert his superiority. A favorite tactic of the whites was to insist that most blacks opposed integrated schools—it was only the self-serving politicians, wild-eyed schemers, and especially the mulattoes who favored integrated schools. The *Times* gave a typical assessment of the proponents of integrated schools on September 3, 1867, when it declared that they were "a selfish set of adventurers" and "a puffed-up tribe of mulattoes and quadroons who, proud of the Caucasian blood which circulates by indirection through their veins, think their children too good to go to 'nigger schools' and set up claims to an equality, the advantages of which would be altogether on their side."

The blacks gave several stock answers to the critics of integrated schools. To those who claimed integration was impossible, they pointed to the integrated schools of Boston, Massachusetts, and Providence, Rhode Island; to those who said such a step was too radical, they asserted that every progressive reform of society was greeted initially with this cry; to those who contended that innocent children should not be forced to try to solve problems their parents had not solved, they asserted that the argument was not only specious, but it also ignored the changes which had occurred in New Orleans' society. Was a child any better than his parents, who sat on juries and the same streetcars with blacks in spite of their deeply ingrained prejudices? Certainly it would be easier for white children, in whom prejudice was yet a small kernel, to attend schools with blacks. If, Negroes asserted, white parents were too prejudiced to send their children to integrated schools, then they should send them to all-white private schools and pay for the privilege of indulging their prejudices.

Given the strong, implacable, and sometimes violent opposition of a majority of the whites to integrated schools, the effort to integrate New Orleans schools would have failed completely had it not been for the rather sizable minority of whites who either were indifferent or had little opposition to sending their children to "mixed" schools. George Washington Cable, the famous Louisiana writer, was the most prominent New Orleans white who rejected the attitudes of most of his fellows. Contending, in several letters to New Orleans newspapers, that not all Negroes were inferior to whites, Cable argued that "the school room neither requires nor induces social equality." Even if Negroes were inferior to whites, the latter had a responsibility to lift the former: "Yes, the black race is inferior to the white. The Almighty has established inequality as a principle in nature. But the lesson it teaches is magnanimity, not scorn." Besides, there was not as much white antipathy to contact with blacks as many of the whites contended; it was illogical for them to oppose integrated schools when their children had been nursed by Negro women. The white children, Cable argued, passed "from infancy to and through the impressible and educable years of childhood still in the nurse's care and frequently in company with the nurse's children."[30] The opposition was also illogical in light of the successful integration of other areas of life in the city.

Finally inaugurated in the autumn of 1869, the system of integrated schools was crippled by opposition from white parents, teachers, students, politicians, newspapers, the White League, and indifferent officials. The most serious obstacle to integration of the schools was the almost unanimous opposition of the white newspapers in the city. Throughout the period from 1869 to 1877, journalists urged whites to resist this step and to boycott the public schools, and they made every effort to keep opposition at a fever pitch. Even violence was almost condoned by many of the newspapers, especially the *Bulletin*. At first many whites applauded the tirades of the *Bulletin* and sent their children to private schools established as alternatives to the mixed schools. Supported by the Catholic, Presbyterian, Episcopalian, and other denominations, by the Peabody fund, and by groups of private individuals, these schools initially attracted thousands of New Orleans whites. In a few years, however, many white parents discovered that such schools were too expensive, and so sent their children back to the public schools.

Many whites expressed their opposition to integrated schools in a violent manner; they threatened to assassinate Thomas W. Conway, the state superintendent who first established the integrated system; and sometimes they attacked school board members who supported Conway's policy.[31] The first concerted effort to abolish integrated schools began in

December 1874. During that month the New Orleans branch of the White League decided on a uniform plan to end integrated schools and urged white students to boycott schools to which blacks had been admitted and to remove them forcibly from their classrooms. The plan was put into operation on December 14, 1874, at the Upper Girls High School, when the white students threatened to boycott graduation and classes unless Negroes were barred from the school. After city superintendent C. W. Boothby met with the students, he was attacked by a band of white men for "insulting" the girls and was forced to sign a pledge opposing integrated schools. Shortly after the demonstration at the Girls High School, a group of white students forced Negro students to leave the Boys High School, and from December 16th to the 19th hundreds of white boys roamed the streets, entered various schools, and expelled black students. After armed Negro parents began marching to the schools to protect their children, and after they fought pitched battles with the boys and their coadjutors, the school board met and closed the schools on December 20th.[32]

Shaken by the threat to law and order posed by the White League outrages, white officials counselled against a repetition of such mob rule, and the schools opened amid relative calm early in January 1875. Things continued this way until September 1875, when whites learned that P. B. S. Pinchback had engineered the appointment of a Negro, E. J. Edmunds, as professor of mathematics at the Central High School for boys. A brilliant graduate of a school in Paris, Edmunds met stiff opposition to his appointment. While the junior class accepted Edmund's tutelage, the eleven senior boys, considering it an insult to be taught by a black man, left the school. When Edmunds left the school at the end of the day, one of the white students accosted him and "began a wordy attack upon him, upbraiding him for having forced himself into the school, declaring that he was nothing but a 'nigger' and otherwise visiting his pent up wrath upon the teacher." After a large crowd of Negroes gathered and urged Edmunds to "kill the man," the student prudently withdrew.[33] The whites held a mass meeting to protest the appointment of Edmunds, and the newspapers castigated Pinchback for his "mischievous" move. But Pinchback stuck to his position that Edmunds was a highly qualified teacher and that if white leaders were sincere in their desire for equality for Negroes they could not oppose his appointment. After the initial excitement, Edmunds was able to settle down quietly to his teaching duties, and he experienced no more interruptions.[34]

The issue of integrated schools involved so much passion and so many difficulties that it is almost impossible to determine how extensive mixed schools were. The difficulties are increased by the inconsistent policies of both the proponents and opponents of integrated schools and because many Negro pupils could and did pass for white. While there were many Negro children who attended "white" schools undisturbed because they were so nearly white themselves, many others were discouraged by the threats of violence or the attitudes of teachers. In one instance in 1870 a Negro boy seeking admission to a white school was beaten so brutally by a white teacher that it was feared he might "be disfigured for life."[35]

In their anxiety over the threat of violence from the whites, many of the school board officials did not push for systematic desegregation of the schools. In effect, the officials left desegregation of the schools up to individual Negro parents. As a result of this, probably a majority of the parents took the easier path of sending their children to Negro schools. The *Republican* asserted that in spite of the school law, "few colored children have availed themselves of it where respectable schools have been furnished them by themselves."[36] The reticence of many black parents and the overly cautious policy of school board officials prevented extensive integration. The *Louisianian* charged that Republican officials, in regard to the school law, had "flagrantly ignored it . . . because they were base hypocrites and not in sympathy with the people whose cause they pretended to espouse." One of these officials, P. B.

S. Pinchback, asserted in 1875 that "we have, in violation of our solemn obligation, refrained to a large extent from forcibly attempting to mix the schools, the result of which is that today a majority of the schools are unmixed."[37]

Remarkably, in spite of lukewarm official support and violent opposition in some quarters, there were several instances of peaceful integration.[38] The principal of Bienville School, where one-third of the children were Negroes, reported in 1872 that it was "but seldom that the usual peace and good order of the school are disturbed by any exhibitions of prejudice on account of race or color. Both classes are equally ready and desirous to learn, and . . . impartial justice [is] meted out to all."[39] There were a number of integrated schools of this character which operated smoothly until "outsiders" interfered. For instance, before the December 1874 outbreak at the Upper Girls High School, a number of Negroes had attended the school and Lower Girls High undisturbed for several years; there were twenty-eight attending the former school in December 1874.

In many of the integrated schools order was maintained only because of the strictness of the teachers and the excellent character of many of the Negro students, a number of whom had transferred from Straight University's elementary school. The ability of the black students sometimes softened prejudices somewhat. For example, on May 8, 1875, the *Louisianian* observed that there were "several colored pupils in quiet attendance at our High Schools. . . . The diligent observance of scholastic duties, and excellence and ability in recitation and deportment of the indubitably colored boys and girls have done much to disarm the foolish opposition to their attendance." At the Mason school three Negro boys who eventually attended Straight University were at the head of their classes in grammar and arithmetic.

While the sterling performances of some black pupils may have won them the respect of their white classmates, the rod was generally more important in preventing conflict between the two groups. Most of the integrated schools were probably as tense as the one Cable visited on Royal Street which, he declared,

suffered much internal unrest. Many a word was spoken
that stung like a club, many a smile stung like a whiplash,
many a glance stabbed like a knife; even in the midst of
recitations a wounded one would sometimes break into sobs
or silent tears while the aggressor crimsoned and palpitated
with the proud indignation of the master caste. The teachers
met all such by-play with prompt, impartial repression and
concentration upon the appointed duties of the hour. . . .
   Not all who bore the tincture of the despised race suffered
alike. Some were fierce and sturdy, and played a savage
tit-for-tit. Some were insensible. A few bore themselves
inflexibly by dint of sheer nerve; while many, generally much
more white than black, quivered and winced continually
under the contumely that fell, they felt, with peculiar injustice
and cruelty upon them.[40]

In spite of such problems, many of the schools had a high percentage of Negro students. From one-sixth to one-third of the students in the Fillmore, Claiborne, Bienville, and Fisk schools were Negroes. A significant number also attended Upper Girls High, Mason, Ramparts, and Bayou Road schools. Apparently the only schools with as many as one hundred Negro students were Bienville (105) and Fillmore (100) boys schools.

Contemporary estimates of the extent of integration vary widely.[41] The *Louisianian* declared on May 25, 1871, that integrated schools were "accomplished facts, which in their very nature are irreversible." In June 1871 Conway asserted that in regard to integrated schools, "The principal [sic] involved has been rigidly enforced."[42] A year later he asserted that "nearly one-half the free schools of New Orleans contain white and colored pupils."[43] Conway claimed in 1873 that "there were colored pupils in every school in New Orleans."[44] When a Northern reporter, Eugene Lawrence, visited the city in 1875, he found that one-third of the public schools in the

city were integrated. Corroborating evidence for these estimates appeared in the editorials of the *Bulletin*. Although
obviously intended to frighten white parents, there may have
been some truth in the *Bulletin*'s claim on January 4, 1871,
that "there is not a single white school in this city, we would
venture to say, that does not contain at least one colored
child." On October 22, 1874, the *Bulletin* reiterated the
charge: "The evil has grown upon us so insidiously, and the
School Board has managed the introduction of negroes into
the schools so ingeniously, that only those who have occasion
to visit them know of the large number of Negroes who to-day
sit in the same rooms with the whites."

The best estimate of the number of Negro children who
studied annually in integrated schools is that of historian
Louis Harlan. After a painstaking check of all the available
sources, Harlan concluded that from 500 to 1000 Negroes
studied in integrated schools annually. The latter figure is
probably more nearly correct. Given the almost unanimous
opposition of white opinion-makers (teachers, ministers, and
journalists) to integration, the movement was remarkably
successful. With one thousand Negroes, or about one-fourth
of all blacks in the public schools, attending about one-half
of the predominantly white schools, large numbers of white
children came into intimate contact with Negro children on
terms of equality for the first time. For many this experience
softened their antipathies toward blacks. Others were unable
to rid themselves of the prejudices engrained in them by their
parents, and they used the experience to strengthen their
hatred of blacks, who they felt had humiliated them. The
greatest failure of the integration movement was that officials
were so cautious that the latter group of white students out-
numbered the former at the end of Reconstruction.[45]

Since the state constitution of 1868 barred discrimination
in schools and the school board did not generally report
statistics by race from 1868 to 1877, it is difficult to determine
how Negro pupils fared during this period. From the city
directories it appears that there were at least twenty-six

Negro public schools in existence at various times between 1868 and 1877. The largest number of Negro public schools in the city appeared in 1873 and again in 1880, when there were seventeen. There were also eleven Negro private schools in the city during this period, with the largest number appearing in 1875, when the board was practically penniless. In spite of the efforts of the Negroes who served on the school board between 1868 and 1880, a disproportionate number of Negro students were shunted off to old, dilapidated buildings.[46]

After the election of 1876 the quality of Negro schools declined as a result of the parsimony of the city officials and the school board's return to the pre-1868 system of segregated education. The school board claimed that it was providing "impartial" education to the Negro students in their separate schools. While this statement may have been an accurate reflection of intention, it was not in accord with the facts. At first glance it appears that Negroes had an equal chance with whites in the race for education. While blacks made up 23 percent of the school-age population, they constituted 25 percent of the student population in New Orleans public schools in 1879. Similarly, while only 28 percent of the whites of school age in 1880 were attending public schools in 1879, 33 percent of the Negroes were. It must be remembered, however, that a much larger percentage of the whites than blacks of school age were attending private schools. Consequently, probably more than 60 percent of the black children never attended any school. It is unlikely that as large a percentage of the whites of school age were unable to obtain an education.[47]

Higher education for Negroes in New Orleans, while limited, probably had more impact on the community than the haphazardly run public schools. The initial impetus for the establishment of institutions of higher learning grew out of the need to improve the quality of Negro teachers and ministers in the city. Dr. S. W. Rogers, the most learned Negro minister in the state, opened the first theology school in 1867. The first institution to train teachers, the Union Normal

Leland University, c. 1880

New Orleans University, c. 1880

School, was established by the Freedmen's Aid Society of the
Methodist Episcopal Church in 1868; two years later the society opened the Fenton Normal School. Despite repeated
appeals, the Peabody Fund did not begin supporting a normal
school for Negroes in New Orleans until 1877, with the official return to segregated education in Louisiana.[48]

The three Negro colleges established in New Orleans during Reconstruction—Straight, Leland, and New Orleans universities—were all supported by religious groups and initially
offered little more than a high school education. The first of
these institutions, Leland University, opened in 1869 after
receiving a $65,000 gift from Holbrook Chamberlain, a re-
tired New York shoe merchant. The Freedmen's Bureau also
appropriated $17,500 for the school, and the American Bap-
tist Home Mission Society gave $12,500. The Home Mission
Society gave annual appropriations to the institution and in
1874 gave $70,000 toward its support. When Chamberlain
died in 1883, he willed $100,000 to Leland. Located at
Chestnut Street and St. Charles Avenue across from Audubon
Park, the campus covered ten acres.

With tuition fees of $8.00 annually, Leland rarely had
more than 250 students enrolled at any point between 1869
and 1880. Small, underequipped, and inadequately financed,
Leland devoted more attention to elementary than to collegiate education; normally, 80 percent of the students were
enrolled in precollege classes. Perhaps it was just as well, for
as late as 1877 the college had only 825 books and 40 pamphlets in its library. Still, in spite of its shortcomings, Leland
provided some professional skills to the Negro community in
New Orleans.[49]

New Orleans University had a history similar to that of
Leland. Chartered in 1873, New Orleans grew out of the
Union Normal School, organized in 1869, Thomson's Biblical
Institute, and an academy in Bayou Têche. At first the campus was situated at 459 Camp Street, but a few years later it
was moved to a four-acre site on St. Charles Avenue near
the present location of Loyola and Tulane Universities and

Audubon Park. Incorporated with provisions for law and medical departments, the school, with I. S. Leavitt, A.M., as president, had 335 students the first year. Three Negroes, William G. Brown (state superintendent of education), James H. Ingraham, and the Reverend J. M. Vance, served on the fifteen-man board of trustees. Supported by the Methodist Episcopal Church, New Orleans University suffered from a lack of scientific equipment, a meager library, and limited finances. The law department never opened, and the medical department opened in 1886 with only a few trained physicians on its staff. By 1875 there were only 110 students attending the school, where four professors taught them ancient languages, natural science, English literature, and music.[50] New Orleans University was most noted for the quality of musical training it provided. It began early trying to preserve Negro spirituals, and by 1880 its "Original New Orleans University Singers" were famous for their renditions of such traditional songs as "The Gospel Train," "This Old-Time Religion," and "Swing Low, Sweet Chariot" and some of their own creations.[51]

The strongest institution for higher education among Negroes in New Orleans was Straight University. Chartered by the Louisiana state legislature in 1869, the school was named in honor of Seymour Straight, the white New Orleans produce merchant who donated the original land for the school. Aided by $20,000 from the Freedmen's Bureau, Straight opened a normal school in a church in 1869, and in 1870 the American Missionary Association began supporting the school and took control of it. The school began with powerful backing: several legislators, Mayor Heath, and Governor Henry Clay Warmouth were on its first board of trustees.

From the beginning Straight figured heavily in the Negro's campaign for integrated higher education. Since Louisiana State University in Baton Rouge adamantly refused to admit black students, Negro legislators and their friends cut off all funds to L.S.U. in 1873 and diverted the money to Straight. Throughout the Reconstruction period Straight was an "integrated" college. Eight of the ten law school graduates in 1878 were white, and the first graduate of the medical school, James P. Hays, was a white alumnus of Queens College in Dublin.[52]

Although one observer remarked that Straight gave "instruction of a good grammar-school grade," it was the only Negro school in Louisiana which was close to university status.[53] It had commercial, medical, law, and theology departments, in addition to the collegiate department. The growth of the Congregational school was phenomenal. In its first year of operation 874 students attended, with 661 of them in the elementary school. In 1870–71 the school had 1,054 students enrolled: 13 in theology, 18 in law, 69 in normal, 51 in commercial, 189 in academic, and 714 in the elementary division. Since many of the applicants could not pay tuition, however, the number of students declined steadily after 1871.

Overwhelmed by students clamoring for admission, the university suffered from inadequate funds in its first few years. In 1873–74, while tuition fees yielded only $1,380, the salaries of the faculty alone amounted to $10,380. After 1874, with increased financial support from Northern whites and a growing number of scholarships, Straight flourished. Then, in February 1877, a fire gutted the main building, destroyed the library, and caused the president and several of the most distinguished faculty members to resign. At the end of 1877 the university had only 223 students taught by seven teachers, with only 14 students in its theology department and 8 in the law department, and with only 200 books in its library.

Despite the university's problems, the instructional staff at Straight was as good as any in Louisiana during Reconstruction. Eighteen of the twenty-six members of the faculty in 1870 (69 percent) had earned more than a bachelor's degree, generally from Northern universities. From 1870 to 1877 Straight probably had one of the strongest medical departments in the state. The department received a $35,000 endowment from the state legislature, and its professors served in the New Orleans Charity Hospital, where students could get practical training. Headed by Dr. C. B. White, a member of the Louisiana Board of Health, the department had seven professors, including Dr. S. C. Russell, graduate of the University of Louisiana and member of the Louisiana Board of Health.

The law faculty of Straight was also highly qualified. It was headed by Rufus Maples, a local lawyer and politician who wrote several books in the 1880s and '90s; he was professor of admiralty, maritime, and international law. Former judge Henry C. Dibble taught civil law and practice, and L. A. Sheldon, A.M., taught common and constitutional law and equity. A few years after the school opened, A. T. Belden, former attorney general of Louisiana, joined the law department. Two years of study in the department led to a bachelor of laws degree, and, according to an act of the state legislature, any graduate of Straight's law department was automatically admitted to the bar without having to undergo an examination.

Standards at Straight were high. Judging by the 1869–70 catalog, it was not easy to gain admission to the college department: "candidates for admission will be examined in the grammar of Latin and Greek languages, Virgil, Cicero, Salust or Caesar, Arnold's Latin Prose Composition, Xenophon's Anabasis, Homer's Iliad, Higher Arithmetic, Algebra and Ancient History."[54] The courses at Straight were similar to those at New Orleans University and at most New England colleges of the period. Students were also expected to master rhetoric and to give public demonstrations of their skill every Wednesday afternoon.

The Negroes in New Orleans followed very closely the fortunes of Straight and had great hopes for the institution. In 1871 the *Louisianian* praised the progress of Straight and declared that it only needed a little more to make it "what we would all like to see it—the Harvard of the South."[55] While Straight never reached this pinnacle, it was patronized "by the wealthiest and most intelligent" Negroes in New Orleans. The Dumases, Isabelles, Dédés, Martinets, Riards, Bouchereaus, Alcés, Desdunes, Clays, Longpres, Metoyers, LaCroix, Pinchbacks, Hubeaus, Antoines, Gaudets, Dejoies, Peyroux, Boyers, Thezans, Sauciers, and Allains all sent their children to Straight. Only 37 of the 119 graduates from the law, theology, classical, and normal departments between 1876 and 1886 were not residents of New Orleans. The most productive division of the university was the law department, which had 81 graduates and 115 students between 1876 and 1886.[56]

Other Negro colleges in New Orleans were not supported as enthusiastically as was Straight. Indeed, almost as soon as white philanthropists and churches established colleges in New Orleans, they began to alienate local Negroes. The major problem was the small or nonexistent roles Negroes played in the administration of the schools and in teaching positions. Throughout the period the chief administrative officers and most of the teachers were white. The staff of New Orleans University and Leland remained lily-white for so long that the *Louisianian* frequently chided them for being too paternalistic and prejudiced to hire blacks. Yet it was obvious, the *Louisianian* contended, that white teachers could not inculcate a sense of manhood in Negro students. The Negro, it maintained, could "only be thoroughly educated, in part, by his own color; for education does not consist in simply mastering what is learned from books. To know and to *feel* that he is a man, the Negro should have the black professor side by side with his white brother. This manhood education can never come from white teachers alone, however competent."[57]

In contrast, Straight University from the outset obtained overwhelming support from the Negro community because it gave Negroes some voice in the direction of the school. Five influential Negroes, Aristide Mary, Lieutenant Governor Oscar J. Dunn, John R. Clay, G. H. Fayerweather, and Fabious Dunn, served on Straight's board of trustees, and two Negroes, Dr. Louis Charles Roudanez and J. Willis Menard, were on the Examining Committee. In its second year of operation five of the seven men on the Trustees' Executive Committee were Negroes. Three Negroes were on the Colle-

giate Division faculty: Reverend C. H. Thompson, D.D., a
graduate of Oberlin; P. M. Williams, A.M., a Dartmouth
graduate; and Louis A. Martinet, a linguist and student at
Straight. Straight University also had Negroes on the staffs
of its professional schools. Dr. J. T. Newman, a New Orleans–
born Negro physician from Chicago who had published several articles in medical journals, was appointed to the medical
department in 1871. One Chicago doctor described Newman
as "an able diagnostician and a bold and skilful surgeon, a
sound practitioner and polished gentleman."[58] In October
1871 Newman became the first Negro physician to be appointed Surgeon and Visiting Physician in New Orleans Charity Hospital, and later he was appointed a member of the
Louisiana Board of Health. Reverend Louis A. Bell, a graduate of the Howard University Law School, joined the faculty
at Straight in 1871. S. S. Ashley, president of Straight in
1873, asserted that Bell was "more literary in his tastes and
culture than any other colored man here to my knowledge."[59]

Straight made a concerted effort to serve the Negro community. For a short while it operated a free medical dispen-
sary with Dr. Newman as resident physician, organized sewing
and homemaking classes for destitute girls, and provided free
public lectures on everything from "Miasmatic Diseases" to
"Far Eastern Cultures." The school offered night classes in
bookkeeping, accounting, commercial law, and business organization in order to train Negro businessmen; furthermore, it
offered courses, free of charge, for local ministers and prospective teachers.

All three universities—Leland, New Orleans, and Straight
—provided a valuable service to the Negro community. A
majority of the Negro teachers, lawyers, and physicians in
New Orleans from 1869 to 1930 were trained in these institutions. During Reconstruction these schools were primarily
interested in providing an education comparable to their New
England models as the best way of ending the ignorance
which shackled the Negro. For years these colleges kept this
ideal before them, but in the 1890s they began to feel the

influence of Booker T. Washington and, unfortunately, made some half-hearted attempts to promote industrial education. However much industrial education was needed in the black belt of Alabama and Mississippi, it was less than useless in New Orleans, where, at least during Reconstruction, Negroes had plenty of opportunities to learn skilled trades. During Reconstruction and for some time afterwards, Negroes in New Orleans insisted that these institutions train a professional cadre to meet the real needs of their community. The alumni of these schools and their achievements stand as a testimony to the respect the founders had for these desires. Because of the efforts of these institutions, not all Negroes sank to or remained at the level of perpetual hewers of wood and drawers of water.

The three Negro colleges also added significantly to the intellectual and cultural life of New Orleans. A number of Negro musicians, artists, poets, and writers studied at these schools. The graduates included six university professors and six editors of journals and newspapers. One of the most impressive of the black intellectuals during this period was John Wesley E. Bowen, a graduate of New Orleans University (A.B., 1878; A.M., 1886) who received a Ph.D. from Boston University in 1887. He taught ancient languages at Central Tennessee College and Hebrew at Howard University, and in 1910 he became president of Atlanta's Gammon Theological Seminary. He also edited *The Voice of the Negro* and *Stewarts Missionary Magazine*, and published several books and pamphlets including *An appeal for negro bishops, but no separation* (1912), and *Africa and the American negro* (1896).

While the colleges helped to strengthen the Negro intellectual class, they were not alone in sustaining it. One of the major barometers and chief spurs to intellectual pursuits in the community was the Negro newspapers. Although there were several short-lived black newspapers established in New Orleans during Reconstruction, the most significant ones were *L'Union*, the *Tribune*, and the *Louisianian*. The first of these

Straight University, c. 1880

journals, *L'Union*, was edited by Paul Trévigne, a language
teacher in a Negro private school, and was written in a florid
style. It carried the poems of local Negro poets and showed
that the editors and correspondents read Pascal, Voltaire,
Rousseau, Montesquieu, Balzac, Commettant, Gregoire, Plato,
and other writers.

For the first two years of its existence, the French- and
English-language *Tribune* was one of the most impressive of
New Orleans papers. Victor Hugo and Garibaldi sent letters
from Europe to the paper; it had regular correspondents in
Mexico, Paris, and Boston, and probably devoted more space
to foreign news than any other paper in the city. It serialized
French novels, published the poems of several local Negroes,
and reported on the social and literary activities in the Negro
community. The character of the paper changed dramatically
and for the worse shortly after Jean-Charles Houzeau, a radical Belgian geographer, took over as the *Tribune*'s coeditor.[60]
After the journal became the organ of the Republican party
of Louisiana and started receiving Associated Press dispatches
in 1866, it degenerated into a typical nineteenth-century political tract with most of its space devoted to ward club meet-

ings and stories reprinted from other newspapers. While the French-language edition continued to publish a few poems, there was almost no social news in the journal.

P. B. S. Pinchback's weekly *Louisianian* varied considerably in quality, primarily because of the frequent changes in the editorial staff. William G. Brown, a native of Trenton, New Jersey, who had been educated in the West Indies, served as editor from 1870 until his election as state superintendent of education in 1872. Then Henry A. Corbin, a graduate of an Ohio college and later secretary of the board of education and a state tax collector, edited the paper from 1872 to 1874. In 1874 George T. Ruby, former Texas politician and editor of the *Galveston Standard*, became editor. After Ruby left the paper, Pinchback became chief editor but hired four graduates of Straight University as associates: Thomas De S. Tucker, H. C. C. Astwood, James D. Kennedy, and A. Lawrence Henderson. The literary quality of the paper also suffered because the paper's chief purpose was to further the political career of Pinchback. When he took over as editor, Pinchback often suspended publication of the journal for months at a time while he went out canvassing.

One of the few Negro newspapers which tried to appeal to whites, the *Louisianian* was similar in makeup to general newspapers. It had regular correspondents in Washington, Philadelphia, Chicago, Mobile, and Cincinnati, and theater, fashion, society, and book review sections. Usually a short melodramatic story from a popular journal was serialized on the front page. Most of the poems which appeared on the front page were written by little-known white poets and were usually innocuous and nostalgic pieces about nature, love, death, and religious faith. Generally about two-thirds of the material in the journal was reprinted from other newspapers and magazines and from the minutes of Republican committees and the reports of the state legislature.

The editors and correspondents of the *Louisianian* were apparently a well-read group of men. They quoted from Shakespeare, Dickens, Burke, Pascal, Justinian, Keats, and

Virgil. While the correspondents were not as deeply read in classics or foreign literature as those of *L'Union* and the *Tribune*, they sometimes quoted Latin and French in their columns. The *Louisianian* frequently noted occurrences in Europe, Africa, and Latin America and closely followed developments in Cuba. The chief interest, however, was in local and national politics. The *Louisianian* also followed literary events. In 1871 it reprinted Frances E. W. Harper's poem on the Fifteenth Amendment, and South Carolina Representative Joseph H. Rainey's "Press On." However, only a few poems of New Orleans Negroes appeared in its columns.

The absence of a literary tradition prevented the production of many pamphlets, books, or poems in the English language by New Orleans Negroes. Most of the poems were generally unsophisticated, sentimental pieces.

The most impressive of New Orleans' English-language Negro poets was J. Willis Menard, a native of Illinois and graduate of Iberia College who taught school and edited a paper, the *Radical Standard*, in New Orleans after his return from the Caribbean in 1865. A number of his poems were inspired by political events and the suffering of his race.[61]

After he moved to Florida, Menard collected and published many of his poems in *Lays in Summer Lands* in 1879. Written in the florid language of nineteenth-century romantics, most of the poems dealt with love and nature or eulogized the race's heroes—Douglass, Garrison, Sumner, Lincoln, and Grant. But in one of them, "The Negro's Lament," Menard rose above the commonplace and explored, with great sensitivity, the black man's painful dilemma in white America. Suffering under Columbia's "ruthless iron hand," which crushed and unmanned him, the Negro felt he was an alien in his native land. America was

> *So fair and yet so false! thou art a lie*
> *Against both natural and human laws,—*
> *A deformed dwarf, dropp'd from an angry sky*
> *To serve a selfish, and unholy cause! . . .*

> *O Liberty! I taste but half thy sweets*
> *In this thy boasted land of Equal Rights!*
> *Although I've fought on land and in thy fleets*
> *Thy foes, by day and by dim camp-fire lights!*
>
> *What more wouldst have me do? Is not my life—*
> *My blood, an all-sufficient sacrifice?*[62]

Declared a vassal by social caste in a land where "manly hopes are only born to fade," the poet teeters on the brink of despair as he considers the "boundless gulf" between America's egalitarian ideals and its racist practices. With all of his blighted, forlorn hopes, he wonders if it were "Far better for me not to have been born." Then, shifting from contemplation of "yearnings crush'd," the poet dreams of brighter days of liberty paid for in blood:

> *New hope is mine! for now I see the gleam*
> *Of beacon lights of coming liberty!*
> *A continent is shock'd—a crimson stream*
> *Of blood has paid the debt, and I am free!*[63]

Only a few literary works were produced in English by New Orleans Negroes. One of the most important of these efforts was Paul Trévigne's "Centennial History of the Louisiana Negro," which was serialized in the *Louisianian* in 1875 and 1876. Trévigne dealt with the literary, artistic, and scientific contributions of the Negro in Louisiana. Apparently Rodolphe L. Desdunes, then a young man, received the inspiration and some of the material for his famous historical work on Louisiana Negroes, *Nos hommes et notre histoire*, from the pioneering venture of Trévigne. Since Trévigne's articles appeared in English, many English-speaking Negroes learned for the first time something of their race's heritage.[64]

The only Negroes in the city with a literary tradition antedating Reconstruction were the wealthy French-speaking Creoles. Before the war a group of them had published a book of poems, *Les Cenelles*, and some of the contributors survived the war and gained fame in Louisiana and Europe.[65] The

most talented of the Creoles found the atmosphere of New
Orleans too oppressive and discovered a more congenial clime
for intellectual pursuits in France. While the work of these
expatriates cannot be classified with that of the New Orleans
Negro, the group was an important part of the literary tradition of the Creoles during this period. Local Negroes followed
the progress of the exiles in belles lettres, and French-language
journals in Louisiana frequently reprinted their work. The
most famous exiled litterateur of the period was Victor Séjour
(b. 1817), who was educated in New Orleans and Paris. An
admirer of Shakespeare, he translated many of the poet's plays
into French. Furthermore, according to a list compiled by
Edward Larocque Tinker, the historian of French literature
in Louisiana. Séjour himself wrote a phenomenal twenty
dramas and comedies between 1841 and 1869. One of his
dramas, *Les volontaires de 1814*, written in 1862, described
the Negro and white victors of the Battle of New Orleans.[66]

Another exile from Louisiana was Camille Thierry (1814–
75), who accumulated a small fortune in New Orleans before
the war and published his first poem, *Les Idées*, in 1843 in
L'Album littéraire. Thierry was the earliest and most prolific
of the Negro poets of New Orleans; fourteen of his poems
appeared in *Les Cenelles* in 1845. After his father's death,
Thierry moved to France, and in 1874 he published a volume
of poetry entitled *Les Vagabondes*. Reflecting the influence
of Lamartine, his poems were carefully composed, charming
and delicate. One of the most famous of these was "Mariquita
La Calentura," which describes the joys and tragedies of a
Spanish family in New Orleans.[67] Most literary historians of
the period would agree with Trévigne's assessment of Thierry:
"His poems are composed with peculiar care, and comprise
all the various rhythms of French prosody. Some of them are
to be classed among the finest poetical efforts of Louisiana's
most gifted writers."[68]

Among the Creole intellectuals who remained in New
Orleans, one of the most popular was the poet Armand Lanusse (1818–67), who taught at the L'Institution Catholique,

loved classics, and exposed his students to the writings of
Fontaine, Boileau, Fénelon, Racine, and Corneille. There
were also several minor Creole poets, novelists, and drama-
tists who wrote during the Reconstruction period. Adolphe
Duhart (d. 1909), who was born in New Orleans and educated in France, published several poems in the *Tribune*, and
in 1867 his play "Lélia D——t" was performed on the stage
of the Orleans Theatre.[69] Victor Ernest Rillieux (1842–95)
wrote several songs, odes, and satires during this period, but
few of them have been found. Historian Charles Rousseve
attributes the unsigned poem "Le docteur noir" to Rillieux.
A story of a Negro slave doctor who refuses to cure his master, the poem reads in part:

> *Je souviens-tu que dans ta rage,*
> *Frappant ma femme et mon enfant,*
> *Sous les coups de ton fouet sauvage,*
> *Tu les fis mourir lentement*
> *Quand je souffrais de ta vengeance,*
> *Tu te riais de ma douleur,*
> *Mais aujourd'hui, vil oppresseur,*
> *Je me ris ton impuissance,*
> *Tremble, et redoute mon pouvoir,*
> *Je suis, je suis le docteur noir.*[70]

In 1868 Michel Séligny, half brother of Thierry, wrote
a novel, *Junius à Octavius*, about Negro life in New Orleans,
but he died before he could publish it. He did, however, publish several poems in *Le courrier de la Louisiana*, *L'Abeille*,
and *Renaissance Louisianaise*.[71] Doctor Joseph Chaumette,
who had been trained in France, wrote a long poem in 1865,
"Les droits de l'homme," in which he denounced slavery and
appealed for abolition. At one point he asserted:

> *Vive la Liberté, la Déesse immortelle:*
> *A la vie, à la mort, nous combattons pour elle!*
> *Le triomphe est à nous, assistés du Seigneur,*
> *Qui protège le faible, et punit l'oppresseur!*[72]

Another minor poet, a wealthy cigarmaker named Lucien
Mansion, wrote "La Folle," a beautiful poem about a woman
who steals bread for her starving child; the poem appeared
in *Comptes-Rendus* in 1886.[73] Louis Nelson Fouche (1824–
86) published a book in 1882 which contained the thoughts
of several authors on such topics as God, truth, reason, conscience, religion, man, woman, love, thought, freedom, education, morality, life, death, and innumerable others. The list
of writers he quoted was impressive and indicated the breadth
of his reading. They included Bossuet, Montaigne, Hugo,
Michelet, Rousseau, Dumas, Voltaire, Balzac, Châtelain,
Robespierre, Virgil, Tertullian, James Fenimore Cooper,
James S. Hosmer, Saint-Rémy, Thomas Paine, Socrates,
Montesquieu, Fénelon, Lafontaine, Considérant, Mirabeau,
Confucius, and several others.[74]

The failure of the *Tribune* in 1869, the decline of private
schools, and the general increase in the use of the English
language in New Orleans during Reconstruction virtually
halted French literary productions by local Negroes toward
the end of the Reconstruction period. The diaspora of the
Creoles which began as conditions became more oppressive
after 1877 further exacerbated conditions. Even so, the talented Creoles established a tradition in the Reconstruction
period which cheered such litterateurs as Alice Dunbar-
Nelson, Rodolphe L. Desdunes, Marcus Christian, Albert E.
Perkins, Charles B. Rousseve, Ernest J. Gaines, and Octave
Lilly in the twentieth century. The spirit of the Reconstruction writers breathes in their beautiful prose and poetry.

In their schools and colleges New Orleans blacks sought
to eradicate ignorance from the community and to promote
intellectual pursuits. They considered integrated public schools
to be the most important positive affirmation of equality and
a tool for softening prejudices in the white community. The
successes in education, while small, were of great significance
in the black man's future claims to justice.

Social Life and Problems

6

Negro social life in New Orleans was varied, rich, and in many ways a reflection of activities in the white community. This social life united the black community while at the same time accentuating class divisions. The class structure was not, however, so rigid as to preclude concerted community campaigns to eradicate such pressing social problems as the high crime and mortality rates among blacks. In spite of the oppressive conditions under which they lived, New Orleans Negroes created several impressive cultural forms and engaged in a wide variety of social activities.[1]

One of the most important and distinctive features of Negro social life was the singing of spirituals and work songs created by slaves. Filled with pathos, joy, pain, and suffering, they were too beautiful, too expressive of the Negro's life and his dreams to remain on the plantations. Several of them were sung in Negro churches in New Orleans and all over the South. These included such traditional favorites as "Before I'd Be a Slave, I'd Be Buried in My Grave," "Swing Low, Sweet Chariot," and others. A number of the plantation songs were set to music by the New Orleans University singers, who appeared at concerts in New Orleans and around the country. Two of the best of these songs were "Jesus, He Mourns for Me" and "We're All Here, Do Thyself a'No Harm."[2]

The freedmen also brought a number of musical skills to the city other than their singing ability. They contributed, for example, to band music. Generally, the freedmen had some knowledge of violins, banjos, fiddles, and especially drums. While the folk tradition contributed to the musical life and style of the New Orleans Negro, it is difficult to gauge the extent of its influence. There were several Negro brass bands in New Orleans during this period, including Thomas S. Kelly's, Charlie Jaeger's, Frank Dodson's, Louis Martin's, Vinet's, Wolf's, and Richardson's. The most famous of them was Sylvester Decker's Excelsior Brass Band. When the band members appeared in a parade in 1879 in their blue Prussian-styled uniforms and long-plumed hats, the *Louisianian* claimed that "everywhere they appeared their approach was heralded with murmurs of admiration."[3] Playing at conventions, in parades, at parties, dances, and funerals, these bands created what is now known as jazz. Later, white musicians pirated their work and made it popular.

Marked by a strong African rhythm, Negro music affected all other forms of music in the city. The writer Lafcadio Hearn, for example, wrote in 1878: "Creole music is mostly Negro music, although often remodelled by French composers. There could neither have been Creole patois nor Creole melodies but for the French and Spanish blooded slaves of Louisiana and the Antilles." A tough critic, Hearn once asserted, in regard to one Negro song: "I would rather listen to it than hear a symphony of Beethoven." In his letters to Henry Krehbiel, a New York music critic, Hearn gave many glimpses of early jazz. In 1881 he wrote: "Did you ever hear Negroes play the piano by ear? Sometimes we pay them a bottle of wine to come here and play for us. They use the piano exactly like a banjo. It is good banjo-playing, but no piano-playing."[4] Much of this original jazz was created for the funeral processions of Negro benevolent societies. After a deceased society member received the last rites, the procession started for the cemetery, and "to the tread of muffled drum and mournful dirge he was carried to his last home on earth."[5] On the return journey the band struck up a happy tune.

In addition to the popular musicians there were several Negroes who, trained in the best classical tradition in France and at the three universities in the city, were noted teachers, composers, and concert artists. Samuel Snaër, Victor Eugene Macarthy, Arthur P. Williams, Charles Vêque, and J. A. Davies were probably the most gifted musicians of the period. Talented Samuel Snaër wrote several musical scores, and when he played one of his overtures in 1865, the New Orleans *Tribune* asserted that it was "a splendid piece of musical composition, of the most elevated and entertaining character." Macarthy, a gifted composer and master of the piano, appeared in several concerts in the 1860s, performing such European pieces as "La Botte secrète," and his own creations.[6] On one occasion the *Tribune* described Macarthy as "one of the most talented men who are an honor for our population and of whom we are proud. He is not only a first rate artist, gifted and endowed with the organs and the sensibility of the musician, his literary acquirements and his enlightened taste secure him a place of distinction in our community."[7]

Probably the only man who rivaled Macarthy as a performer was Arthur P. Williams. College professor, public school principal, and choir director, Williams was undoubtedly the most active of the musicians. He performed in and directed most of the concerts given during the Reconstruction period. Remarkably, he also found time to teach piano, organ, and voice. In a characteristic comment, the *Tribune* wrote that in one of the concerts, Williams "executed a very difficult piece, and displayed in its execution a remarkable talent. As an amateur, Mr. W. has few if any superiors."[8]

There was also one small Negro symphony orchestra in the city. Organized by Louis Martin, the orchestra began playing at concerts in 1877. The *Louisianian* was enthusiastic about this sign of musical progress. It asserted that the twenty-man orchestra's playing "of several difficult overtures, symphonies, etc., evidenced careful training, and reflected credit upon their accomplished leader, Prof. Louis Martin."[9]

In their numerous concerts Negro performers sang many of the popular American and European songs of the day. The most popular singers were Ada and Emma Stackhouse, J.

Henri Burch, Arthur Williams, Louise De Mortie, Geraldine
Nolaso, Amanda and Sallie Perkins, George H. Fayerweather,
and Samuel Snaër.[10] The French-speaking, or Creole, Negro
population was more cosmopolitan in its musical taste than
the English-speaking Negroes. They often sang popular songs
of the French, Italian, German, and Spanish languages, as
well as arias from several operas.

The most notable operatic event in the Negro community
occurred in 1875 when a French opera troupe was stranded
in New Orleans. The Creole Negroes organized several concerts in May to raise money for the troupe and even took
roles in some of the scenes from the operas which the troupe
performed. Led by Aristide Mary and other opera fans, large
crowds attended the performances and requested that the
company include on the program selections from "La Travi-
ata," "Rigoletto," "La Muette de Portica," "La Juive," "La
Favorita," "La Reine de Chypre," and "Guillaume Tell."[11]

Those blacks who had not absorbed European tastes
shunned the opera but engaged in a number of other activities. They watched the opening of the state legislature, listened
to the debates, lounged around the assembly's hall, crowded
into the recorder's court, and watched magic lantern shows
for diversion. Similarly, attending minstrel shows and vaude-
ville acts at the Academy of Music and the St. Charles Theatre also furnished amusement to many Negroes. Sometimes
Negroes performed in minstrel shows of their own. When the
local Negro company, the Crestiani Comedians, performed
in 1871, the *Louisianian* observed that "The songs, dances
and jokes of the minstrels created a great deal of merriment
among the guests, and some of the performances were received with rapturous applause."[12]

Sports also provided much entertainment for blacks. Negroes participated in contests at the roller-skating rink, re-
gattas of the Saratoga Rowing Association and the Antoine
Rowing Club, rifle matches, or horse races. The most notable
of the latter was the 1871 match race for a $400 purse be-
tween C. C. Antoine's "Nellie" and W. B. Barrett's "Frank."

Another of the Negro's favorite sports was baseball, which provided the chance for active participation for some and spectator enjoyment for many more. The first Negro baseball clubs were mentioned in newspapers in the early 1870s, and by 1875 there were thirteen in the city. In September 1875 the Negro clubs met and formed a citywide league and had a state championship game.[13]

Another form of entertainment, an old sport which grew in popularity during Reconstruction, was gambling. In the dives and houses on and near the Rue Royale, Negroes and whites eagerly tried to beat Lady Luck. Negroes, just as almost everybody else in the city, eagerly visited the ubiquitous shops of the Louisiana Lottery Company. Some of the agents of the company were Negroes, and blacks often risked their all in the hope of winning a fortune. Undoubtedly the lottery had a demoralizing effect on the Negro as well as on the white community. One observer declared that the lottery company had

established policy shops and petty gambling dens around the markets and other public places in New Orleans, which perpetually demoralize the laboring class, and particularly negro men and women, over which the city government has no control; and they have agents and solicitors all over the state, tempting the poor and ignorant to gamble, providing for this end what they call a "combination game," which can be played even by the owner of a ten-cent piece.[14]

In spite of almost continuous losses, the individual was lured by the lottery's promise of a big fortune. Besides, some Negroes did win in the drawing presided over by former Confederate Generals P. G. T. Beauregard and Jubal Early. On one occasion a Negro man allegedly won $15,000.

Negroes celebrated several important occasions with mass meetings and giant parades. Thousands of Negroes gathered at Congo or Lafayette Square to celebrate the issuance of the Emancipation Proclamation and the anniversary of the abolition of slavery in the West Indies, to honor Lincoln and to

Musicians

mourn his death, to celebrate a mass for John Brown, and to hear the reports of delegates to national Negro conventions.

The societies, clad in bright uniforms, often paraded through the streets and joined the funeral processions of famous residents. The procession which followed the body of Oscar J. Dunn in November 1871 was the largest and most impressive one ever seen in New Orleans. It included Masonic lodges, benevolent societies, Governor Warmouth, Mayor Benjamin Flanders, General Augustus Longstreet, city administrators, Republican ward clubs, state legislators, judges, 500 metropolitan police, and 840 militiamen.

Another form of recreation in which large numbers of Negroes participated was excursions. Negro societies chartered special trains and steamboats, hired bands, and went to such places as St. Louis, Pass Christian, Mobile, Bay St. Louis, Bonnet Carré, Biloxi, Baton Rouge, and even Virginia. These excursions usually included about 900 people and on occasion as many as 2,000.[15] If they were unable to go on excursions during the spring and summer, Negroes enjoyed large picnics at City Park, Oakland Riding Park, and the Fair Grounds. At these picnics they had foot races, military drill competition, baseball games, band music, competitive dancing, shooting matches, croquet, buggy races, raffles, sack races, and fencing matches. Often as many as 1,500 people attended these picnics. Throughout the Reconstruction period this was one of the most important forms of communal recreation encouraged by schools, churches, and social organizations.[16]

It was natural, in a city that was famous for its Mardi Gras, that the carnival would be important in Negro social life. Large numbers of them viewed the annual parade in the 1860s and began to join in the processions in significant numbers and to hold balls during the season in the 1870s. Englishman George A. Sala wrote that during the carnival, "the negroes have gone extensively into masquerading on their own private account. They have been capering about the streets arrayed in the most absurd dresses, and cutting the most ridiculous capers."[17] The Mardi Gras season was inaugurated by a series of masked balls late in January. At one of these in 1880 the costumed revelers bore names such as "Italian Peasant," "America," "Butter Cup," "Folly," "German Maid," "Scotch Queen," "Duke of Wellington," and "Charles VII." The last masked balls of the season were usually held on St. Joseph's Eve (March 18) at Geddes, Globe, Economy, Union, and other halls.[18] In a characteristic comment, the *Louisianian* asserted on March 19, 1872, that on St. Joseph's Eve the halls "were thronged with masquerade parties, and the festivities lasted till a late hour."

Measured by the newspaper space given such activities, dancing was the most popular pastime in the Negro community. By paying $1.00 for himself and $.50 for his date, a young man could attend any of a number of dances at Geddes, Globe, Brown, National, Economy, Union, and Francs Amis halls. Large dances were also held at Mechanics Institute, the meeting place of the state legislature. The dizzying round

BRISTOL POLYTECHNIC
ST. MATTHIAS LIBRARY
FISHPONDS

of quadrilles, waltzes, continentals, Prince Imperials, varieties, New Yorks, pinafore lancers, polkas, mazourkas, valses, cotillions, grand marches, and schottisches often lasted until early in the morning. Practically every private party ended with dancing.

Those Negroes who rejected dancing and other "frivolities" in favor of more serious intellectual engagements could attend at least one lecture in the city almost every week as well as the Wednesday afternoon lectures at Straight University. Probably the most notable event of the period occurred in 1872 when Frederick Douglass lectured at Mechanics Institute on "Self-Made Men."[19] The most impressive Negro women who delivered lectures in New Orleans were Louise De Mortie and Frances E. W. Harper. Both women had received rave notices for their readings in other cities. The *Liberator* declared that in her appearances in Boston Miss De Mortie, "in reading 'Leap from the Long Bridge,' exibited [sic], in some of its passages, traits that called to mind the finest display of Fanny Kemble, Miss Glinn, or Mrs. Barrow." When she gave a "Patriotic and Sentimental Reading" in New Orleans in March 1865, Miss De Mortie received "immense applause."[20] Frances E. W. Harper, the Negro poet whose lectures had been compared by Northern newspapers to those of Emily Dickinson, took New Orleans by storm in April 1871 with a series of lectures on "The Work Before Us," "The Great National Opportunity," and other topics. In one lecture in which she urged Negroes to use their intellect and physical and political power to obtain their rights she drew repeated applause from her audience. William G. Brown asserted that no female lecturer was as impressive in "the command of language, the graceful and easy flow of words, the power of reasoning united with an ability to infuse burning satire and cutting sarcasm, as . . . this lady."[21]

Local Negroes often delivered orations from classical works, and many attended the theater. The *Louisianian* frequently reviewed the plays which appeared at the St. Charles and varieties theaters, and amateur Negro drama companies also presented many of the familiar works of Shakespeare as well as popular plays. The latter included "Vespers of Palermo," "Pocahontas," "Hiawatha," and others.[22]

Practically every aspect of social life other than commercial entertainment such as was furnished by the theaters was dominated by Negro social clubs. Between 1862 and 1880 there were more than 226 Negro societies which were listed in the Signature Books of the Freedmen's Bank or were frequently noted in the newspapers. Since only the most prominent and active clubs received public notice, in all probability at least a third of them never appeared in the newspapers. Included among the organizations were benevolent associations; militia companies; rowing clubs; masonic, Odd Fellow, Eastern Star, and Knights Templar lodges; religious societies; social and literary clubs; orphan-aid associations; racial improvement societies; and baseball clubs. Ranging in size from 20 to 175 members, many of these organizations were short-lived; only thirty-eight (16.8 percent) survived until the twentieth century. During the Reconstruction period at least 82 (36.2 percent of the total number) of the societies had bank accounts. A number of the societies also built halls during this period. In 1880 ten Negro societies owned a total of $11,480 in real estate, with the Société d'Economie et d'Assistance Mutuelle possessing the most property ($4,000).[23]

The hundreds of social clubs in the city provided status and entertainment to their members. Four of the most important of these clubs were the Mignonette, Athenaeum, Louisiana, and Americus clubs. The Americus Club, one of the most exclusive in the city, was founded in 1874 by James D. Kennedy to cultivate literary tastes, to promote rational discussion, and to sponsor public debates and lectures. A number of the club members were graduates of Straight University, and in 1879 6 of the 37 members were delegates to the state convention of the Republican party. The club house, which opened in 1879, was one of the most impressive in the city. Even more impressive than the Americus Club was the Louisiana Progressive Club, organized in 1874; among its 36 members were the most influential Negro politicians, wealthy Negro creoles, and a few white politicians. William G. Brown, P. B. S. Pinchback, C. C. Antoine, P. G. Deslonde, James Ingraham, J. Sella Martin, Henri Burch, A. E. Barber, James Lewis, and other prominent Negro politicians belonged to the club.[24]

For many Negroes the church was the most important social institution in the community. Here the Negro could find a refuge and some hope of escape from his earthly hell. With emancipation the Negro began to enjoy some religious liberty and the right to control his own churches; almost immediately after Union troops occupied the city in 1862, Negroes began to form new churches. There were several reasons for the growth in the number of Negro churches. First, there were many Negroes who received no religious instruction in the city, and the number of churches which welcomed them was limited. Second, Negro communicants felt that they could not remain in the white churches they had attended before the war. Too many of their white fellow communicants treated them as pariahs. Besides, they remembered vividly that their white pastors had been in the forefront of those defending slavery and insisting that in the natural order of things this was the only place the Negro could enjoy.[25]

After the war the white churches continued their paternalistic treatment of Negroes, forced them to remain in the balconies, barred them from participation in church government, and urged them to establish separate congregations. Understandably, Negroes had little desire to continue their affiliation with those white denominations "that recognized slavery as a divine institution."[26] Repelled by discrimination in the white churches and desirous of controlling their religious destiny and exercising authority, Negroes began to leave the white churches at the first opportunity. There were still a few Negroes, however, in a number of white congregations in the 1870s. Most of the Negro Catholics continued to attend integrated churches throughout the Reconstruction period. At the same time there was a mass exodus of Negro Methodists from the Methodist Episcopal Church South. By 1863 about 3,000 of them had joined the Methodist Episcopal Church North. Throughout the period the strength of Catholicism among Negroes blunted the drive to expand Protestant churches in New Orleans.[27]

The strongest Protestant church in the Negro community was the African Methodist Episcopal. The number of churches belonging to this denomination grew from four in 1860 to ten in 1873. Many of these churches were small and fought a losing battle with the Catholic Church for members. The largest A. M. E. congregation in the city was St. James, which in 1880 built a parsonage, a hall for meetings, debates, and concerts, and a private school.[28]

The Congregational Church fared poorly in New Orleans. At first it was difficult to attract Negro Catholics because of the Protestants' reputation for emotionalism. S. S. Ashley, American Missionary Association representative in New Orleans, complained about this in 1873: "It is becoming more and more evident that the Roman Catholics (colored) are repelled from Protestantism by the wild, turbulent and distracting scenes of the colored churches. Unless we can show them a better view we labor in vain."[29] The A. M. A. found it difficult to present a different view because of the ignorance of many of the Negro pastors. In fact, many of the churches were initially Congregational in name only. Since the pastors had an imperfect understanding of Congregationalism, they generally held services which were a mixture of Baptist, Methodist, and Congregational practices. When A. M. A. representatives insisted that they become full-fledged Congregationalists, whole churches joined the Baptist or Methodist denominations. As a result of these problems, there were only five Negro Congregational Churches in New Orleans in 1879, with a total of 465 members and 300 students in Sabbath schools.[30]

As soon as the war ended, Negro leaders began to call upon the churches to appoint competent men to lead their flocks. Northern missionaries were especially adamant on

Mardi Gras

this point: one of the first things they did after the war was
to open Bible schools which Negro ministers could attend
free of charge. Apparently the campaign was relatively successful; by the 1870s, many of the churches had highly trained
ministers. The quality of the A.M.E. ministers is indicated by
two of those who served at St. James. The Reverend John
Turner, who was pastor from 1865 to 1868, was a highly
literate man and served as chaplain of the state senate in 1868.
The Reverend M. M. Clark, who had been educated at Jefferson College (Pennsylvania), became pastor of St. James
in 1868. He had gone to England in 1846, had attended the
Royal Medical College at Dublin, and had spent eighteen
months in Africa. The best-trained ministers in the city were
those of the Congregational Church, and especially at the
Central Congregational Church. The first pastor of Central
was C. H. Thompson, chaplain of Straight University and a

graduate of Oberlin College. In 1874 he was appointed president of Alcorn College, and he later became an Episcopal priest and rector of St. Phillips Church. After Thompson's tenure at Central, Reverend M. E. Cole, secretary of the State Board of Education, and W. S. Alexander, president of Straight University, served as pastors of that church.[31]

There were two very different kinds of religious services in the Negro churches. In upper-class churches religion was more form than passion. Lower-class churches, composed primarily of former slaves and illiterate migrants from the parishes, had an entirely different form of religion. These people had a strong belief in the presence and power of God in everyday life; they emphasized revelations, visions, dreams, and inward expressions of the Divine presence. Their services, a mixture of grief and sadness about their weary life on earth, provided an emotional release for them. The sermons and songs about their bondage, and the passionate prayers for Divine aid, gave to their services a reality, vividness, and emotionalism which created a sense of shared suffering and hope which caused the congregations to shout, cry, and raise a joyful noise to the Lord. In spite of the emotion, there was a deep practical strain running through sermons which usually compared the Negro's lot with that of the Jews and which urged him to protect and to enlarge his freedom. These men were devout, their prayers were earnest appeals to God, and their songs were narratives of their sufferings.[32] Most observers were impressed by the earnestness of the prayers and songs in these services. Surgeon Harris Beecher felt that the Negro's religious services were "the most singular and impressive sights imaginable, consisting of weird songs, incoherent, irreverent shouts, mingled with violent contortions, wails and moans, quaint prayers and responses."[33]

Upper-class Negro church services were generally less passionate than those in lower-class churches. Long-time residents of the city, both the ministers and members of these churches were literate. They had fewer Hell-fire-and-damnation sermons, more intellectual appeals, attention to the social problems of the community, and less of the emotionalism which characterized the lower-class churches. This was especially true of Negro Congregational, Presbyterian, and Episcopal churches and some of the A.M.E. churches. The sermons at St. James A.M.E., for instance, were listened to "with marked attention and a deap spiritual interest by a very large and intelligent audience."[34]

The Negro churches established missions on the plantations near New Orleans, acted as clearing houses for lost wives and family members or for those seeking aid in times of disaster, and led in the formation of benevolent societies and private schools for blacks. The major social and religious events in the churches were the annual revivals, baptisms, excursions, fairs, camp meetings, and Sunday school exercises.[35]

Most churches, organizations, and social activities in the Negro community were divided along class lines. The class structure in New Orleans was so complex and was related to so many factors, however, that it is difficult to analyze. Most historians of the period have focused on the social divisions between the primarily mulatto free Negroes and the predominantly black freedmen as the explanation for the social structure in the Negro community. Most contemporaries not only divided the community along these lines but also insisted that the mulattoes looked down on blacks. B. Rush Plumly, Thomas Conway, General Stephen A. Hurlbut (Commander of the Department of the Gulf), and others made this charge. Plumly wrote in 1864 that the free Negroes, slaveholders themselves, were part of the "rebel party" and were "rich, aristocratic, exclusive, and bitterly hostile to the black, except as a slave."[36] The *New Orleans Times* and other white newspapers repeatedly made the same claim. Jean-Charles Houzeau, the Belgian coeditor of the *Tribune*, claimed that the mulattoes were too aristocratic and too impressed by their own respectability to be interested in the freedmen. Apparently a number of blacks felt this way about the mulattoes, for in 1865 they established a newspaper, the *Black Republican*, to represent those Negroes allegedly ignored by the *Tribune*. In the pages of the *Black Republican*, the editor claimed, "the poor as well as the rich, the freedmen as well as the freemen will be heard."[37] One black man, Dr. R. I. Cromwell from Wisconsin, was so bitter against the mulattoes that he argued that they were "unfit to be his 'public associates.' "[38]

While there was some truth to the charges of color prejudice in the Negro community, many of the contemporary witnesses were impeachable. Conway, Plumly, and Hurlbut fumed against the mulattoes and especially against the editors of the *Tribune* because the latter were the principal leaders of the fight against Banks's labor policy. Conway was among the most important men who were intrumental in establishing the *Black Republican* as a pro-Banks counter to the *Tribune*. And in spite of the paper's apparent opposition to the free mulattoes, several mulattoes, including C. C. Antoine and Thomas Isabelle, signed its prospectus. The white newspapers highlighted racial exclusiveness in the Negro community in order to divide and nullify its political strength. Houzeau's criticism of the mulattoes was apparently based as much on the fact that they were not as revolutionary as he was as it was on their color prejudice.[39]

In reality many of the mulattoes were aristocrats and were somewhat paternalistic toward freedmen. They felt that their education entitled them to a natural position of leadership in the Negro community. In 1864 a fairly large number of the mulattoes supported a motion in the Constitutional convention for an extension of the franchise which would have permitted only the wealthy and well-educated mulattoes to vote (a motion which was primarily the result of the machinations of Banks and his coadjutors). Similarly, the mulattoes gained much more than the blacks from the provisions of the Louisiana Civil Rights Bill: the right to attend the opera, theater, or expensive restaurants was of little practical importance to black men too poor to afford such luxuries.

Many of the mulatto leaders were realistic enough to see that they were wedded to the blacks on a common level of oppression from which they could rise only as a result of the strength of numbers which the blacks provided. The New Orleans *Tribune* summed up this philosophy perfectly on December 29, 1864:

These two populations, equally rejected and deprived of their rights, cannot be well estranged from one another. The emancipated will find in the old free men, friends ready to guide them, to spread upon them the light of knowledge, and teach them their duties as well as their rights. But, at the same time, the free men will find in the recently liberated slaves a mass to uphold them; and with this mass behind them they will command the respect always bestowed to number[s] and strength.

There is abundant evidence that the mulattoes cooperated with the blacks to achieve common goals. The *Tribune*, for instance, claimed that it fought for "the oppressed, whether black, yellow or white." One Creole asserted in 1865 that "the old free colored people of this city and State have done and are doing all that is in their power to morally and physically improve the condition of the new freedmen." In this regard, the mulattoes were prominent in the freedmen's aid associations and cooperated with the blacks to organize orphanages, schools, and old folks homes. The mulattoes dominated politics during Reconstruction but did not try to exclude blacks from leadership positions. For instance, at a mass meeting in December 1864 Oscar J. Dunn, a mulatto, opened the meeting by declaring: "We regard all black and colored men as brothers and fellow sufferers." At Negro conventions held between 1864 and 1867 former slaves and former slaveholders, rich and poor, mulattoes and blacks, and "all the classes of society," according to the *Tribune*, "were represented in a common thought: the actual liberation from social and political bondage." As a result of such views, the editors of the *Tribune* led a spirited campaign against the "quadroon bill" because it largely excluded blacks from the franchise. Expressing similar concern for blacks, mulattoes argued that although wealthy Negroes would receive most of the practical benefits from a public accommodations law, all Negroes would be relieved of the psychological burden that segregation imposed on them.[40]

Color per se was more apparent than real as the underlying cause of social divisions in the Negro community. The association of color with a certain social class was due primarily to historical accident and was not immutable. There were, of course, striking and readily identifiable differences between blacks and mulattoes. The mulattoes, because of the patronage and aid of their white fathers before 1860, had an overwhelming majority of the wealth and education in the Negro community after the war. Because of the distinctions between black slaves and mulatto freemen in the Black Codes, the encouragement by whites of a feeling of superiority among mulattoes, and their ownership of slaves, many of the mulattoes looked down on the former bondsmen after the war, as much because of the bondsmen's previous condition as because of their color.

There was also a historical nexus between occupational skill and color. Before the war the free mulattoes had become skilled craftsmen, and after the war they continued to dominate certain trades to the exclusion of the black freedmen, who had learned few skills in slavery. As a result of historical developments, most of the educated, refined, wealthy, and skilled Negroes in New Orleans were mulattoes, and, just as most men who are differentiated from the mass by these qualities have generally done, they formed associations among their own kind.

The most important cause of social division in the Negro community was cultural differences. This area, as with wealth, education, and occupations, was to a degree linked with color and previous condition. The free mulatto was French in thought, language, and culture while the black freedman was English-speaking and Afro-American in culture. This distinction was mentioned in the newspapers more often than any other factor as a cause of class-division in the Negro community. Because the Creole Negroes used French in their

daily affairs, vacationed and were educated in Paris, deliber-
ated in French at their club meetings, and read French novels,
poems, and newspapers, English-speaking blacks were generally barred from associating or communicating with them.
One of the primary reasons for the establishment of the *Black
Republican* was that the free Negroes initially paid little attention to the English-language edition of the *Tribune*. According
to the editors of the *Black Republican*, their paper would be
"printed in the English tongue, the tongue that brought us
freedom. . . . It will be the true organ of the American colored
people of Louisiana."[41]

Color aside, the language barrier alone was sufficient to
make the French-speaking, Creole Negroes an exclusive
group. But considering the Creoles' pride in their French background, and their wealth, education, and occupational skills
too, the barriers to social intercourse with blacks appear to be
almost proscriptive. Given these barriers, the surprising thing
is that there was any social intercourse between the American
and the Creole Negro communities. Occasionally there were
marriages across cultural lines, and representatives from both
groups often went to the same parties, banquets, lectures,
picnics, and excursions and supported each other in the
political canvass. It is notable that as the popularity of the
French language declined in the 1870s, the cultural barriers
to social intercourse between the two groups decreased.[42]

The Creoles had several exclusive organizations. The
Louisiana Association for the Relief of Colored Orphans,
Amis Sincères, Creole Association, Dieu nous Protège, Francs
Amis, Jeunes Amis, Frères Amis, Société d'Economie, Société des Artisans and others were composed almost exclusively of the Creoles. The standards of membership in these
organizations were wealth, education, and a speaking knowledge of French. Color, however, was no bar to membership;
wealthy French-speaking blacks also belonged to them.

The only way to identify individuals by class in the Negro
community is to accept the dual social structure in the community. But there have been so many oversimplified analyses

of the class structure in Negro communities that it is almost
impossible to find models to use in analyzing social class in
New Orleans. Historians have traditionally used objective
criteria (wealth, occupation, and so on) in studying class
structure. While this method is relatively easy to apply, it
ignores the subjective factors used by contemporaries in rank-
ing their fellows (personableness, intelligence, dependability,
special skills, and so forth). To the extent that social position
depends on the evaluation of contemporaries, objective criteria, when used alone, are unreliable indices of social structure.

One way of determining the social position of individuals
is to find out how often they were chosen to fill positions of
trust and honor by people who knew them. In an effort to
discover the socially prominent Negroes in New Orleans
during Reconstruction, a list of all officers in Negro organizations was compiled from the newspapers and from the signature books of the Freedmen's Bank. The persons who held the
largest number of the most prestigious offices were accepted
as the most prominent individuals. On this basis the social
leaders (those elected to more than five offices) in the English-
speaking Negro community were James Lewis and his father
John Lewis, William G. Brown, J. Henri Burch, Oscar J.
Dunn, Alfred E. Barber, Calvin F. Ladd, William Mulford,
William Thompson, Arthur P. Williams, Henry A. Corbin,
Edward J. Holmes, James H. Ingraham, and William G. Johnson. Several persons who held fewer than five offices should
be included in the upper class because they appeared fre-
quently as guests at banquets and were continuously desig-
nated as social leaders by the newspapers. They include P. B.
S. Pinchback, A. Lawrence Henderson, George D. Geddes,
James D. Kennedy, Thomas J. Boswell, Thomas Isabelle, J.
T. Newman, S. W. Rogers, J. W. Roxborough, Frederick
Simms, and James M. Vance.

The individuals who held the largest number of offices
(more than three) among French-speaking Negroes were
Felix and C. C. Antoine, Charles Aubert, Ludger Boquille,

C. L. Boise, Firmin C. Christophe, Manuel Camps, Louis de
Grug, George H. Fayerweather, Henry François, J. B. Gaudet,
J. P. Lanna, Ernest C. Morphy, J. A. Norager, Jordan B.
Noble, Lawrence Quanders, Isidore Pieras, Louis Charles
Roudanez, Paul Trévigne, William Vigers, and Benjamin
Xavier. Those individuals who held less than three offices but
whose names frequently appeared in the newspapers as social
leaders included Thomy Lafon, Aristide Dejoie, P. G. Des-
londe, Aristide Mary, and Eugene Macarthy.

A social profile analysis of the 500 individuals listed in the
census who served as officers in Negro organizations revealed
several characteristics. According to the manuscript census of
1870 and various city directories, the social leaders were engaged in 46 different occupations, among which were 26
policemen; 19 clerks; 19 laborers; 14 porters; 10 merchants;
9 cigarmakers; 7 draymen; and 6 brokers, carpenters, and
shoemakers, government officials, teachers, and ministers each.
The social leaders also included editors, tailors, coopers, lottery agents, jewelers, doctors, dentists, druggists, engineers,
and a fencing master. The average age of the social leaders in
1870 was about 36 years. Although it is difficult to obtain
accurate figures, apparently about one-third of the leaders had
been free before the war and 90 percent were natives of Louisiana. The social leaders who could be identified as property
holders possessed 1/8 of all property held by blacks in 1870
($302,250), or an average of $4,322 in property. Ten men
owned between $10,000 and $100,000 worth of property. In
a community with relatively few wealthy individuals and in
which most of the people were illiterate, education was the
most important determinant of social class position. While
rarely could any other single factor guarantee one a leadership post in a social organization, literacy could.[43]

Apparently there was a connection between social class
and political preferment. The precise nature of the relationship, however, is not clear. On the one hand, it could be
argued that certain Negroes were elected to important
political posts because of their social prestige. On the other,

it could be argued that social prestige was based on political standing. While there were some Negro clubs which excluded politicians from membership, for the most part political honors were translated into higher social standing. In 1879, for instance, the society reporter of the *Louisianian* lamented the fact that political standing was used as a basis for social exclusiveness: "Political distinction is the sure step to social favor."[44]

The style of life of the Negro upper-middle and upper class was comparable to that of the same classes among whites. An analysis of the household effects of thirty-seven wealthy Negroes who were listed in the manuscript census, for example, showed that most had mahogany furniture, sofas, mirrors, clocks, carpets, marble-topped tables, silverware, china, books, pictures, and jewelry. Some upper-class families also owned diamonds, candelabras, pianos, oil paintings, statuettes, engravings, chess sets, swords, and chandeliers.[45]

In 1872 a New Orleans *Times* reporter described the interior of the home of P. B. S. Pinchback, which was typical of those of upper-class Negroes. The parlor, he asserted,

was found highly respectable, if not elegant, in all its appointments. A fine brussels carpet covered the floor, and it was furnished with a plain black hair-cloth set of furniture. The windows were draped with handsome curtains. An upright piano on one side gave evidence of musical capacity in the household and a marble topped centre table, bearing a silver ice pitcher and goblets on a salver, gave evidence of the occupant's popularity in the shape of a testimonial from somebody. The walls were hung with numerous pictures, evidently selected with both taste and discrimination. Among them a large engraving of Napoleon caressing the young King of Rome, another picture, called "The Prison Window," a rather indifferent oil painting of a falconer, hung on the pier over a large "etagere," which was covered with a profusion of photographs, principally those of colored statesmen. In a rear room, divided by folding doors, was a library and sideboard.[46]

Several forms of recreation were typical among upper-class Negroes. Birthdays, anniversaries, baptisms, weddings, Christmas, Thanksgiving, and testimonials were occasions for banquets, dinners, and parties. On a number of occasions small bands were hired to furnish music for these private parties. Parties and dinners given by P. B. S. Pinchback, J. Henri Burch, C. C. Antoine, William G. Brown, P. G. Des-londe, and A. E. Barber were attended by members of the local Negro upper class, as well as by such national Negro politicians as J. C. Napier of Tennessee and Blanche K. Bruce and James Hill of Mississippi, and such local and national white politicians as Governors Warmouth and Kellogg and Senators Howe, Morton, and Cameron. Many of the private parties were elegant affairs to which the women often wore evening dresses, diamonds, and pearls.

For the most part, however, these social gatherings were informal affairs where friends gathered for an afternoon or evening of chess, checkers, croquet, card-playing, dining,

The Cakewalk

drinking, dancing, singing, demonstrating paintings and crayon drawings, and discussing contemporary books. Piano-playing and singing were the indispensable ingredients in most informal gatherings. For example, at one of William G. Brown's parties, a "Mrs. H. . . . [favored] the company by playing one of Offenbach's operas."[47]

The wealthy Negroes of New Orleans often spent their vacations in such places as Cincinnati, Chicago, Baltimore, Charleston, Washington, D.C., Saratoga and Glen Falls, New York, and even Canada. Wealthy Creoles, such as Louis Charles Roudanez and Francis E. Dumas, often returned to Paris for short visits. There were also popular local spas: Bay St. Louis; plantations in the parishes; Biloxi, Mississippi; and resorts on Lake Pontchartrain.[48]

Another characteristic of the upper-class Negroes was a great deal of intermarriage: wealth tended to wed wealth. Wealthy families which were related by marriage included the Bettingers and Royeres, Dumases and Thezans, Rouzans and

Lavignes, Montforts and Lomines, Christophes and Metoyers, Bouttes and Lavignes, Perraults and Clays, Glaudins and Bonseigneurs, and the Thezans and Deslondes.[49]

The upper-class Negroes often demonstrated a strong sense of noblesse oblige, commitment to racial uplift, and social conscience in regard to the black lower classes. Their desire to aid their less fortunate fellows was often frustrated, however, by the ignorance, poverty, and superstition which pervaded the community and by the effects of slavery and discrimination—social problems which were so endemic to New Orleans that they almost defied solution. This was apparently true, for example, in regard to the Negro crime rate.

While there are no uniform crime statistics by race for New Orleans during the Reconstruction period, the crime rate was apparently very high in the Negro community. For instance, according to the 1870 census, 150 (30 percent) of the 500 inmates in the Orleans parish prison on June 1, 1870, were Negroes, although blacks constituted only 25 percent of the total population. Even this figure was probably lower than the general crime rate among Negroes. In October and November 1867, for example, Negroes accounted for 38 and 35 percent of the total number of persons arrested in New Orleans. By the 1870s the crime rate of Negroes had apparently increased: in September 1874 Negroes made up 43 percent of the total number of prisoners in Orleans parish.[50]

Nevertheless, it is practically impossible to draw any firm conclusions from the figures cited above. First of all, they refer to arrests and not to convictions. Secondly, given the widespread corruption in the New Orleans police department, the fact that white policemen were more likely to arrest and white judges were more likely to sentence Negroes than whites, the statistics may be deceptive. Most Negroes were arrested for disturbing the peace, assault and battery, and petty larceny. There were also a few allegations of murder, rape, counterfeiting, vagrancy, and illegal possession of weapons.[51]

Before the installation of the Reconstruction government, Negroes rarely obtained justice in New Orleans courts or

protection from the police. In fact, the white policemen frequently attacked Negroes without provocation. As a result of
this, blacks on occasion mobbed the police when they attempted to make arrests. There were so many unprovoked
attacks on Negroes by whites, so little protection from the
police, and so much injustice in the courts that in June 1867
General Joseph A. Mower ordered his Freedmen's Bureau
agents to arrest the offending whites. After Negro policemen
were added to the force by the Republicans, after some of the
most conservative judges were replaced, and after juries were
integrated in 1867, blacks had a better chance of receiving
justice.[52]

A much more serious social problem than crime was the
generally unhealthy condition of the Negro population during
the Reconstruction period. Negro morbidity and mortality
rates were so frightfully high that they were destructive of
family stability and economic growth, and touched nearly
every individual and institution in the black community. Between 1860 and 1880 the annual death rate of Negroes fluc-
tuated between 32 and 81 per thousand, exceeding that of
whites by from 5 to 39 per thousand. The infant mortality
rate of Negroes was especially high: 450 per thousand in
1880. The differential in mortality is, of course, reflected in
the lower life-expectancy of blacks. While a white child at
age one had a life expectancy of 46 years, a Negro child at
age one had a life expectancy of only 36 years.

There are several possible explanations of the high Negro
death rate in New Orleans. So many of the Negroes were
crowded into dilapidated huts and tenements that they were
easy prey for pulmonary consumption, smallpox, and pneu-
monia. Living in overcrowded and frequently badly ventilated,
uninhabitable tenements, surrounded by filth, drinking unsanitary water, subsisting on insufficient diets, Negroes were
naturally the major victims of such communicable diseases as
smallpox and cholera. Until 1879 the Board of Health was
unsuccessful in its efforts to prevent outbreaks of smallpox
because Negroes not only refused to be vaccinated, but also

concealed smallpox cases from officials and refused to go to the hospitals. The fatalism of the blacks and their trust in God were the primary reasons for their obstinate refusal to be vaccinated.[53]

While many of the deaths among blacks can be attributed to the unsanitary conditions, faulty drainage, and poor water supply which plagued New Orleans throughout much of the nineteenth century, the excess of Negro deaths over whites can only be explained by the greater poverty, superstition, and ignorance of the blacks. According to the 1880 Board of Health report, the high Negro mortality rate was caused by "(a) improvidence in living, irregular habits; poor diets; (b) neglect of the sick; indifference to medical aid; neglect of vaccination; (c) crowding and imperfect ventilation; (d) less vital power or capacity to resist the ravages of diseases; (e) ignorance of, and violation of, physiological and sanitary laws."[54]

Undoubtedly the poor state of medical knowledge, the inability of blacks to pay for medical attention, discrimination in health services, and the fact that superstitious blacks put so much faith in folk cures and untrained "Indian" or voodoo doctors, all contributed to the high mortality rate. The rapid decline in the medical services provided by the Freedmen's Bureau to poverty-stricken blacks in New Orleans effectively prevented many of them from receiving the attention of trained physicians. In addition, the relative scarcity of Negro physicians seriously undermined efforts to provide medical services for blacks. In 1870 there were only ten Negro doctors in New Orleans, or one Negro physician for every 5,094 blacks. The situation had improved little by 1880: in that year there were only thirteen Negro doctors listed in the census, or one for every 4,434 Negroes. The problem was exacerbated because many of these doctors had received little training; four of them were listed as "Indian" doctors in 1880. Of the five registered Negro physicians listed by the Board of Health in 1882, only one, Louis Charles Roudanez, had graduated from medical school. A graduate of the Medical

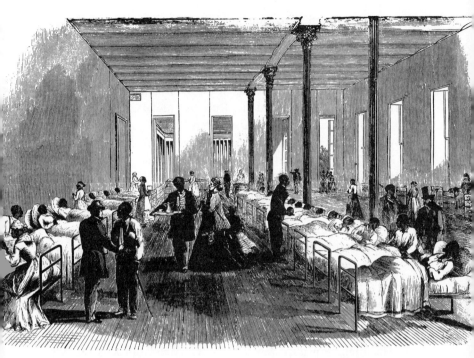

Marine Hospital

Faculty of the University of Paris and Cornell University, Roudanez was one of the best-trained physicians in New Orleans and had a lucrative practice among blacks and whites in the city. Other trained Negro physicians included Alexander Chaumette, graduate of the Medical Faculty of the University of Paris; Thaddeus T. Walker, 1885 graduate of Meharry Medical College; Isaiah Mullen, 1883 Meharry graduate; and J. T. Newman, instructor in Straight's Medical School, visiting physician at New Orleans Charity Hospital, and member of the Louisiana Board of Health.

The most formidable barrier to the provision of adequate health services was the fact that many of the blacks were too poor to afford the medical attention they needed. The only solution to the problem was free medical services. Bureaucratic inefficiency and inadequate funding by the Union army and the Freedmen's Bureau, low pay for physicians, and the high rate of turnover in the personnel in the Freedmen's Hospital in New Orleans prevented the provision of adequate health care for indigent blacks in New Orleans. In 1866 and 1867 the Freedmen's Hospital in New Orleans employed an average of only five physicians. Bureau officials, insisting that health care was an individual responsibility, were never seriously committed to free medical service for blacks.

In an effort to offset the failures of the bureau to provide health care for indigent Negroes in New Orleans, Elisha Hathaway, a businessman from Rhode Island, gave $25,000 to Straight University, part of which sum was designated for a free medical dispensary for blacks providing that the Louisiana legislature would match it. The medical dispensary lasted for only a short while, because the legislature appropriated only $5,000 for it in 1871. After 1871 there were few opportunities for poverty-stricken Negroes to receive medical attention except at the overburdened Charity Hospital.[55]

The high mortality rate left heavy social burdens on the Negro community. Because of the sex differential in the death rate, many Negro families were suddenly left without breadwinners, and there were many Negro orphans and aged and poverty-stricken dependents. In spite of this, the rate of public dependency in the Negro community during Reconstruction was apparently low. Initially, after the Civil War, the Freedmen's Bureau encouraged this by refusing to give rations except to prevent starvation, and then rarely to able-bodied Negroes. Generally there were more destitute whites than Negroes on the bureau's relief rolls in New Orleans. In March 1868 there were 149 whites and 29 blacks receiving bureau rations; in April, 151 whites and 71 blacks; in July, 709 whites and 411 Negroes receiving rations. Most of these Negroes had come to the city from the neighboring parishes. Since aged and infirm New Orleans Negroes were usually cared for by their friends and relatives, few of them lived in the Dependents Home organized by the Freedmen's Bureau;

only 154 Negroes were admitted to the home between May 1867 and December 1868. Most of the paupers in New Orleans during Reconstruction were foreign born. In 1870, 1,178 of the 1271 paupers in the city were foreign born; only 31 were native-born blacks.[56]

There were probably three reasons for the apparently low rate of public dependency in the Negro community. First of all, New Orleans whites were generally unwilling to support Negro paupers. Secondly, Negroes had an abhorrence of public relief. Whites had contended so vociferously and continuously that Negroes would not work, that most New Orleans Negroes shunned public relief as a matter of racial pride. Negro newspapers tried to discourage their readers from going on relief even in times of public disaster. A white resident of New Orleans, Elizabeth Baker, wrote in 1878 that many Negroes refused charity: "the negroes, as a class dislike the insinuation of applying to Charitable institutions. . . . destitution is rife in the city and many prefer starvation to charity."[57] A third factor which kept Negroes off public relief was the activities of Negro benevolent societies and the desire of Negroes to care for their friends and relatives. In this regard, Friedrick Gerstäcker asserted that in New Orleans "the Negro is kind-hearted toward people of his own color and would not lightly abandon one in need of help."[58]

The Negro societies and benevolent associations were the most important agencies involved in organized efforts to solve community social problems. Negro societies in the days before the rise of Negro insurance companies provided the major form of social security against sickness, death, and poverty. They aided orphan asylums, Negro veterans, and the indigent; gave religious education to children; and fought against segregation and for racial uplift. For individual Negroes the societies provided status, a sense of belonging, some form of organized social life, a guarantee of aid to the sick and to the children and widows of deceased members. They also assured members an impressive and proper burial by paying for the bands to lead funeral processions, taking care of burial expenses, holding special rites over the body, marching in special regalia in the funeral procession, and wearing mourning badges for the deceased. Two societies, the Good Samaritans and the Union Benevolent Association, even had cemeteries for their members. Usually the societies held wakes over the bodies of deceased members and fined those members who did not attend the wake and funeral.[59]

Many of these societies were miniature life and health insurance companies. The Young Female Benevolent Association, for instance, for an admission fee of from $2.50 to $5.00 and monthly dues of from $.25 to $.50, guaranteed members from $2.00 to $4.00 per week in sick benefits, $1.00 for each doctor's visit, $50.00 for burial expenses, and $3.00 for wakes. Les Jeunes Amis, organized in 1867 and composed primarily of French-speaking Negroes, was even more like an insurance company. It assisted sick members, paid for drugs, doctor's fees, and burial expenses, and furnished cash relief for sick members. Charging admission fees of $1.00 to $2.00 for those who could pass a medical examination and from $.50 to $1.00 monthly dues, the society's benefits also extended to the immediate family of members. In each of the districts in which its members lived, the society established a relief committee to visit and aid the sick and to make sure they received their sick and burial expenses. Les Jeunes Amis elected three physicians and one druggist annually to care for its members. One of the physicians was the medical examiner of the society, and each of the physicians could receive up to $50 per month based on the record of their attendance on the sick. The druggist was paid according to the prescriptions he filled for members monthly. Sick members received a cash relief of $3.00 weekly; the money for burial expenses was $55 for members and from $10 to $40 for a member's relative. In addition, a member's beneficiary received from $20.00 to $50.00 upon his death. The members of the burial committee were required to attend the funeral of deceased members, at which they were to be dressed in the regalia of the society.

Les Jeunes Amis was one of the most substantial and elite societies in New Orleans. Any member could be expelled for a "dishonorable act," and ten members could bar any applicant from the society. Certain classes of people were automatically barred from membership. According to the constitution of the society, "No concubine or mistress can be registered as passive [family] member."[60]

Another society similar in character to Les Jeunes Amis was La Concorde. Organized by 65 French-speaking Negroes in 1878, the society had grown to 103 members and their families by 1884. Between 1878 and 1884 the society paid out a total of $1,838 for burial expenses for 55 members, $2,453 in fees for doctors and druggists, and $1,085 for pensions for aged and infirm members.[61]

A number of societies were organized to provide relief for indigent, aged, and suffering persons in the Negro community. Many of these were started by wealthy Negroes, for whom the care of their fellow blacks was a matter of noblesse oblige and racial pride. If blacks were to prove their capacity as free men, the community had to provide for those Negroes who were unable to care for themselves. The New Orleans *Black Republican* summed up this feeling perfectly on May 20, 1865: "It is indispensable that the people of color indicate ability to seize upon all the avenues that are open to any people. We must have of our own whatever of intellectual activity, of collective organization, in churches, asylums, or secular organizations, that makes up society and reveal[s] the capacity of government in a people."

The most important relief agencies were the Negro orphanages. Negro newspapers and churches led the campaigns for these orphanages, and Negro benevolent associations raised money for them. One observer noted in 1865 that Negroes were enthusiastic in their support of these institutions: "From the poor people of this city, destitute themselves, and troubled by the high prices of everything to provide for their own wants, we have raised near fifteen hundred dollars by appeals to our churches and benevolent societies for our orphans."[62]

One of the first orphan-aid organizations, the American Arts Association, was formed in 1864 among Negro Baptists. Later, the orphanage it established, the Union Sisters Asylum, was taken over and suported by the National Freedmen's Relief Association. On May 10, 1865, the N. F. R. A. also took charge of the Jefferson City Asylum, which had been established by General Banks on October 1, 1863. Negro churches, especially the Baptists, made clothing, furnished nurses, and made repairs on the Jefferson City asylum. The asylum received rations, clothing, wood, and hats from Union Army officials, and clothing, furniture, and $100 per month for salaries from the N. F. R. A. By July 1866 the N. F. R. A. had distributed $4,686 worth of clothing to the sick, destitute, and orphans in the city. From October 1863 to May 10, 1865, the asylum had an average of 50 inhabitants and placed 23 orphans in the homes of Negro families.[63]

There were several orphan-aid associations supported entirely by Negroes which operated during the Reconstruction period. The most important of these was the Louisiana Association for the Benefit of Colored Orphans, which was founded by the wealthy French-speaking Negroes early in 1865. The association's first orphanage was established by Louise De Mortie of Boston in March 1865, when General Stephen A. Hurlbut permitted the association temporarily to use the beautiful mansion of Pierre Soulé as an orphanage. Several fairs were held to raise money for a permanent orphanage. A Frenchman contributed $10,000 for this purpose, and in 1866 Thomy Lafon gave the association two lots as a site for the building, and a number of Negro workers donated two days of labor a week toward its construction. From concerts, fairs, and contributions from March to June 1865, the association raised $2,002 for the orphans and spent $918. Between September 1865 and December 1866 the balance in the association's treasury fluctuated between $641 and $1,300. The congregation of the St. Louis Cathedral collected $214

for the building fund, and Louis Charles Roudanez gave
the money to lay the foundation of the building for the association's Providence Asylum, which was completed in the fall
of 1867. In 1870 there were 21 orphans in the asylum, and
there were 40 in it in 1880.[64]

There were also several other associations to aid indigents.
In 1867 the Louisiana Relief Association raised $357 to
educate indigent Negro children. A Negro order, the Sisters
of the Holy Family, opened a home for the aged in 1875 and
an orphanage in 1880, both of which were supported by
several benevolent associations. In 1880 there were twenty-
three orphans (one white) cared for by thirteen sisters of the
order in its orphanage, and twenty-two Negroes ranging in
age from 40 to 95 in its home for destitute old people.[65]

The relatively small number of wealthy Negroes, the widespread poverty and ignorance, and the discrimination in
public services made it impossible for Negroes to eradicate all
of the social problems facing the community. Yet they made
a strenuous effort to support black orphans and to provide
mutual aid in time of sickness and death. Finding sustenance
for their spirit in their churches, Negroes drew upon their
African and European heritage to create the spirituals and
jazz, and engaged in several different kinds of social activities
which helped to unite the black community.

Race Relations

7

Relations between blacks and whites in New Orleans swung like a crazy pendulum back and forth between integration and segregation during the Reconstruction period. One steamboat admitted Negro and white passengers without discrimination to its cabins, while another, traveling the same route, herded all blacks into a section known as the "Freedmen's Bureau." While Negroes and whites sat indiscriminately in city streetcars, blacks were barred from hotels with a white clientele. Saloons serving all customers without regard to race often operated on the same street as soda shops which would not admit any black man. Integrated social clubs and churches existed side by side with segregated ones. These confusing swings of the race relations pendulum occurred in spite of the almost unanimous publicly stated desire of whites for complete segregation between the races and the equally unanimous desire of Negroes for integration in places of public accommodations. The mixture of Anglo-Saxons and Latins in the white population, varying degrees of commitment to equality among local and federal officials, and the sometimes servile and sometimes militant attitudes of Negroes created a mosaic in race relations without design.[1]

Most caucasians in New Orleans vigorously applauded the assertion by the New Orleans *Bulletin* that "The white race rules the world—the white race rules America—and the white race will rule Louisiana—and the white race shall rule New Orleans."[2] Blacks and whites were so dissimilar, whites argued, that it was impossible for them to interact on terms of equality. Could one mix oil and water? Blacks were afflicted with so many vices and were so inferior to whites that they should be kept in a subordinate position socially, politically, and economically.

The chief defenders of white supremacy in the city were the white-owned newspapers which continually vilified and ridiculed the Negro. Describing blacks as "niggers," "darkies," and "Sambos," white journalists generally depicted Negroes as speaking in almost incomprehensible dialect, and as an instinctively stupid, immoral, criminal, debased, dishonest, lazy, brutal, and lustful subhuman species. According to whites, there was nothing in the historical record of blacks which proved their capacity for advancement; they had contributed nothing to civilization or to the art of government.[3]

Humiliated by their defeat in a war in which the blacks had marched in the legions of the victors, southern white men returned from the field of battle to find the Negro in places which they felt were their own. The white man had hoped for so much in his "war for Independence," and had lost so much —his right to self-government, his right to hold office, the respect of his women, his self-respect, his property—at Appomattox, and the burden of defeat and humiliation hung so heavily on him, that he was forced to grasp any straw that promised some relief for the pain. The Negro, the property the white man went to war to preserve, was the ubiquitous reminder of his folly, guilt, humiliation, and defeat. The change in the Negro's status threatened to undermine his status. Most whites were bewildered, angered, and humiliated by the change. One of the rebel soldiers who returned to New Orleans in 1865 typified the attitudes of many whites: "It is very hard to get back home after four years of hardships and find niggers with arms in hand doing guard duty in the city and to see a white man taken under Guard by one of those black scondrels [sic]." Later he declared: "I hope the day will come when we will have the upper hand of those black scondrels and we will have no mercy for them[,] we will kill them like dogs. I [was] never down on a nigger as I am now."[4]

Throughout the Reconstruction period many whites advocated killing the Negroes "like dogs" in order to force them back into their subordinate position. The *Bulletin,* for instance, on December 16, 1874, urged the whites to "rebel and resist all attempts to join that which all experience has declared must be kept asunder."

When they were not advocating violence, New Orleans whites were adopting several devices in an effort to maintain white supremacy. Change in the Negro's position, they contended, should not be precipitous; the slow working of time would cure all ills. Besides, why was the South being singled out for special treatment when caste existed everywhere and even the radicals did not practice what they preached? It was better for the radicals to recognize that God had created whites superior to blacks and that the prejudice which was based on this fact was an instinct, an immutable law of nature. Nothing could change the natural antipathy between the races.[5] Since they could not completely blunt the demands that blacks were making to alter the Heaven-designed relations between the races, whites adopted a policy of divide and conquer. It was, they declared, only the mulattoes who wanted to associate with whites. They were simply using the blacks, whom they hated, to advance their own selfish designs.[6]

However much whites screamed about black inferiority, the Negro, in spite of his past enslavement, was the "coming man" in New Orleans. He had the heady feeling, a few years after he had been languishing in the dark night of slavery, of making and executing laws for all men, of being flattered by politicians (even his old masters) who sought his vote, of holding his dances in the legislative halls, and of being protected by a government he had helped to preserve with his own blood. His psychological security was enhanced by all of the promise inherent in Reconstruction: black was now fashionable; it symbolized power and influence.[7]

The changes in the Negro's status were so breathtaking, so hopeful, that it was cheering for blacks and their friends. The change in status did not, of course, mean an automatic change in Negro attitudes toward themselves and in their conduct toward whites. Some observers argued that the Negro continued his slavish conduct and obsequiousness when dealing with whites long after the war.[8] Because they recognized that there were feelings of helplessness, dependency, and self-depreciation in the black community, Negro leaders formulated an ideology to combat them. The Negro, they insisted, had to be upright and moral in his deportment, unselfish in his devotion to his race, and self-reliant. J. Willis Menard represented the views of many Negroes when he declared in 1867: "Our first step should be to dispel that servile hereditary fear which slavery has so deeply implanted in our natures, and learn to look at the white man as a mere common human being, and not as a ruler or superior."[9]

One of the most consistent themes of Negro racial ideology was the demand that whites respect black manhood. Manhood had to be exalted and preserved; a Negro had to be as bold in his actions as any man. Because he felt that he was a man and an American citizen, the Negro demanded equality of treatment and opportunity with whites. But his demands went beyond the question of integration and segregation. He wanted to be respected by whites, to have justice, a fair chance in life, and a recognition of his manhood.[10] What Negroes wanted, the *Tribune* argued, was for whites to "deal justly by us, respect our humanity, honor our aspirations, throw open to us the avenues of life. . . . The spirit of Christianity demands the recognition of our common brotherhood, and an equal opportunity for us with the rest of the human race, to develop our manhood." New Orleans Negroes wanted the schoolhouses and places of public accommodations open to all; they wanted equal justice, and an end to all "invidious discriminations." As Americans, blacks wanted to share all the privileges that other citizens enjoyed. "We wish," the *Tribune* declared, "to be respected and treated as men—not as Africans, or negroes, or colored people, but as Americans and American citizens."[11]

New Orleans Riot, 1866

A just appreciation of his manhood demanded that the Negro control his own destiny and institutions. No white man could understand the black man's sufferings, fight for the black man's rights, or transmit the ideal of citizenship, independence, and self-reliance to the black man's children.

Blacks had been sold out too often by whites to trust them to lead their fight for equal treatment; blacks had to battle in their own cause and make their own decisions because they were men. The *Tribune* asserted that although the Negro was thankful for his white friends, he had to control his own destiny:

If we are men—as our friends contend we are—we are able to attend to our own business. There is no man in the world so perfectly identified with our own interest as to understand it better than we do ourselves. . . . We must deliberate and decide for ourselves. . . . We need friends, it is true; but we do not need tutors. The age of guardianship is past forever. We now think for ourselves, and we shall act for ourselves.[12]

Many Negroes were proud of their racial origin. They generally referred to themselves as "colored," and "Negro," and sometimes as "black," "African," and "Africo-American." In 1878 New Orleans blacks joined with others in the campaign to capitalize "Negro"; the small "n," they contended, was a mark of inferiority fastened on them by white printers.[13] New Orleans Negroes, according to the *Tribune,* were men who were "proud of their origin, and who like the fiercest Roman would use the term, will tell you, 'I am a citizen.' " Pinchback spoke for many blacks in 1876 when he asserted that Negroes were "proud of our manhood and perfectly content to stand where God has placed us in the human scale; and would not lighten or darken the tinge of our skins, nor change the color nor current of our blood."[14] The vulgar and disgusting scurrility and contempt of the white press held no terrors for Negroes who were proud of the property they held, their successes in literature, and the offices they held and the character of the men holding them. Until recently enslaved, they felt that their progress was little short of remarkable. The *Louisianian* voiced this attitude in its April 11, 1874, editorial on the "Progress of Our Own Race." Negroes, it asserted, "have achieved, under the conditions precedent of centuries of trial and contact with civil liberty and a Christian civilization, in a decade of years—a progress and development that came

to our Anglo-Saxon citizens only after more than a thousand
years of conflict, civil wars and revolutions."

For years after the Civil War, New Orleans Negroes
fought against the attempt of whites to maintain segregation
in transportation and places of public resort. The practice of
segregation, blacks contended, stamped the mark of inferiority
on them; it was humiliating, inconvenient, crushing, and an
abridgment of their liberties. The word "humiliation" appeared more frequently than any other in Negro catalogues
of the impact of segregation on them.[15] The *Louisianian* contended that Negroes as a race, being "denied the rights of
men," and placed under a ban, were "made to feel the sword
piercing our souls, at every turn, and in every avenue of life."[16]

Negroes argued that prejudice, because it was based on
selfishness, arrogance, pride, and a spirit of caste, was a
cancer eating away at the vitals of American society, a fester-
ing sore on the body politic blocking progress, reform, and
civilization. Closed to reason, prejudice led to the belief that
a man had a right to wrong another because he did not like
him. It was un-American, un-republican, and un-Christian.[17]
Compared to foreign countries or judged on the basis of universal principles, America was a moral wasteland, a criminal
in the morally ordered universe.[18] The moral insensitivity of
America began with its birth and continued throughout its
history. The founding fathers and subsequent statesmen were
"little men" who applauded or acquiesced in the oppression
and enslavement of Negroes, in spite of the lofty words of the
Declaration of Independence and the Constitution. America
had been so demented by prejudice, one Negro declared, that
it drew "its line of recognition of humanity at *white men*, and
. . . tells the negro applying for civil rights: 'You must try
some other establishment sir. We couldn't do it here.' " And,
although it abolished slavery, in its place it "attempted in the
forms of democracy to establish the most preposterous and
impossible of aristocracies—*une aristocratie de la peau*" which
doomed the Negro "to a Pariah-like position on earth" and
assigned him "to an equivocal position in heaven."[19]

Since Negroes felt that prejudice was not innate, they fought to eradicate it from the minds of whites. They appealed to the white man's conscience, sense of fair play, reason, and justice. They pleaded for whites to put themselves in the Negro's place and imagine how they would feel if they were kicked out of a hotel or theater simply because of the color of their skin and regardless of their wealth and culture. Negroes also tried to show that there were no superior or inferior races. While there were different races, the *Tribune* asserted, none could be declared superior to the others: "one race may excell in one respect, but be inferior in another. No one race combines in itself all the separate excellencies of the rest. Differences are also very largely the result of circumstances, and will in time vanish or be materially modified."[20]

Discrimination, Negroes argued, cast doubt on the superiority of the Southern white. If the white man was so superior in intellect, physical strength, and morality, why was he so intent upon handicapping his "inferior" in the race of life? If he belonged to such an elite race, why should he be demeaned by contact with his "inferior"?[21] "The pride of race which would be damaged by such propinquity," the *Tribune* declared, "must be of a very shallow character." In fact, reasoned the *Tribune,* all of the proscriptions and bombast indicated that the white man was not as sure of his superiority as he claimed: "This perpetual and feverish cry of superiority is a clear mark of weakness. The bully is proverbially a coward, the braggart a shallow prated ignoramus. True worth, intellectual or moral, is modest and unpretending. It does not blow its own horn. It is not intensely sensitive of any invasion of its sacred dignity. It fears not contact with inferiors."[22]

Whites, blacks asserted, could not point to the condition of the Negro or his enslavement to prove his inferiority. Whites had been enslaved before Africans had: the Britons had enslaved the Saxons and Normans, and the Romans had made slaves of them all. At some point in their history all Americans had been savages, so what right did whites have to point to the savagery of Africans as proof of the Negro's

John Willis Menard

inferiority? Besides, the degradation of the contemporary
population of Ireland showed that "similar circumstances
have the same effect upon a white race that they have upon
the colored people of the South."[23]

To those who counseled patience, the Negro answered
"now!" To those who called upon Negroes to wait for the
slow but sure operation of time to cure racial animosities, they
asked, "What has time ever cured?" The *Tribune* declared
that the Negro could not wait for time to wear away prejudice
while whites were busy increasing it: "If our white editors and
politicians, and neighbors generally, would stop pelting us
with stones, would stop abusing and deriding us, their talk
about leaving everything to time would have some reason in
it." Time alone would not, the Negroes contended, soften
prejudices. The white man could counsel patience because he
did not feel the pain of discrimination. But patience was not
a virtue to the Negro; it was absolute folly.[24]

If blacks waited for the slow operation of time, they
would never obtain their rights. If left to time, caste lines

would harden, segregation would be enshrined in law and custom, and two separate nations, one white, one black, would develop in America. The only way for the races to learn to live together peacefully was to begin their integrated life during Reconstruction. If not during their lifetimes, Negroes asked, when would the time come for equality? On July 31, 1867, the *Tribune* summed up these arguments perfectly and made a prophetic statement about the dangers of waiting:

The objection 'too soon' is but laughable. It is repeated at each and every reform to be accomplished. It only evinces a lack of courage to carry out the reform itself. When will the right time come? Is it, per chance, after we will have separated for ten or twenty years the two races in different schools, and when we shall have realized the separation of this nation into two peoples? The difficulty, then, will be greater than it is to-day. A new order of things, based on separation will have taken root. It will, then, be TOO LATE.

It was not patience but agitation which would reform society. Negroes protested strongly against segregation and called for a redress of their grievances. As men, felt the *Tribune,* they could not do otherwise: "We can and must show ourselves men, conscious of our rights and resolute to assert them. . . . If we tamely submit to indignity, without even a remonstrance, we prove ourselves to be unworthy of anything better." Agitation had to be the order of the day, regardless of the costs. According to the *Louisianian,* Negroes would struggle to obtain their rights, "And we will agitate, and agitate, and struggle for the enjoyment of our rights at all times, under all circumstances and at every hazard. We know our rights, and we will dare maintain them even if we do have some broken heads."[25]

Historically it was true, Negroes contended, that barbarous practices were rooted out by a positive act, by the application of the power of the state. Consequently they began at an early date to demand legislative protection for equal access to all public institutions and places of public accommodation in Louisiana. They rejected the old adage that custom made law and that no legislation could change custom. On the contrary, the *Louisianian* argued, "custom must yield to statute law whereof it is a contravention. Custom makes habit, and as we are all creatures of habit to a greater or lesser extent, the reform of bad customs must necessarily precede the acquirement of good habits."[26]

The best way to end the custom of segregation and the whites' habit of looking down on blacks was to have equality before the law. No citizen should be allowed, the *Louisianian* asserted, to oppress another citizen because of his prejudices. Negroes urged the legislature and the 1867 constitutional convention to make it impossible for whites to continue the savage policy of exclusion. The rights of all citizens had to be protected, the *Tribune* declared, and the community had to be organized "in such a way that every man, woman, and child have [sic] the same rights, immunities, and privileges, in all public concerns, as any other man, woman or child."[27]

One of the most controversial positive laws was the one forbidding discrimination in places of public resort, passed by the legislature in 1869. White businessmen protested that as owners of private establishments they had a right to refuse to serve any customer. They felt it was wrong for Louisiana to be a pioneer in this area. Besides, they argued, if they served Negroes, their white customers would desert them because they did not believe in social equality. Negro leaders answered these charges in various ways. Any business which was licensed by a public agency, they contended, had, in effect, signed a contract to serve the public. And since Negroes and whites constituted the body politic, a licensed business violated its contract by treating any segment of the public with contempt. Any merchant who offered goods or services to the public was bound to sell them to everyone without distinction.[28]

To those businessmen who feared that a swarm of Negroes entering their establishments would chase away white customers, Negro leaders tried to reassure them. First of all, since the law applied to all businesses, where would the whites run? And even if boycotts started, they would be brief; whites simply could not do without the services the businesses provided. The second reason for the painlessness of instituting equality in public accommodations, Negro leaders promised, was that probably few blacks would visit white businesses. Too may Negroes were too poor to visit the more expensive places and too religious to attend many of the places of public amusement. Consequently, Negroes would not stampede these places. Those who did come would be the "respectable," well-educated, wealthy Negroes. The poor black laborer, the *Tribune* assured whites, would not even "pretend to come and pay the price charged by the whites."[29] Essentially, then, Negro leaders tried to assure upper-class whites that they were in no more danger of being inundated by lower-class blacks than they were of rubbing shoulders with lower-class whites: equals would associate with equals.

Did practice conform to the accommodations law in New Orleans, or was the law negated by customary segregation? While there is no simple answer to the question, the racial ideology of blacks and the social, economic, and political milieu of the period apparently made it difficult for a white businessman to evade the law. The large number of white small businessmen generally operated on such a small profit margin that they could not lightly disobey the law and risk the possibility of an expensive lawsuit and having to pay a large fine. If they did go to court, their cases might be heard by city recorders and judges, many of whom were married to Negro women or had Negro concubines and who might not be entirely sympathetic (even the attorney general of Louisiana had a Negro family). In addition, there were Negroes on the city council and in the state legislature who granted and revoked charters of the businesses. Then, too, the civil sheriff of Orleans parish was a Negro, and many blacks served on the police force and could not be expected to be enthusiastic in enforcing a custom which discriminated against them.

In their dilemma white businessmen reacted in various ways to the public accommodations law. The most recalcitrant refused initially to serve any blacks. Those who did serve them tried to discourage them from returning by adopting several devices. As soon as a Negro entered an establishment, the price of a soda would suddenly jump from five cents to one dollar. If the Negro persisted, the proprietor might add castor oil or pepper to his drink.

There is a great deal of evidence which suggests that a number of businessmen refused to obey the public accommodations law. In 1871, for example, the managers of the Metairie Race Course built a separate viewing stand for Negroes. The complaints of Negroes indicate that throughout the period there was much discrimination in other places of public accommodations. One Negro, deeply angered by discrimination against blacks in New Orleans, argued that because of their "pride of person," Negroes should boycott discriminatory businesses and refuse to "submit to *pay* for self-degradation."[30]

Many Negroes tried to end discrimination by suing the businessmen who refused them service. They filed at least fourteen suits against soda shops, saloons, theaters, and the opera in New Orleans between 1869 and 1875. Negroes adopted the practice of demanding a large amount of money in damages to discourage other white businessmen from discriminating against blacks. Two of the suits were for $10,000; one for $5,000; and one for $500. The businessmen were fined from $30 to $1,000 when found guilty of violating the law. In one of the most important of these cases, C. S. Sauvinet, civil sheriff of Orleans parish and former cashier of the Freedman's Savings and Trust Company, sued a saloon keeper for $10,000 in 1871 for refusing to sell him a drink because he was a Negro. Sauvinet won the case and was awarded $1,000 in damages by a New Orleans judge. Similarly, Emily Lobe and William Smith were awarded $250 and $30 respectively when they were refused service in soda

shops. In 1874 the manager of the Academy of Music was
fined $1,000 for ejecting Peter Joseph from his seat after he
had purchased a ticket.[31]

Apparently the successful suits against some proprietors
forced many others to serve all customers without distinction.
After the Lobe case the *Louisianian* observed: "Suits of this
kind prosecuted under our State laws have proved very beneficial in causing the abandonment of the absurd conduct prac-
ticed so largely by these and similar places."[32] The effect of
lawsuits is indicated clearly in the efforts Negroes made to
have integrated seating arangements at the opera house and
theaters. The campaign also disclosed the strange twists which
efforts to enforce the accommodations law often took.

The first suit against the St. Charles Theatre was filed by
Victor Eugene Macarthy, a mulatto who was so nearly white
that he often obtained seats in the section reserved for whites.
But when Macarthy went to see the opera *Figaro Bravo* in
January 1869, the manager discovered he was in the section
set aside for whites and asked him to leave. Macarthy asserted
that it was "an indignity that he, a colored man, should be
thus treated in a civilized community." When the manager
tried to return his fare, Macarthy began to use "some rather
uncomplimentary language . . . and finally to threaten that
gentleman with corrections by slaps in the face and kicks
a posteriori."[33] Macarthy immediately filed suit against the
manager in the district court. Even after this suit, however,
the St. Charles did not relent. As a result, Negroes boycotted
the theater until the national civil rights law was passed in
1875. In March 1875 state senator T. B. Stamps and tax
assessor Aristide Dejoie decided to test the law by purchasing
tickets to the dress circle. At first the proprietor tried to steer
them to the old Jim Crow section, but when they insisted on
the seats they had paid for, they were directed to them.[34]
Apparently this act ended Jim Crow seating in the St. Charles.
The *Louisianian* urged blacks to attend, and one of its editors
went to the theater and reviewed many of the plays presented
in it.

Negroes were even more persistent in their efforts to end
Jim Crow seating arrangements in the New Orleans Opera
House than in theaters. Initially, after the passage of the state
civil rights law, the opera house had ended its policy of
segregated seating. In fact, the manager, L. Placide Canonge,
had been so congenial that in the spring of 1874 a group of
Negro opera lovers bought him a silver service as a testimonial. The white newspapers were enraged by these developments. The *Bulletin* took the occasion to launch a long tirade
against Negroes and to deliver a veiled threat to Canonge:
"the issue must be met boldly, and managers of theatres must
not be the recipients of silver service as testimonials from
Negroes for relaxing the rule of exclusion in favor of a
favored few of their race."[35] The result was that Canonge
bowed to pressure from the whites and resumed Jim Crow
seating arrangements.

Negroes immediately filed three separate suits against the
opera house and generally boycotted it. First, Aristide Mary
and John E. Staes, a Negro lawyer who was the son of one
of the white recorders in the city, sued the manager in December 1874 for denying them seats which they had formerly
occupied. Later in the same month, a Negro with the same
name as Canonge, with Staes as his attorney, sued the opera
house. Apparently the boycott had been effective, because
the manager complained that very few Negroes had been attending and certainly not enough of them to justify the risk
of losing his white customers by "promiscuous" seating arrangements. After these suits and the passage of the national
civil rights law, Negroes returned to the opera and were
seated "promiscuously" among the whites.[36]

There is a practical difficulty involved in any attempt to
prove how widespread were the integrated facilities in New
Orleans. Generally, those white businessmen who obeyed the
law were not mentioned in the newspapers of the period. It
is obvious, however, that there were many of them who did
obey it. For instance, several of the white newspapers, conscious of the defections among the white businessmen, repeat-

Jim Crow Gallery

edly urged white proprietors of places of public resort to
refuse service to Negroes. By March 1875 the *Bulletin* had
become so exasperated that it urged white patrons to boycott
those businesses which served Negroes and whites without
distinction. Apparently there were few white businessmen who
bowed to this pressure. The *Louisianian* was proud of their
record in this regard and asserted on June 13, 1874, that the
"Catholicity of spirit" in New Orleans "has expressed itself
by the recognition in our midst of the civil and public rights
of the colored race more fully than has been the case in any
other Southern city."

    A few of the places where equality of treatment was a
fact were mentioned in the newspapers. Many of the saloons,
for instance, apparently served black and white customers
alike. In Redwitz's beer saloon, accoring to the *Louisianian*

in 1874, Pinchback had "repeatedly for the last two or three years, accompanied by white and colored citizens, been waited upon and served in the same saloon and that without insult."[37] When Redwitz refused to serve Pinchback in May 1874, even the *Bulletin* castigated him for seeking cheap publicity. Negroes also were served along with whites at the Maison Blanche restaurant and at public resorts on Lake Pontchartrain. In regard to the latter, on August 9, 1879, the *Louisianian* urged Negroes to visit Spanish Fort and advised them that "there is no distinction." In January of the same year Senator William P. Kellogg had an integrated dinner party at Antoine's Restaurant.

The longest and one of the most bitter of the Negro's campaigns for equal treatment involved public transportation. The first issue which arose involved the "star cars" which were exclusively for Negroes on the streetcar lines in New Orleans. Negroes complained that there were so few of the specially marked cars that they experienced great difficulty in traveling about the city. Actually, about one-third of all the streetcars were set aside for Negroes, but, in practice, so many whites crowded into them that there was little room left for Negro passengers.[38]

In their campaign to abolish the star cars, Negroes insisted that the exclusion of Negroes from the "white cars" was not only an inconvenience and a barbaric relic of slavery, it was a public insult and mark of inferiority placed on blacks. In an effort to remove this brand Negroes petitioned military officials for redress from 1862 to 1867, and the Negro newspapers urged blacks to enter the cars set aside for whites and to sue the companies for their exclusion. The Negro journals also reprinted as models for the emulation of New Orleans blacks the news of every successful suit or campaign to integrate street cars in San Francisco, Mobile, and Philadelphia.[39]

Animosity toward the "star cars" was apparently widespread in the Negro community. From 1862 until the spring of 1867 blacks frequently boarded the "white cars" and refused to leave. Almost as frequently they were beaten up by the passengers and drivers and thrown off. They then lodged complaints with the city recorders, provost marshals, and U.S. commissioners. On occasion Negroes reacted violently to discrimination; in September 1862 and May 1867 groups of Negroes stopped the white cars and beat up the drivers. Squads of Negro soldiers sometimes leveled their rifles on white drivers who refused to pick up Negro passengers.

On this, as on other issues, military officials were inconsistent. The employment of Negro troops and their subsequent aggressive demands for impartial admission to all streetcars forced military officials to take some steps to end the potentially explosive situation. Butler ordered that Negro troops in uniform be admitted to the cars, but military officials were not enthusiastic in enforcing the order. And even when they were admitted to the cars, complained the Negro soldiers, their wives and children were excluded. They demanded that the privilege they enjoyed should be extended to all blacks. In May 1867, after General Philip H. Sheridan refused to sustain the policy of exclusion, the streetcar lines ordered their drivers to admit impartially to all the cars all persons who purchased tickets. Although there was some resistance from the drivers at first, by midsummer integrated streetcars had become an accepted pattern in New Orleans; they remained integrated throughout the Reconstruction period.[40]

Negroes could not abolish discrimination on railroad trains and steamboats as easily as they did on streetcars. The railroads were especially offensive in this regard. Many of the companies relegated Negroes to the smoking cars, refused to sell them pullman berths in spite of Louisiana's law forbidding such practices, barred them from cars in which white ladies were riding, and forced them to occupy the car nearest the engine.[41] Some of the railroads discriminated against Negroes so consistently that the *Louisianian* asserted on February 25, 1872, that "flagrant violations . . . have been, and are being daily perpetuated by our railroad companies." In regard to the law forbidding discrimination, the *Louisianian* declared, "At present this is a dead letter." When a special

committee of the legislature investigated charges of discrimination against three railroads, they found that the New Orleans, Mobile, and Texas Railroad had violated the civil
rights law. In fact, the committee reported, "the testimony
before us shows clearly that . . . persons have been ejected on
account of color from the first class passenger cars of the
company, and were compelled to go into the second class cars
(smoking cars) by order of the conductors of the train . . .
the same distinction and discrimination is enforced at the
present time."[42]

The attempts Negroes made to prohibit segregation on the
railroads were far more sophisticated than any of their other
campaigns. Unlike their fight for equal treatment in places of
public resort, blacks filed few suits against the railroads. Instead, Negro legislators insisted that each act chartering a
railroad must contain a provision prohibiting racial discrimination, and they extracted explicit promises from company
officials to provide equal accommodations to all passengers.[43]
Pinchback, for instance, wrote that he had voted for the
charter of the Jackson Railroad only after he had "received
. . . positive assurances" that "it would be run on just and
liberal principals [sic], making no distinction on account of
color."[44] These promises and charter provisions were important
because it gave the Negro legislators a weapon to use against
the railroads which adopted Jim Crow practices. Each case
of discrimination led to a threat of legislative review of a
company's charter.

These threats and the few suits which were filed were
generally effective in forcing the railroads to provide equal
accommodations. Negroes adopted a novel and very effective
procedure in filing suits against the railroads. For example,
in 1871, when Pinchback purchased a pullman ticket for his
wife on the Jackson Railroad, and the company refused to
honor the ticket, he filed a $25,000 damage suit against the
company, threatened to try to have its charter revoked, and
argued that it was senseless to exclude blacks from a pullman
"when colored people *sit* with white people in the cars." Com-

pany officials were profuse in their apologies, and H. S. McComb, the president, wrote Governor Warmouth that his agents were acting under the rules of the old company and had he known of Pinchback's application for a pullman berth he would have honored it. And although it was not possible to change the Jim Crow arrangements immediately, McComb asserted, he was "desirous of doing everything I can in that way." Pinchback shrewdly refused either to drop or to prosecute his suit, holding it as a threat over the company to insure equal accommodations.[45]

By and large, these tactics worked. When the legislative committee condemned the New Orleans, Mobile, and Texas Railroad in February 1872, it did not have cause to censure either the Louisiana and Texas Railroad or the Jackson Railroad. Of the latter company, the committee reported that it had "examined, with great care, the Jackson railroad. . . . We find that this company has conformed in all things to their chartered rights."[46] There are several other indications that Jim Crow rail cars were infrequent during the 1870s. The *Louisianian* frequently complimented the Louisiana and Texas Railroad and the New Orleans, St. Louis, and Chicago Railroad for their courteous treatment of Negro passengers in both day and pullman coaches.[47] While there was some change after the Democrats returned to power in 1877, the *Louisianian* could still commend the latter company on November 30, 1878, "because of the courtesy of its attaches and eating-house keepers all along the line—which is in marked contrast with those of any other route outside of the city." Another indication of equal access to railroad cars during this period was the outcry which was raised when a Louisiana railroad took the unusual step of providing separate cars for a Negro excursion to Mobile in 1880. The *Louisianian* complained about this and urged Negroes to boycott the railroad: "What an outrage, and how long will such continue? Of course decent colored people will leave those special cars alone." As late as 1885 George Washington Cable asserted that "In Louisiana . . . in the trains a Negro or mulatto may sit where he will."[48]

The steamboat companies were more adamant than the railroads in their opposition to providing equal accommodations to Negroes. Cable wrote that while the Louisiana Negro was not segregated on trains, "on boats he must confine himself to a separate quarter called the 'Freedmen's bureau.' "[49] Several suits were filed by Negroes because of this treatment. State Senator Edward Butler of Plaquemines parish filed a $25,000 suit against the officers of the *Bannock City* when he was refused admission to a first-class cabin, beaten with an iron bar, and stabbed by the crew. In 1872 Josephine DeCuir, a plantation owner in Pointe Coupée parish, sued the owners and officers of the *Governor Allen* for $75,000 because they refused her a cabin and would not serve her dinner until after all of the white passengers had dined. Eventually the Eighth District Court awarded her $1,000, and the decision was overturned by the U.S. Supreme Court. Louisa Chevalier filed a similar suit against the *Seminole* in 1875. In 1879, while on the steamer *Frank Pargoud*, T. T. Allain, an Iberville parish planter, was refused a drink of water by the bartender who told him the water was not intended for "niggers."[50]

The most effective means Negroes devised to obtain equal accommodations on the steamboats was the boycotting of offensive companies. Many of the steamboats, realizing that they would lose the freight of large Negro planters, did not discriminate against blacks. Edward Butler asserted that even on the *Bannock City* he had not been Jim Crowed before 1871. He declared that "he had frequently travelled on steamboats under the identical officers, and had enjoyed undisturbed access to every part of their boat, and never until this wanton outrage had been subject to any annoyance."[51] Occasionally the companies provided steamers for excursions by integrated groups.

While it is obvious that the steamboat companies were inconsistent in their treatment of black passengers, the general rule apparently was segregation. When the companies obeyed the law, of course, they did not make the headlines. There are a number of indications, however, that there was a great

P. B. S. Pinchback

deal of segregation. In 1870, for example, Pinchback and several other Negroes attempted to launch a steamship line partly because they were dissatisfied with the treatment of black passengers by white-owned companies. Apparently things changed little in the next two years, for on December 21, 1872, the *Louisianian* commented that a new boat which provided equal accommodations for blacks was "the first boat that was ever shown a colored passenger respect."

This same pattern of inconsistency appeared in practically every area of public accommodations except the streetcars. There were too many Negroes who were too ignorant, too timid, or too poor to fight against discrimination, and too many whites who insisted on it, for things to be otherwise. Even when Negroes were able to prohibit discrimination in Louisiana, their efforts were undermined by the Jim Crow patterns which existed elsewhere in the South. One example of this occurred in 1871 when several Negroes rode to Mobile in a railroad car with whites on the Chattanooga Railroad but were forced to occupy the smoking car on their return trip over the same line. When they complained about this they were informed that "they were not in Louisiana, but in Alabama, where they would not be permitted to mix as they liked with white people."[52]

Such events as these convinced many blacks that they could never have equal access to places of public resort as long as Jim Crow was a national figure. The *Louisianian* argued that the only recourse for Negroes was a national civil rights bill, because blacks had learned that in spite of the various state laws, they could "expect no effectual remedy of these evils from the respective State governments."[53] Since so much discrimination occurred in interstate travel, Negro leaders urged New Orleans Negroes to join national campaigns to halt the practice. In 1872 and 1873 New Orleans Negroes held mass meetings and sent petitions to Congress in support of Senator Charles Sumner's civil rights bill.

It is not exactly clear what impact the passage of the national civil rights act in 1875 made on race relations in New Orleans. The New Orleans *Picayune* asserted on March 6, 1875, that there was little change in racial patterns in the city because Negroes realized that under the act they could only obtain slow and expensive remedies through the courts. C. C. Antoine told a northern newspaper reporter the same thing. In an effort to minimize conflict and quiet the fears of whites, Negro leaders apparently tried to discourage their followers from descending en masse on white businesses. They felt that, since the law had been passed, time and the power of the state would eventually overcome white resistance to equal accommodations. Pinchback was probably more insistent on this point than any other prominent New Orleans Negro.[54] In a speech in March 1875 he advised the Negroes that they "should so prudently and courteously exercise the rights it gave us so as not to make the measure an irritant and aggravation of the evils and prejudices it was intended to correct."[55] Many New Orleans Negroes, having always rejected calls for patience, felt Pinchback's position was untenable. They realized that they had to begin exercising their rights immediately while the whites were still demoralized and unsure of how they should react. Acting on this premise, they obtained equality of treatment in the opera house, theaters, and other places. Unfortunately there were many Negroes who took Pinchback's advice and lost a golden opportunity to integrate many of the places which had defied the state law.

Some of the businesses were so overwhelmed by the pressure of state and national legislative threats that they capitulated and served all customers without distinction. Others, however, made it so unpleasant for blacks or were so inconsistent in their policies that few Negroes frequented their establishments. Apparently the most implacable foes of the provision of equal accommodations were the white hotel owners. While this proved to be a boon to Negro boarding-house keepers, it seriously undermined the effectiveness of the state and national civil rights laws. A number of the upper-class white restaurants were also apparently able to evade the law. But this was a result more of the poverty of Negroes and the fact that few of them dined out than of the ineffectiveness of the law.

The public opposition of whites to extending equal privileges to Negroes in places of public resort pales in comparison to the almost insane fears which they expressed over the possibility of intimate contacts with blacks in public institutions and in social relations. Every right granted equally to Negroes and whites, they screamed, made an irreparable breach in the barriers to social equality. "Promiscuous mixing" of the races in places of public resort conjured up horrifying visions of the angelic white woman in the arms of a savage black Lothario. Consistent with this fear, most whites were publicly violently opposed to integrated schools, churches, and social functions, to mixed marriages, or to equality of the races in any public institution. Almost every demand that blacks made in these areas was viewed as an attempt to force themselves on white folks, a violation of the sacred principle that every man had a right to choose his associates, and a contravention of the Divine Law ordaining the separation of races.

Since racially exclusive social organizations, functions, and public institutions were so sacrosanct, the charge of attempting to enforce "social equality" was the most difficult problem Negroes had to overcome in their fight for equality. Generally the blacks gave two answers to their detractors. First, they almost always denied any desire for social equality with whites. Second, they contended that legislation had nothing to do with social relations, and, for that matter, neither did equal access to public institutions: even among whites, attendance of all-white schools and other public institutions did not involve social acceptance of all those who attended. J. Sella Martin gave a typical answer to such charges in 1874: "Social equality is a humbug. There are many men of my own race with whom I would not associate, and not a few whites. We must determine for ourselves the positions to which we are entitled and obtain them if we can." Negroes also chided whites for being so presumptuous as to think that blacks were especially desirous of their company.[56]

Most public institutions, except schools, affected so few individuals that they rarely made news. Consequently it is practically impossible in many cases to determine whether they were ever integrated during this period. Take, for instance, the matter of cemeteries. It is clear from the reports of the sextons of many cemeteries that both whites and blacks were buried in the same cemetery. Apparently, however, Negroes and whites were often buried in separate sections. Since so many of the different nationalities and religious denominations had privately owned separate cemeteries, Negroes generally accepted the pattern and established cemeteries of their own. On the other hand, Negroes did protest the exclusion of their race from insane asylums and orphanages, especially if such institutions received appropriations from the state. In regard to asylums, Mayor Monroe asserted in 1866, "All persons temporarily insane are, without reference to race and color, admitted to the City Insane Asylum." When a correspondent of the New York *Herald* visited the asylum in July 1871 he found "white and black, old and young, pure and

BRISTOL POLYTECHNIC
ST. MATTHIAS LIBRARY

impure, . . . all huddled together."[57] Apparently, however, Negroes were excluded from privately financed white orphanages and were relegated to a separate ward of Charity Hospital. Negroes did, however, admit a few white children to their own orphanages and were admitted along with whites to the municipally operated Boys' House of Refuge for orphans, delinquents, and abandoned boys.[58]

The same mixed pattern of segregation and integration prevailed in social relations as in public institutions. For the most part whites were opposed to any public social intimacy with Negroes. Because of the resistance of whites and because of the Negroes' desire to manage their own affairs and to achieve status, most of the blacks were also opposed to intimate relations with whites unless they were on terms of perfect equality. Even so, the two groups did occasionally interact on intimate terms. There was one integrated social and political organization, the Louisiana Club, and one of the white clubs sometimes invited Negroes to attend its receptions. Early in 1880 Negro and white baseball clubs began competing against each other. Occasionally, Negro and white veterans of the Battle of New Orleans had dinner together, and local and national Republican black and white leaders socialized or attended banquets together.[59]

The most successful integration of a social organization was among the Masons in New Orleans. In 1867 Eugene Chassignac, Grand Commander of the white Scotch Rite Masons of Louisiana, began to organize integrated lodges in the city. Over the strenuous objections of Oscar J. Dunn, Worshipful Grand Master of the all-black Free and Accepted Masons in Louisiana, Chassignac engaged in "the noble task of obliterating the distinction of race and color in the Masonic fraternity." Most of the Negroes who joined the two integrated lodges which were subsequently established belonged to the old Creole community. Initially most of the officers were white, but by the mid-1870s more and more Negroes were being elected to leadership posts. A Parisian lodge elected Chassignac an honorary member, and lodges in Italy, Bel-

gium, and Rhode Island commended the whites in New Orleans for their successful efforts "in abolishing all prejudices
based on color and in recognizing no other gradations of
society but those marked out by personal virtues and merits."[60]

Generally speaking, the churches in New Orleans maintained the patterns which had existed before the Civil War.
Negroes continued to be relegated to galleries and to be taught
in separate Sunday schools when they attended white Protestant churches; the color line was tightly drawn in the house
of God. On May 25, 1871, the *Louisianian* complained that
"It is still true, as in the olden time that the doors of the
house of God are shut in our face, except upon the condition
that some imp of proscription shall open them, and colonize
us in the galery [sic] of the church." One Negro complained
in 1871 because black children were first accepted in a separate Sunday school class at the Fourth Presbyterian Church
and then excluded and told to go to a Negro church. Describing such actions as "a wicked senseless antagonism to
the principle of equality in God's Church," he felt that eventually the church would be so "purified as not to seek for
fitness for scriptural teaching in a Sunday school in the color
of a skin."[61]

The most noteworthy conflict over segregation in the
churches occurred at Ames Methodist Episcopal Church. In
1869 Ames had twenty Negro members who apparently sat
where they wished in the church. In that year, however, one
of the trustees objected, and Negroes were relegated to the
balcony, with the approval of the pastor. In 1875, after a
spirited controversy in the religious press in the city, the
church adopted a nondiscriminatory policy.[62] The Reverend
J. C. Hartzell, editor of the *Southwestern Christian Advocate*
and an elder in the Methodist Church, could then report in
March 1875 that "Ames Church . . . has colored members
who sit with the congregation where they choose."[63]

The Catholic church was the only denomination which
fought consistently against the proscriptive pew. Many observers noted the lack of color distinctions among the com-

Oscar J. Dunn

municants at the St. Louis Cathedral. In 1863, for instance, Silas E. Fales, a Union soldier, wrote that he saw all classes entering the cathedral, "from the purest white donor through all the different shades to the blackest negro."[64] The most convincing account of integration in the Catholic church came from a Methodist minister, the Reverend Hartzell, who declared that "In her most aristocratic churches in this city, lips of every shade, by hundreds press with devout kisses the same crucifixes, and fingers of as great variety in color, are dipped in the 'holy water,' to imprint the cross on as varied brows. In the renting of pews colored families have a chance, and we have seen them sitting as others in every part of the house."[65]

In spite of its lofty principles, the Catholic church was not immune to pressure from prejudiced whites. This was especially true of the White League. In 1875 some of the Catholic priests publicly supported the league, and in the same year they attempted to segregate parishioners in the St. Louis Cathedral. As a result of the latter practice, the *Louisianian* reported on December 4, 1875, many Negroes were boycotting the cathedral. As the White League turned more of its attention to politics and as the boycott by the Negro parishioners became increasingly effective, the cathedral quietly returned to its traditional nondiscriminatory policy.[66]

The most controversial aspect of race relations in nineteenth-century New Orleans was the question of interracial sexual contacts. By the time Reconstruction began, miscegenation had been going on for so long that more people of both the "white" and "Negro" populations in New Orleans and Louisiana had ancestors in the other race than did the residents of any other city or state in America. In fact, the population was so mixed that it was virtually impossible in many cases to assign individuals to either group. Silas E. Fales, a Union soldier, wrote in 1863 that "it is hard telling who is white here[,] the Creoles are blacker than some of the mulattos [sic]."[67] Many of the Italians, Spanish, and Portuguese were, of course, dark because of their contact with Africans for several centuries in Europe. Other "whites," who had originally come from the West Indies, also had Negro ancestors. Then, too, some of the quadroons had "passed" for and were accepted as white. As conditions became more oppressive in the mid-1870s, more and more Negroes who were white in appearance passed for "white." Louisiana officials reported that hundreds of mulattoes recorded themselves as "white" in the 1875 state census. In all probability, from 100 to 500 Negroes became "white" every year from 1875 to the 1890s.[68]

The meaninglessness of racial distinctions and the extent of miscegenation and social intimacy are revealed clearly in the 1880 manuscript census of New Orleans. Several Negro and white couples had adopted children or had stepchildren, godchildren, and grandchildren of the opposite race living with them. The census takers' attempts to classify people according to skin color often led to rather strange things. Two mulattoes, John Antoine and his wife, were listed as the parents of one "white" and four mulatto children. A. Delespard, white, and his Negro wife were listed as the parents of a "white" son; Eugenia Marchand, mulatto, appeared as the mother of one white and two mulatto children; sixty-five-year-old Myrtle Cassanda had one white son and one mulatto daughter; Joseph Sauvinet, mulatto, lived with his mother, white sister, and two white nieces; and mulatto Pauline Dupasse was listed as the mother of four mulatto and two white children.[69]

Much of the miscegenation which occurred in New Orleans during the Reconstruction period was a continuation of the old antebellum pattern of concubinage. Although emancipation, the improvement of the economic standing of many Negro families, and the decrease in the number of quadroon balls and in the control which white men exercised over Negro women led to a decline in miscegenation, it still occurred frequently in the city. For a while even the traditional social functions of quadroon women and white men continued. For instance, on July 18, 1867, the quadroons gave a picnic at City Park which was attended by "distinguished" white men. Furthermore, without regard to politics, nativity, class, or occupation, a large number of white men kept Negro concubines throughout the Reconstruction period. Included among these men were laborers, judges, lawyers, businessmen, and state officials.[70]

The sexual liaisons between white men and Negro women which occurred during Reconstruction are far more difficult to explain than those which occurred during the antebellum period. Slavery had ended, so Negro women could not claim that they were forced into these liaisons. Similarly, since the sex ratio in the white population had completely reversed itself, with white women outnumbering white men by 1870, the white male could not claim that the Negro woman was the only sex object available to him. In many cases white men

chose Negro mates during this period because they had enjoyed the sexual contacts they had had with them when the
women had been slaves and because of the myths which surrounded the Negro woman. The white man was often attracted to the Negro woman because of her beauty, her reputation for sensuousness and passion, and because her color
contrasted so strongly with that of his pale paramours.

During the Reconstruction period, in spite of all the
ostracism, there were also frequent sexual contacts between
white women and Negro men. Many white women had lived,
played, and interacted with Negroes for so long during the
antebellum period that they had no antipathy to them. Besides, the change in the Negro's position after the war, his
service as a soldier, his wealth, his political power, and his
confidence enhanced his status in the eyes of many white
women. Since the black man was no longer browbeaten and
servile, he was no longer viewed as a vile, contemptible thing
undeserving of the respect of the lowest white woman. As L.
Seaman, an opponent of miscegenation, observed in 1864:
"Cuffy's good time is come—his millenium is at hand." William H. Dixon agreed; in the South, he declared, "the fact is,
the Negro here is the coming man."[71]

The change in the sex ratio among whites contributed to
the increase in sexual contacts between white women and
Negro men. So many New Orleans white males were killed
during the war that there were now many more white women
than white men. In many cases white females competed openly
with Negro women for the sexual attentions of black males.
Other white women had assignations with Negro men because
the white man, by constant repetition of allegations of the
black male's extraordinary strength, and exhaustless sexual
desire and passion, had created a virtual black Apollo in their
minds.[72]

While the white public tolerated concubinage and even
casual liaisons between black men and white women throughout the nineteenth century, most whites opposed marriage
across racial lines. In fact, such marriages had been legally

impossible before the Civil War. Moreover, judging from
newspapers published during Reconstruction, most whites
were almost maniacal in their opposition to interracial marriages. They were enraged at every advance the Negro made,
because they felt that each step brought him closer to the
marriage bed of their daughters. William Helpworth Dixon
wrote that in the South the idea of a black man's marrying a
white women "excites the wildest rage" among white men.[73]
This rage lay at the foundation of almost all white opposition
to the Negro's acquisition of civil and political rights. Voicing
this rage, the *Crescent* screamed on October 27, 1868, that
the radicals had brought out "the mad excitement of every
savage instinct, of every brutal lust, before latent or subdued,
in the nature of the negro population. . . . Hence rape, pillage,
arson, murder." The Negroes' barbaric thirst for power was a
sure sign that they were preparing for a saturnalia in which
they would fulfill their carnal lust by the "simple and direct
methods of savage impulse." If the authorities, the *Crescent*
complained, could not protect their "persons from violence,
our property from pillage, our houses from the torch, our
homes form invasion, our wives and daughters from outrage
and pollution," then whites should take matters into their
own hands.

The interracial marriages which occurred in Louisiana
were rarely mentioned in white journals except as the last
salvo fired in the character assassination of a radical politician.
The newspapers, however, frequently returned to the major
image of the *Crescent* editorial: that of savage black men
raping angelic white women. White editors generally felt that
a quick lynching was the most important deterrent to such a
heinous crime.[74] The purity of the white woman had to be
protected at all costs. A branch of the White League in
Opelousas spoke for many whites when it declared, "above all
things our families must be excluded from them—this bastard
miscegenation of races . . . should be stopped."[75] Because of
such sentiments, the all-white Louisiana legislature in 1864

refused to repeal the antebellum law banning interracial marriages in the state.

When blacks obtained political power, however, they demanded the repeal of the law banning interracial marriages. Negroes argued consistently that every man had a right to choose his own mate, regardless of custom or law to the contrary. Laws which banned interracial marriages abridged a man's civil rights.[76] On March 7, 1872, the *Louisianian* questioned whether it was "anybody's business whether a white man cho[o]ses to . . . [marry] a colored woman, or vice versa? Is it not one of those transactions in which individuals should preeminently consult their own tastes?"

To those whites who strenuously and sometimes violently opposed racial intermarriage, Negroes declared that it was a matter that Nature would decide. In spite of all the claims of racial antipathy, history showed that whenever different races had come into contact, there had been race mixing— so much so that only the most isolated of groups were racially pure. The *Tribune* frequently reiterated this theme. On July 26, 1867, it asserted:

Should history teach something, we would say that the
African and Caucasian populations will mix together, as they
did in Egypt, in Abyssinia, in the malayan Islands, and in
every country where they had been for a long time in contact.
Prophesies and selfish wishes have no influence on the issue.
Nature will regulate the future relations of both races in
America; far from presuming to dictate laws to nature, we
stand ready to abide by her decrees.

Not only had there always been race mixing, the *Tribune* claimed, but the most heterogeneous races were the most brilliant and progressive. On the other hand, pure races were "very apt to degenerate." According to the *Tribune*, studies in Switzerland demonstrated that races "marrying only among themselves, soon degenerate and become inferior, morally and physically, to miscegenating communities. . . . Intercourse and conjugal alliances from town to town, from nation to nation, from race to race, is the condition of strength and progress."[77]

Regardless of the attitudes of whites toward Negroes, many white men married Negro women after both the Civil Rights Act of 1866 and a Louisiana statute of 1870 permitted interracial marriages. A number of these unions were consummated because the Negro concubines, with their Oriental-like devotion, love, and attention, had won the love of their white paramours during the antebellum period. Almost immediately after the passage of the law, these men took advantage of its provisions and married the Negro women they loved and made their children legitimate. A number of these partners had lived together faithfully for twenty years or more.

According to the census of 1880, there were 176 white men who were married to Negro women in New Orleans. An analysis of these families is very revealing. The average age of the white males was 50.14 years; of the Negro females, 38.61 years. The average size of these families was 3.7 persons. A majority of them had boarders in their homes, because the average number of people in their dwellings was 6.2 persons. In regard to the marriage partners, 97 (55 percent) of the white husbands were foreign-born males (29 percent of which were from France). Only 17 (9 percent) of the white husbands were illiterate, and the 176 men were engaged in 59 different occupations. The largest categories of occupations were laborers (25), clerks (11), cigarmakers (11), sailors (10), carpenters (8), merchants (7), and brokers (5). The white males who were married to Negro women also included tailors, teachers, engravers, engineers, policemen, druggists, doctors, grocers, planters, printers, bookkeepers, lawyers, and architects. Most of them were skilled craftsmen or professional men; only 15 percent of them were unskilled laborers. Little is known about the females in these marriages, though we do know that at least 42 (23 percent) of them were illiterate.

There were fewer marriages between white women and Negro men during Reconstruction than between white men and Negro women. This reflected the deep opposition to such liaisons on the part of white men, who, fearful of the sexual prowess of the black man, tried to shield the white woman from him. They insisted that the white woman preserve the purity of the race. Most white women accepted their enforced cloistering and, along with it, the white man's view of the undesirability of such unions. Such were the views related by Thomas L. Nichols, who reported that in the South "the last and vilest thing that could be charged upon the lowest and most abandoned white women would be having such relations with a negro." W. Laird Clowes, an English traveler, agreed; he reported in 1891 that in spite of all the miscegenation in the South, "the Southern white woman has had no part in it. In her opinion it is, in all circumstances and conditions, loathsome and abominable." Many of those white women who chose black partners were ostracized in the white community, treated as moral degenerates, arrested when discovered by white policemen, or saw their lovers attacked by enraged whites.[78]

In spite of all of the ostracism, some white women loved black men so passionately that they were willing to marry them. According to the 1880 census, 29 white women were married to Negro men in New Orleans. The average age of the black men was 40 years; of the white women, 35 years. Ten (33 percent) of the white women were foreign-born, and only 4 (12 percent) were illiterate. Three of the black males were foreign-born, seven of them were illiterate, and sixteen of them were listed as "black" in color. Seven (24 percent) of the Negro men were laborers. Others were engaged in such occupations as cigarmaker, broker, merchant, drayman, minister, and gardener. The average size of these families was 3.7 persons.

The burdens on the partners in mixed marriages were great; they were almost crushing in the case of black men and white women. White employers shunned the black men in such unions. For instance, S. S. Ashley wrote in 1871 of one New Orleans Negro man, who had been born in Scotland and had married a white woman there: "He can get no employment here. The fact that his wife is white is unfavorable. I do not think that in any family or hotel when that fact is known they could obtain, or retain employment." While white male partners of interracial marriages were socially ostracized, their complexion guaranteed them employment, and sometimes their wealth and social standing led to a degree of acceptance for their Negro wives. For example, in 1864 a resident of Abbeville, Louisiana, wrote that one of her white friends had given a sewing bee which was "quite a select affair judging *by some* she sent for—a negro woman who has a white husband, and lives here in town."[79]

Both blacks and whites who were involved in interracial sexual liaisons indicated, in a sense, their rejection of their own color. Many of the blacks had heard so much about the superiority and beauty of whites that they enthusiastically entered into liaisons with them. Negro women often united with white men because by doing so they gained more financial security than they could get with many Negro men. The Negro sought out white women in the houses of prostitution, casual liaisons, and as marriage partners to taste of the forbidden fruit—the mythological angelic white woman—and to improve his status.

Such extensive interracial sexual contacts are inexplicable when the rhetorical opposition to such relations is considered. Several demographic, historical, and psychological factors, however, suggest some of the reasons for this phenomenon. Generally, interracial sexual contacts occur where there is social and spatial propinquity and where there are similarities of culture between different races. Integrated housing in New Orleans and the anonymity that city life afforded created many opportunities for interracial sexual contacts and the softening of racial antipathies. Then, too, there were so many Negroes on the police force that it lost its effectiveness as an agency to enforce this social taboo. An important general factor in interracial marriages which was present in New Orleans was a large foreign-born population. With far less antipathy to blacks than native-born whites, especially Anglo-Saxons, immigrants were much more willing to have sexual relations with and to marry Negroes. This is reflected in the relatively high percentage of the foreign-born among white partners in interracial marriages in New Orleans.[80]

Undoubtedly the "liberal" attitudes of the white residents of French and Latin descent contributed to the widespread interracial sexual contacts. Similarly, the social atmosphere in which those of Latin background had sexual relations with blacks may have led many Anglo-Saxons to follow suit. These facts do not, however, explain the wide disparity between profession and practice among Anglo-Saxons. For instance, 25 of the 29 white women who were married to Negro men in 1880 were Anglo-Saxons, and 14 of them were natives of Louisiana. Similarly, 110 of the 176 white males married to Negro women were Anglo-Saxons. And in spite of the threats of violent reprisals which whites repeatedly vowed to make against persons in interracial unions, there were few occasions when this actually occurred. Even in a city as large as New Orleans, it was impossible to hide these interracial unions from the view of many white men. For instance, at least 105 of the mixed couples shared houses with whites of every class and nativity or had them as next door neighbors. In all probability, then, the most important reason for the lack of violent reactions to interracial sexual contacts was the rather amazing, but psychologically necessary, selective inattention of white men regarding this matter. The newspapers, by ignoring the interracial marriages which occurred, could hold on to the myth that innate antipathies prevented such unions. On the other hand, when they did report such unions, they described the white partners (especially women) as poor whites who were degraded, morally insensitive beings.

Nothing is more indicative of the strange twists and turns which the color line took in New Orleans than the sexual intimacy between whites and blacks. In this area, as in many others, Latin practices belied Anglo-Saxon ideology. This is not to say, of course, that there was no painful discrimination against Negroes in public institutions and social relations. As a matter of fact, this was the customary pattern.

Most places of public resort at least occasionally served Negroes along with other customers without distinction. And, in spite of the reticence of some Negroes, the implacable resistance of some whites, the lax enforcement of some provisions of the laws, and the numerous instances of discrimination, there was undoubtedly more integration of places of public resort in New Orleans than in any other southern city (and some northern ones) during Reconstruction. This came about primarily because of several conditions: blacks had enough political power to pass and, on occasion, to enforce civil rights laws; enough of them were wealthy enough to sue businesses which discriminated against them; some whites overcame their prejudices; and Negroes used their sophisticated (almost modern) knowledge of history, logic, government, economics, and psychology to build up their own racial pride and to struggle against the degrading effects of racism and prejudice.

In New Orleans, as perhaps in no other American city, there were many cracks in the color line. Negroes frequently interacted on terms of perfect equality with whites in public institutions and in social relations. Jim Crow did not erect a monolithic barrier between the races; instead, race relations in the city presented a very complex and varied pattern of complete, partial, or occasional integration and intimacy in several areas.

Conclusions

Slavery and the antebellum proscriptions against blacks were heavy burdens for the Negro community in New Orleans during Reconstruction. Surprisingly, Negroes succeeded in many areas in spite of their antebellum legacies. Many of them not only survived the dehumanization of slavery, but retained enough manhood to escape from the plantations and contribute significantly to the Union victory in the Civil War. However submissive they had been as slaves, they rarely flinched in combat with their former masters. Union occupation of New Orleans gave the Negroes an opportunity (in spite of inconsistent official policies) to raise their self-esteem and cease to cower before whites.

In the political area, blacks gained relatively few lasting benefits from Reconstruction. Even so, the role of blacks in New Orleans politics was distinctive in many ways. Shortly after the Union occupation of New Orleans, Negroes began a brilliant campaign to obtain the franchise. They castigated Lincoln for attempting to reconstruct the state on the basis of white manhood suffrage; they called upon whites to live up to the lofty principles of the Declaration of Independence; and they constantly reiterated their right to vote because of the guarantees in the treaty ceding Louisiana to the United States, their roles in the War of 1812 and the Civil War, and their wealth and literacy. Practically every state convention held by Negroes in Louisiana between 1863 and 1867 ended with a demand for the franchise.

The campaign for political rights did not, however, end with such demands. In an effort to influence national Republican policies, blacks sent copies of *L'Union* and the *Tribune* to congressmen, and in 1864 J. B. Roudanez and Arnold Bertonneau delivered to Lincoln a petition calling for the right to vote which contained 5,000 signatures. When this move failed, Negroes began contending that the rebel-dominated state government was illegal and that Louisiana had therefore reverted to territorial status. Acting on this premise, Negro leaders united with local white "radicals" to form the Friends of Universal Suffrage and, later, the Louisiana Republican Party; they registered voters, held a convention, and induced 16,512 people to vote for a territorial delegate to Congress in September 1865. Congressional refusal to seat the delegate appeared to halt the drive of the blacks for a time. Then, the local police rioted and killed dozens of blacks and white radicals attending a convention in July 1866, and Negro leaders used the incident to renew their demand for the franchise.

After they obtained the right to vote in 1867, Negroes moved quickly to protect their interests. First, they insisted that at least one-half of the delegates to the first Republican nominating convention be Negroes. Then, led by the Roudanez brothers, the Creole Negroes began a campaign to block the efforts of Henry Clay Warmouth, Thomas W. Conway, and Benjamin F. Flanders to control the party. Initially the *Tribune* supported Thomas J. Durant, a Southern Unionist and former slaveholder, for governor. After Durant withdrew from the campaign on the eve of the convention, the Creole Negroes worked furiously to get the nomination for Francis E. Dumas, who had been one of the largest Negro slaveholders before the war. Their campaign almost succeeded: Dumas came within two votes of being nominated for governor on the second ballot on January 14, 1868.

Although New Orleans Negroes failed to elect one of their own as governor, they did obtain other political plums. There were several common features in the roads which they took to political power. An overwhelming majority of black elected officials were native-born, young, literate, property-holding veterans of the Civil War who had played a leading role in state civil rights organizations and in the Republican party before 1867 and who were of free ancestry. Many of them, such as Pinchback, Antoine, Menard, George T. Ruby, and William G. Brown, established or edited newspapers to further their political careers. Because of the weaknesses of the Protestant churches, few Negro politicians were able to use the church as a springboard to political power. Generally those Negroes elected to prominent state and local offices had served a short apprenticeship in the constitutional convention in 1868, the Freedmen's Bureau, local appointive office, or community organizations.

In spite of their literacy and status in the community, Negro politicians in Louisiana never obtained more than the semblance of power. Although two Negroes, Oscar J. Dunn and C. C. Antoine, were elected to the office of lieutenant governor, only one, Charles E. Nash, ever served in Congress. Generally, blacks were restricted to small roles in the drama of Louisiana politics. Several factors contributed to this. In general, black leaders in New Orleans were too young, inexperienced, friendless, and poor to achieve much success in the political arena. In fact, blacks never had any real voice in the Republican party from the outset. For example, because of a lack of organization skills, only one Negro, Pinchback, was president of a ward club in New Orleans before 1867. Whites almost universally held the positions of president and secretary of the clubs and thus were able to elect their own delegates to the first Republican nominating convention. As a result of this, Dumas had already lost the nomination for governor before the balloting began. Since the major federal offices in the Customs House, Post Office, and Marshal's Office went to whites, blacks had no control over federal patronage in the state. National politicians consistently refused to consider blacks for such posts, and when the white Republicans in the U.S. Senate refused to seat

Pinchback in the early 1870s, blacks lost their last chance to build a real power base.

Prospects were even worse in the city of New Orleans. Since blacks constituted only about one-fifth of the total population, they never had an opportunity to play a large role in municipal politics after military Reconstruction ended. Realizing this, blacks worked with white Republicans to take away effective home rule for the city—the city police and schools were controlled by state-appointed boards. Negro leaders were also hampered by the fact that most of their constituents were illiterate and thus subject to manipulation and fraud. Even as late as 1880, 62 percent of the Negro voters in New Orleans were illiterate (only 0.6 percent of the whites were illiterate).

The heaviest political burden the blacks bore was the fickleness of their "friends." Warmouth, Conway, Flanders, and most other white "radicals" were not only white supremacists, but also self-seeking, avaricious, and power-hungry men. Most Louisiana historians, however, have not been objective in dealing with the radicals. Generally speaking, the orgy of corruption that was Reconstruction was characteristic of nineteenth-century Louisiana politics. The apparent distinctiveness of the period is primarily a result of the disruption of the traditional channels for giving bribes (or what some call lobbying). Because so many of the postwar leaders were "new men," the lobbyists found it difficult to locate the one or two men they needed to bribe in order to obtain official favors. Instead, they often had to bribe everyone. It was, of course, inevitable that this would become public knowledge. The public nature of the corruption tainted every move blacks made to use their political power and enabled whites to defeat their efforts to bring about meaningful economic and social changes in the position of blacks.

Blacks were far more successful in the economic than in the political realm. Negroes in New Orleans often used the skills they had developed in the antebellum period to compete successfully against whites. The most important source of skilled labor during this period was the old free Negro class. While Negroes were prepared to compete against whites in many trades, antebellum proscriptions prevented them from developing the business acumen and accumulating the capital necessary for large-scale economic enterprises. This is clear when the complex occupational structure of blacks is compared with the small number of different kinds of businesses owned by Negroes and the relatively small amount of wealth they possessed. Again, the free Negroes, as a result of legacies from their white fathers, led in this area. Still, most Negro businesses were short-lived, small, one-owner concerns. They were strongest in those areas requiring the smallest amount of capital investment and the least cooperation from whites, particularly in those areas largely monopolized by Negroes before the war. Initially the most important economic institution for Negroes was the Freedman's Savings and Trust Company. After a few years, however, the criminal mismanagement of the bank wiped out the painfully accumulated capital reserve of the Negro community and made it practically impossible for blacks to improve their economic position in the late 1870s. Even so, considering the proscriptions Negroes faced, their tenacious grip on certain occupations, the few sizable businesses they operated, their unions, and the property they held, the economic adjustment of the Negro was one of the most hopeful signs of the Reconstruction period.

The positive changes which occurred in black family life were even more encouraging than black economic successes. Although slavery had almost completely destroyed the patriarchal Negro family, it had also bequeathed some positive things to the black community. In the first place, slavery was unique among closed institutions because it permitted its members some form of family life. The form that emerged in Louisiana was the monogamous family. Since the sex ratio among slaves was balanced in Louisiana (unlike Latin America), the monogamous family became the cultural norm for Negroes during the antebellum period. Unfortunately, some

of the most hellish practices of slavery were also concentrated
on the family. As a result of the high rate of slave mortality
and the arbitrary rule of the planters, the slave family was
the most unstable institution in America. In all probability,
less than 20 percent of the slave families were intact when
bondage ended. Consequently, the norm in the black community in 1865 was serial monogamy: a man would live with
one woman at a time, but he might live with several of them
in his lifetime.

The long, persistent campaign of Negro ministers, teachers, and editors, and of white missionaries, army officers, and
Freedmen's Bureau agents, coupled with the desire of the
former slaves for more stable family relations, led to a remarkable adaptation of Negroes in New Orleans to American
mores regarding the family. By 1880 the Negro family had
become a strong, stable institution dominated by males. As
long as Negroes were able to escape from the socially disorganized central city, the family was stable. The most important contributor to family instability was the differential in
the mortality rates of Negro males and females.

Throughout the period under review, the heads of Negro
families made unusual sacrifices in order to educate their
children. In spite of the Negro's sacrifices, the educational
history of the Negro in New Orleans is as full of failures as
achievements. Beginning during the war, Negro schools were
crippled by inadequate funds. Astutely insisting upon and
getting a degree of integration in the schools, Negro leaders
were able to obtain at least a semblance of quality in education for Negro children in the schools. There was so much
corruption, however, that about three-fourths of the black
children did not get the opportunity to attend schools. Consequently, the illiteracy rate was still distressingly high in 1880.

The record in higher education was much better than that
of the public schools. The Freedmen's Bureau, local and
Northern philanthropists and churches, and Negro legislators
united to establish and maintain several normal schools, semi-
naries, and colleges in New Orleans. Most of these institutions

were organized like their New England models. This was probably the best approach in such a cosmopolitan city as New Orleans. Given the occupational structure among Negroes and their need for professional training, industrial education similar to that provided by Hampton and Tuskegee institutions was generally unnecessary in New Orleans. Because of the character of the Negro colleges, and especially of Straight University, Negroes did not fight as hard to integrate Louisiana State University as they did to desegregate the public schools. The quality of education furnished by all of the Negro colleges except Straight was about comparable to that furnished in the academies of the period or contemporary junior colleges. The colleges' most important function was to furnish Negro teachers for Louisiana public schools. In this area there was a significant advance over the antebellum period, when only the wealthiest of Negroes could obtain higher education.

The campaign of Negroes to integrate the public schools is only one indication of the complexity of race relations in New Orleans. In fact, antebellum patterns in race relations and the increased political power of blacks led to an almost unbelievably complex pattern in relations between the races in New Orleans during Reconstruction. While segregation was the norm, there was some integration in places of public accommodations, transportation, and social relations. Integrated schools, large-scale miscegenation, and integrated housing patterns existed at the same time that many institutions were segregated. In spite of the rhetoric of whites, there was a significant amount of integration. In spite of the rhetoric of blacks, however, segregation was the customary pattern in most areas of their lives. Two vastly different racial ideologies (with blacks insisting on equality of treatment and whites on total segregation), a large Catholic population of Latin origin, and the political power of blacks laid the foundation in New Orleans for Jim Crow's strangest career in nineteenth-century America.

Appendix

Table 1. Population of New Orleans, 1860–80.

Districts	1860		1870		1875		1880	
	Negro	White	Negro	White	Negro	White	Negro	White
1	6,226	51,129	13,991	42,565	12,464	39,939	14,126	43,282
2	8,956	30,218	13,158	29,475	12,087	27,278	13,301	31,241
3	6,052	38,273	11,466	29,270	15,214	30,984	11,856	33,727
4	2,840	24,981	5,737	28,101	6,213	29,684	6,910	30,592
5	......	......	3,017	3,802	4,604	4,531	3,835	5,020
6	......	......	3,126	7,710	4,471	10,570	4,078	11,954
7	......	......	......	......	2,594	2,806	3,125	3,043
Totals	24,074	144,601	50,495	140,923	57,647	145,792	57,647	158,859

SOURCE: *Louisiana Board of Health, Annual Report, 1883. The population of 1880 is slightly smaller than the figure reported in the 1880 census, but I have accepted it in most cases because the board reported the population by districts.*

Table 2. General Population, 1875

Districts	Males	Females	Totals	Foreign-born	Can't read and write	Native-born, La.	Native-born, other states	% Foreign-born	% Native-born in La.	Males to 100 females	Persons temporarily absent
1	24,604	27,799	52,403	13,006	18,183	26,541	12,856	24	67	88	576
2	18,419	20,946	39,365	9,394	11,265	26,464	3,507	23	88	87	376
3	22,253	23,945	46,198	9,288	17,281	30,198	6,712	20	81	92	604
4	16,824	19,073	35,897	7,542	12,444	19,606	8,749	21	69	88	644
5	4,508	4,627	9,135	1,124	5,352	6,328	1,683	12	78	97	283
6	7,390	7,651	15,041	2,511	6,009	9,927	2,603	16	79	96	192
7	2,684	2,716	5,400	847	2,492	3,590	963	15	78	98	134
Totals	96,682	106,757	203,439	43,712	73,026	124,654	35,073	21(a)	78(a)	90(a)	2,809

SOURCE: *Report of the Louisiana State Census of 1875*
[a]Averages

Table 3.   Negro Males,
Occupations, 1860

OCCUPATIONS

Occupation	No.	Occupation	No.
Carpenters	257	Barkeepers	4
Bricklayers	223	Clothiers	4
Cigarmakers	171	Milkmen	4
Shoemakers	151	Bakers	3
Laborers	145	Hucksters	3
Draymen	101	Hostlers	3
Sailors	84	Sawyers	3
Tailors	51	Traders	3
Painters	48	Policemen	3
Coopers	42	Sailmakers	3
Clerks	39	Doctors	2
Barbers	36	Farmers	2
Servants	30	Vegetable dealers	3
Whitewashers	22	Shipwrights	2
Porters	20	Jewelers	2
Plasterers	19	Boatbuilders	2
Cooks	18	Butlers	2
Grocers	17	Kettle setters	2
Hunters	17	Hairdressers	2
Caulkers	16	Engineers	2
Tinsmiths	15	Bookbinders	2
Gardeners	14	Preacher	1
Slaters	13	Stevedore	1
Teachers	12	Fruit stand proprietor	1
Butchers	10	Chemist	1
Blacksmiths	10	Undertaker	1
Printers	9	Engraver	1
Apprentices	9	Wood and coal dealer	1
Fishermen	8	Dyer	1
Brokers	8	Wagonmaker	1
Coffeehouse proprietors	7	Inspector of weights	1
Mattressmakers	7	Oyster dealer	1
Cotton weighers	6	Paperhanger	1
Waiters	6	Hat cleaner	1
Merchants	4	Jockey	1
Warehousemen	4	Meat inspector	1
Machinists	4		
Cabinetmakers	4	Total labor force	1,732
Bookkeepers	4		

SOURCE: *Compiled from Census of Population, Orleans Parish*

Table 4.   Negro Males,
Occupations, 1870

OCCUPATIONS

Occupation	Count	Occupation	Count
Laborers	4,941	Engineers	17
Servants	1,687	Printers	17
Steamboatmen,		Laundrymen	16
sailors, etc.	785	Cabinetmakers	16
Carpenters	716	Teachers	14
Draymen	605	Screwmen	14
Masons	449	Stablemen	13
Cigarmakers	397	Doctors	12
Bakers	338	Mattressmakers	12
Shoemakers	249	Custom officers	12
Sawyers	233	Bookkeepers	11
Clerks	187	Sailmakers	10
Porters	181	Rag pickers	10
Policemen	177	Fish dealers	10
Painters	165	Cotton samplers	9
Barbers	155	Coffeehouse proprietors	8
Coopers	154	Government officials	8
Gardeners	144	Marble and stone cutters	8
Blacksmiths	89	Fishermen	8
Plasterers	88	Hostlers	7
Waiters	84	Watchmen	7
Farmers	82	Musicians	7
Peddlers	70	Nurses	7
Whitewashers	65	Jewelers	7
Slaters	57	Clothiers	6
Apprentices	57	Lamplighters	6
Tailors	38	Stevedores	6
Cotton pressers	35	Scavengers	6
Grocers	35	Dentists	6
Butchers	31	Machinists	5
Warehousemen	31	Milkmen	5
Factory workers	30	Soldiers	5
Tinsmiths	29	Builders	5
Clergymen	28	Brokers	5
Merchants	24	Coal rollers	5
Caulkers	25	Moulders	4
Wood and coal dealers	22	Cotton weighers	4
Barkeepers	21	Firemen	4
Dairymen	19	Furniture repairers	4

Mailmen	4	Bar owner	1
Hunters	4	Rent collector	1
Collectors	4	Newspaper dealer	1
Liquor dealers	3	Varnisher	1
Hatters	3	Cakemaker	1
Sextons	3	Waterman	1
Wheelwrights	3	Gunmaker	1
Pantrymen	3	Water works employee	1
Sugar factory workers	3	Fruit dealer	1
Distillers	3	Confectioner	1
Inspectors	3	Inspector of weights	1
Telegraph operators	3	Paperhanger	1
Soda dealers	3	Poultry dealer	1
Packers	3	Herb dealer	1
Moss pickers	3	Florist	1
Lottery agents	3	Legislator	1
Sugarmakers	3	Plant foreman	1
Pilots	2	Vendor	1
Roofers	2	Gunsmith	1
Ice cream dealers	2	Weigher	1
Officemen	2	Meat inspector	1
Boiler cleaners	2	U.S. government employee	1
Boxmakers	2	Coffin maker	1
Cotton brokers	2	Bookbinder	1
Framemakers	2	City officer	1
Stockkeepers	2	Brewer	1
Undertakers	2	Ice dealer	1
Vegetable dealers	2	Cattle inspector	1
Basketmakers	2	Banker	1
Travel agents	2	Cigar store owner	1
Landlord	1	Shoe dealer	1
Speculator	1	Huckster	1
Cisternmaker	1	Agent	1
Boilermaker	1	Photographer	1
Veterinarian	1	Editor	1
Sheet sprinkler	1		
Coffee sampler	1	Total labor force	12,992
Pipe fitter	1		
Bill collector	1		

SOURCE: *Compiled from Census of Population, Orleans Parish*

Table 5.   Negro Males,
Occupations, 1880

OCCUPATIONS

Laborers	6,534	Barkeepers	29
Servants	739	Policemen	27
Steamboatmen	595	Caulkers	26
Carpenters	567	Factory workers	25
Cigarmakers	524	Engineers	20
Draymen	492	Grocers	19
Bakers	330	Firemen	19
Masons	301	Merchants	19
Shoemakers	279	Butchers	19
Gardeners	278	Mattressmakers	19
Cotton Pressmen	255	Postmen	18
Farmers	222	Rag pickers	18
Clerks	220	Doctors	16
Waiters	199	Mechanics	15
Coopers	195	Customs officers	13
Sawyers	175	Printers	12
Porters	167	Weighers	12
Painters	156	Brokers	11
Barbers	155	Elevator operators	10
Plasterers	119	Cotton samplers	9
Blacksmiths	99	Claims agents	9
Slaters	78	Sextons	9
Ministers	71	Sailmakers	9
Apprentices	62	Watchmen	9
Wood and coal dealers	58	Dentists	8
Screwmen	57	Dairymen	8
Fishermen	53	Lottery agents	8
Hostlers	47	Vegetable dealers	8
Tailors	46	Bookkeepers	7
Whitewashers	45	Lamplighters	7
Musicians	45	Marble and stone cutters	7
Warehousemen	42	Fish stand operators	6
Stevedores	34	Officers	6
Peddlers	34	Inspectors	5
Cabinetmakers	33	Undertakers	5
Hucksters	33	Vendors	5
Tinsmiths	29	Collectors	5
Teachers	29	Brickmakers	5

OCCUPATIONS

Lawyers	5	Distillers	2
Music teachers	4	Turners	2
Stockkeepers	4	Wheelwrights	2
Landlords	4	Capitalists	2
Horse traders	4	Chimney sweeps	2
Coffee stand proprietors	4	Paperhangers	2
Shoeblacks	4	Chairmakers	2
Gamblers	4	Oil mill workers	2
Basketmakers	4	Druggists	2
Roustabouts	4	Pawnbrokers	2
Newsboys	4	Furniture repairer	1
Organ-grinders	4	Variety store proprietor	1
Sugar makers	4	Law student	1
Swampers	4	Clothier	1
Ice dealers	3	Veterinarian	1
Inspectors of houses	3	Dyer	1
Builders	3	Striker	1
Pilots	3	Coppersmith	1
Fruit dealers	3	Artist	1
Gravediggers	3	Moulder	1
Hatters	3	Coffinmaker	1
Jewellers	3	Sculptor	1
Confectioners	3	Fencing master	1
Milkmen	3	Banker	1
Telegraph repairers	3	Galvinizer	1
Hairdressers	3	News dealer	1
Broommakers	3	Skinner	1
Hunters	3	Furniture store proprietor	1
Gas fitters	2	Potter	1
Traders	2	Bottle dealer	1
Coal rollers	2	Carpet layer	1
Janitors	2	Journalist	1
Laundry owners	2	Brass finisher	1
Restauranteurs	2	Cowboy	1
Moss pickers	2	Cabbon roller	1
Shinglemakers	2	Harnessmaker	1
Saddlers	2	Contractor	1
Horse trainers	2		(Cont.)

(Cont.)

Table 5.   Negro Males,
Occupations, 1880 (Cont.)

OCCUPATIONS

Glazer	1	Coffee inspector	1
Glass washer	1	Dealer in china	1
Ice cream dealer	1	Jockey	1
Photographer	1		
U.S. Mint employee	1	Total labor force	14,027

SOURCE: *Compiled from Census of Population, Orleans Parish*

Table 6.   Negro Males, Selected Occupations, 1860, 1870, 1880

Occupations	1860[a]	1870	1880
Laborers	145	4,941	6,534
Servants	30	1,687	739
Steamboatmen	84	785	595
Draymen	101	605	492
Shoemakers	151	249	279
Masons	223	457	308
Bakers	3	338	330
Butchers	10	31	19
Cabinetmakers and upholsterers	4	20	33
Carpenters and joiners	257	716	567
Cigarmakers and tobacco workers	171	397	524
Coopers	42	154	195
Fishermen and oystermen	8	8	53
Machinists	4	5	15
Painters and varnishers	48	166	156
Plasterers	19	88	119
Tailors	51	38	46
Tinners	15	29	29
Wheelwrights	. . .	3	2
Blacksmiths	10	89	99
Printers	9	17	12
Dentists	. . .	6	8
Clergymen	1	28	71
Barbers and hairdressers	38	155	158
Gardeners	14	144	278
Apprentices	9	57	53
Totals	1,732	12,992	14,027

[a]*Free Negroes only.*

Table 7. Negro, White, and Foreign-Born Males, Selected Occupations, 1870

Occupations	Total labor force	Negro	Foreign	% Negro	% Foreign	% OF LABOR FORCE IN EACH OCCUPATION		
						Total	Negro	Foreign
Labor force	50,116	12,992	24,831	25.9	49.5			
Laborers	9,499	4,941	3,503	52.0	36.8	18.9	38.0	14.1
Servants	2,972	1,687	a	56.7	a	5.9	12.9	
Steamboatmen	1,700	785	544	46.1	32.0	3.3	6.0	2.1
Draymen	1,611	605	738	37.5	45.8	3.2	4.6	2.9
Shoemakers	1,154	249	744	21.5	64.4	2.3	1.9	2.9
Masons	696	457	119	65.6	17.0	1.3	3.5	0.4
Bakers	641	338	a	52.7	a	1.2	2.6	
Brick and tile makers	20		4		20.0			
Butchers	767	31	600	4.0	78.2	1.5	0.2	2.4
Cabinetmakers and upholsterers	307	20	218	6.5	71.0	0.6	0.1	0.8
Carpenters and joiners	2,357	716	917	30.3	41.1	4.7	5.5	3.9
Cigarmakers and tobacco workers	728	397	244	54.5	33.5	1.4	3.0	0.9
Coopers	596	154	238	25.8	39.9	1.1	1.1	0.9
Fishermen and oystermen	109	8	70	7.7	64.1	0.2		0.2
Harness and saddlemakers	128		70		56.2	0.2		0.2
Machinists	244	5	98	2.0	40.1	0.4		0.3
Painters and varnishers	841	166	356	19.7	42.3	1.6	1.2	1.4
Plasterers	206	88	54	42.7	26.2	0.4	0.6	0.2
Tailors	701	38	a	5.4	a	1.3	0.2	
Tinners	249	29	137	11.6	55.0	0.4	0.2	0.5
Wheelwrights	58	3	41	5.1	70.6			0.1
Blacksmiths	625	89	356	14.2	56.9	1.2	0.6	1.4
Printers	324	17	94	5.2	29.0	0.6	0.1	0.3
Dentists		6						
Clergymen	126	28	61	22.2	48.4			

Barbers and hairdressers	416						0.1
Launderers	2	16	a		0.6	0.1	0.1
Lawyers	310		39	12.5			0.3
Musicians and teachers of music		7					
Physicians	284	12	95	4.2	33.4	0.5	0.1
Teachers	196	14	a	7.1		0.3	0.1
Saloonkeepers and bartenders		21					0.4
Apprentices		57					1.1
Gardeners	410	144	190	35.1	46.3	0.8	0.7

Sources: *United States Census Office, Ninth Census, 1:792; Census of Population, Orleans Parish.*
aWomen included in tabulation.

Table 8. Negro, White, and Foreign-Born Males, Selected Occupations, 1880

Occupations	Total labor force	Negro	Foreign	% Negro	% Foreign	% OF LABOR FORCE IN EACH OCCUPATION		
						Total	Negro	Foreign
Labor force	59,173	14,027	19,565	23.7	33.0	24.9	46.4	17.3
Laborers	14,777	6,534	3,394	44.2	22.9	2.0	5.2	a
Servants	1,221	739	a	60.5	a	2.8	4.2	2.2
Steamboatmen	1,694	595	437	35.1	25.7	2.9	3.4	2.7
Draymen	1,743	492	533	28.2	30.5	1.9	1.9	2.7
Shoemakers	1,177	279	530	23.7	45.0	1.0	2.1	0.5
Masons	603	308	98	51.0	16.2	1.2	2.3	1.6
Bakers	722	330	329	45.7	45.5			
Brick and tile makers	29	5	2	17.2	06.8	1.2	0.1	1.0
Butchers	738	19	206	2.5	27.9	0.5	0.2	0.8
Cabinetmakers and upholsterers	325	33	176	10.1	54.1	3.8	4.0	3.3
Carpenters and joiners	2,257	567	647	25.1	28.6	1.7	3.7	1.3
Cigarmakers and tobacco workers	1,010	524	258	51.8	25.5	1.1	1.3	0.8
Coopers	702	195	168	27.7	23.9	0.3	0.3	0.3
Fishermen and oystermen	178	53	74	29.7	41.5	0.3		0.3
Harness and saddlemakers	212	3	73	1.4	34.4	0.4		0.6
Machinists	274	15	126	5.4	45.9	1.4	1.1	1.2
Painters and varnishers	858	156	241	18.1	28.0			
Plasterers		119				1.0	0.3	
Tailors	638	46	a	7.2	a	0.5	0.2	0.5
Tinners	314	29	109	9.2	34.7	0.1		0.2
Wheelwrights	79	2	43	2.5	54.4	0.9	0.7	1.0
Blacksmiths	544	99	201	18.1	36.9	0.9		0.5
Printers	535	12	109	2.2	20.3	0.1		0.1
Dentists	75	8	24	10.6	32.0	0.3	0.5	0.2
Clergymen	229	71	65	31.0	28.3			

Boarding and lodginghouse keepers	36	4	a	11.1	a			0.1
Launderers	58	2	a	3.4	a			0.6
Lawyers	374	5	35	1.3	09.3	0.6	0.3	0.3
Musicians and music teachers	228	53	127	23.2	55.7	0.3	0.1	
Physicians	283	16	75	5.6	26.5	0.4	0.2	
Teachers	228	29	a	12.7	a	0.3	0.2	
Saloonkeepers and bartenders	954	29	330	3.0	34.5	1.6		1.6
Apprentices	514	62	33	12.0	06.4	0.8	0.4	0.1
Gardeners	896	278	384	31.0	42.8	1.5	1.9	1.9

SOURCE: *United States Census Office, Tenth Census, 1:891; Census of Population, Orleans Parish.*
[a] *Women included in tabulation.*

Table 9.   Negro Males, Unemployed, by Selected
Occupations, 1880

Occupations	Total	Number un- employed	% un- employed	Avg. no. months unemployed
Labor force	14,027	2,600	18.4	..
Laborers	6,534	1,645	25.1	4.6
Painters	156	39	25.0	4.6
Masons	308	74	24.0	5.4
Shoemakers	279	24	8.6	5.6
Coopers	195	35	17.9	5.1
Carpenters	567	131	23.1	5.6
Blacksmiths	99	8	8.0	4.5
Plasterers	119	23	19.3	5.3
Barbers and hairdressers	158	4	2.5	3.5
Bakers	330	23	6.9	5.2
Servants	739	30	4.0	4.4
Steamboatmen	280	57	20.3	4.9
Cigarmakers	524	63	12.0	5.7

SOURCE: *Compiled from Census of Population, Orleans Parish*

Table 10. Number and Percentage of Negro Males in Selected Occupations, 1890, 1910, 1930

Occupations	1890		1910		1930		% OF NEGRO WORKERS		
	Total	Negro	Total	Negro	Total	Negro	1890	1910	1930
Labor force	69,635	17,760	106,600	28,014	143,280	39,512	25.4	26.2	27.5
Gardeners	772	198	251	51	......	......	25.6	20.3	....
Barbers and hairdressers	672	200	1,148	289	1,223	297	29.7	25.1	24.2
Boatmen	1,298	458	866	491	2,939	863	35.2	56.6	29.3
Draymen	2,493	1,096	2,583	1,324	739	454	43.9	51.2	61.4
Apprentices	701	123	981	123	......	......	17.5	12.5	....
Shoemakers	1,469	366	492	322	......	......	24.9	65.4	....
Carpenters and joiners	2,698	603	3,782	1,075	4,140	1,153	22.3	28.4	27.8
Coopers	835	235	661	323	256	158	28.1	48.8	61.7
Masons	756	495	681	485	565	368	65.4	71.2	65.1
Painters	1,150	200	1,376	286	2,651	573	17.3	20.7	21.6
Plasterers	349	239	530	436	384	69	68.4	82.2	17.9
Tobacco workers	971	530	378	211	......	......	54.5	55.8	....
Longshoremen	......	......	2,478	1,461	4,847	3,647	....	58.9	75.2
Firemen (manuf.)	......	......	697	290	794	238	....	41.6	29.9
Sawmill operators	247	110	648	453	326	240	44.5	69.9	73.6
Roofers and Slaters	......	......	......	......	303	205	....	....	67.6
Mailmen	......	......	......	......	315	207	....	....	65.7

SOURCES: *United States Census Office, Eleventh Census,* 16:702–3; *Thirteenth Census,* 4:570; *Fifteenth Census,* 4:628–30.

Table 11.   Negro Families, 1880

Districts	Total house-holds	Head of Household Male	Head of Household Female	% of male heads	Female heads, widows	% of female heads that are widows	% of male heads, widows not counted	Avg. family size
1	3,160	2,435	725	77.0	556	76.6	93.5	3.39
2	2,634	1,853	781	70.3	614	78.6	91.7	3.91
3	2,489	2,047	442	82.2	397	89.8	97.8	4.22
4	1,594	1,218	376	76.4	316	94.0	95.3	3.71
5	925	831	94	89.8	87	92.5	99.1	3.89
6	906	738	168	81.4	139	82.7	96.2	3.73
7	744	654	80	87.9	64	80.0	97.6	3.83
Totals	12,452	9,776	2,666	78.5[a]	2,173	81.5[a]	95.1	3.79[a]

Source: *Compiled from Census of Population, Orleans Parish*
[a]*Averages*

Table 12.   Negro Family Organization, 1880

Districts	% of male heads	Divorcees	Adopted children	Unwed mothers	Males	Females	Males to 100 females
1	77.0	23	71	40	5,955	8,171	72
2	70.3	29	57	65	5,755	7,546	76
3	82.2	25	24	7	5,324	6,510	81
4	76.4	15	13	14	2,829	4,081	69
5	89.8	6	26	4	806	890	90
6	81.4	5	21	6	2,731	3,486	78
7	87.9	7	19	2	1,501	1,624	92
Totals	78.5[a]	110	241	138	24,921	32,310	77[a]

Source: *Compiled from Census of Population, Orleans Parish*
[a]*Averages*

Table 13. Property and Dwellings, 1880

Districts	Stores and factories	Rooms in dwellings	Avg. no. persons per room	Dwellings occupied by Negro families	Persons in Negro family dwellings	Avg. no. persons per Negro family dwelling	Boarding houses and hotels	Value of property (millions of $)
1	3,240	48,997	1.06	2,170	15,083	6.9	513	68
2	1,805	33,243	1.21	1,918	13,580	7.0	282	28.7
3	459	28,172	1.12	2,035	11,415	5.6	26	12.5
4	1,258	37,761	1.14	1,275	7,011	5.4	3	15.1
5	....	......	....	734	3,484	4.7	4	....
6	255	11,561	1.32	807	3,851	4.7	0	7.2
7	31	4,346	1.12	602	3,000	4.9	4	1.4
Totals	7,048	164,080	1.16[a]	9,541	57,424	6.0[a]	832	134.8

SOURCES: *Louisiana Board of Health*, Annual Report, *1880; Census of Population, Orleans parish, 1880;* Report of the Louisiana State Census, 1875.

[a] *Averages*

Table 14. The Negro Family and Employment, 1880

Districts	MARRIED WOMEN		MALES		Married men, un-employed	NEGRO LABORERS		Unemployment rate among Negro males (%)	% of women working
	Employed	At home	Total	Unemployed		Total	% of total labor force		
1	509	1,140	3,697	441	285	1,965	53	11	30
2	463	715	3,068	149	79	842	27	04	39
3	473	1,006	2,595	688	449	1,129	43	26	31
4	219	894	1,636	295	230	675	41	18	19
5	198	487	1,105	609	384	731	66	55	28
6	187	361	1,051	203	146	629	59	19	34
7	138	378	875	252	187	560	64	28	37
Totals	2,187	4,981	14,027	2,637	1,760	6,531	46.5[a]	18.7[a]	30.5[a]

SOURCE: *Census of Population, Orleans Parish*
[a] *Averages*

Table 15. Mortality by Race and Sex at Selected Ages, 1880

	AGES				
	15 to 44	15 to 54	15 to 64	20 to 54	20 to 64
Population					
Negroes					
Male	11,365	13,885	15,191	12,154	13,460
Female	16,446	19,652	21,408	16,930	18,686
Whites					
Male	35,129	42,432	46,390	35,061	39,019
Female	40,346	48,150	52,166	38,957	42,973
Deaths					
Negroes					
Male	303	418	477	394	453
Female	262	324	390	297	363
Whites					
Male	545	864	991	764	951
Female	405	552	675	517	640
Death rates per 1,000					
Negroes					
Male	26.66	30.10	29.98	32.41	33.65
Female	15.93	16.48	18.21	17.54	19.42
Whites					
Male	15.51	20.36	21.36	21.79	24.37
Female	10.03	11.46	12.93	13.27	14.89

SOURCE: *United States Census Office*, Tenth Census, Vital Statistics, *2:783*

Table 16. Negro and White Families, 1880

	DISTRICT					
	1	2	3	4	5	6
Males						
Negro	5,955	5,755	5,324	2,829	806	2,73
White	20,702	14,806	16,104	13,671	2,382	5,63
Females						
Negro	8,171	7,546	6,510	4,081	890	3,48
White	22,617	16,526	17,708	17,043	2,641	6,55
Males to 100 females						
Negro	72	76	81	69	90	7
White	91	89	90	80	90	8
Families						
Negro	3,160	2,634	2,489	1,594	925	90
White	1,689	1,169	1,183	1,044	178	42
Male heads						
Negro	2,435	1,853	2,047	1,218	831	73
White	1,336	926	965	817	145	36
Female heads						
Negro	725	781	442	376	94	16
White	353	243	218	227	33	6
Percentage of male heads						
Negro	77.0	70.3	82.2	76.4	89.8	8
White	79.1	79.2	81.5	78.2	81.4	8
Mixed marriages	32	108	50	11	11	

SOURCE: *Census of Population, Orleans Parish*
[a]*Averages*

7	Totals
501	24,921
524	74,848
524	32,310
578	84,801
92	77[a]
90	88[a]
744	12,452
131	5,819
654	9,776
98	4,649
80	2,666
33	1,170
87.9	78.5[a]
74.8	79.8[a]
7	227

Table 17. Mortality in New Orleans, by Race, 1845–80

Years	POPULATION		
	Negro	White	Total
1845	34,744	79,698	114,442
1847	32,360	88,530	120,890
1849	29,978	97,362	127,340
1850	28,787	101,778	130,565
1852	27,845	110,342	138,187
1853	27,374	114,624	141,988
1856	25,961	127,470	153,431
1857	25,489	131,753	157,242
1858	25,017	136,036	161,053
1859	24,545	140,319	164,864
1860	24,074	144,601	168,675
1861	26,716	144,233	170,949
1863	32,000	143,497	175,497
1864	34,639	143,129	177,768
1865	37,282	142,761	180,034
1866	39,925	142,393	182,318
1867	42,568	142,025	184,593
1868	44,411	141,657	186,068
1869	47,853	141,290	189,143
1870	50,495	140,923	191,418
1871	50,717	142,695	193,412
1872	51,969	144,437	196,406
1873	52,721	146,179	198,900
1874	53,473	147,921	201,394
1875	54,225	149,663	203,888
1876	54,976	151,406	206,382
1877	55,727	153,149	208,876
1878	56,479	154,892	211,371
1879	57,230	156,635	213,865
1880	57,761	158,379	216,140
Totals	1,207,341	4,059,777	5,267,114

	NUMBER OF DEATHS, BY RACE			DEATH RATE PER 1,000, BY RACE	
Negro	White	Total	Negro	White	Total
782	2,001	2,783	22.50	25.10	24.32
,225	6,274	7,499	37.08	70.86	62.03
,886	7,976	9,862	62.91	81.92	77.44
,500	6,319	7,819	52.10	62.08	59.88
,199	7,499	8,693	43.04	67.91	62.90
,341	14,292	15,633	48.98	124.68	110.09
926	4,274	5,200	35.66	32.98	33.89
988	4,593	5,581	38.07	34.86	35.49
,236	9,474	11,710	89.37	69.64	72.70
,135	4,712	6,847	86.98	33.58	41.53
,271	6,070	7,341	52.79	41.99	43.51
993	4,456	5,449	37.16	31.58	31.87
,905	5,353	7,258	59.53	37.30	41.35
,832	6,032	8,864	81.75	42.14	49.86
,264	4,756	7,020	60.88	33.31	38.99
,518	5,236	7,754	65.56	36.77	42.52
2,030	8,066	10,096	47.80	56.79	54.69
,731	3,612	5,343	38.97	25.49	28.60
2,144	3,857	6,001	44.80	27.29	31.73
2,636	4,755	7,391	52.20	33.74	38.61
2,169	3,890	6,059	42.76	27.26	31.32
2,179	3,943	6,122	41.93	27.29	31.17
2,711	4,794	7,505	51.42	32.79	37.73
2,430	4,368	6,798	45.44	29.53	33.75
2,183	3,934	6,117	40.25	26.28	30.00
2,340	3,917	6,257	42.56	25.87	30.31
2,732	3,976	6,708	49.02	25.96	32.11
2,256	8,062	10,318	39.94	52.05	48.81
1,855	3,267	5,122	32.41	20.85	23.95
1,986	3,637	5,623	34.38	22.96	26.01
7,383	163,390	220,773	49.27	42.03	43.57

SOURCE: *Compiled from Louisiana Board of Health, Annual Report for 1884 (New Orleans, 1885), p. cccxviii. The mortality records from 1860 to 1876 give a certain number of deaths as "Color not stated." These have been divided in the above table by estimating two-thirds to be white, and one-third Negro.*

Table 18. Deaths From Principal Diseases, by Race.

	1877		1878		1879		1880	
	Negro	White	Negro	White	Negro	White	Negro	White
Smallpox	662	437	82	69	..	..	..	1
Measles	2	9	1	2	..	..	40	57
Scarlet fever	..	10	..	1	..	1	7	49
Malarial fevers	132	277	143	634	58	151	102	234
Pulmonary consumption	375	513	373	507	352	472	346	517
Pneumonia	150	205	165	178	155	151	143	164
Diarrhea	62	113	61	109	43	101	130	201
Dysentery	49	102	41	79	35	82	..	..
Diphtheria	9	24	4	55	10	48	6	75
Bright's disease	48	57	39	68	34	70	39	68
Cancerous disease	27	78	26	89	30	75	27	102
Suicides	..	3	2	14	1	20	1	19
Yellow fever	..	..	183	3863	..	19	..	2

SOURCE: *Compiled from Louisiana Board of Health*, Annual Report, *1877, 1878, 1879, 1880.*

Table 19. Mortality in New Orleans, by Age and Race, 1880

Ages	Population[1]			Deaths[2]			Death Rates		
	Negro	White	Total	Negro	White	Total	Negro	White	Total
Under 1 yr	1,288	3,753	5,041	473	774	1,247	367.2	206.2	247.3
1 to 2	1,005	2,835	3,840	133	240	373	132.3	84.6	97.1
2 to 5	4,156	11,725	15,881	144	244	388	34.6	20.9	24.4
5 to 10	6,514	18,454	24,968	69	142	211	10.5	7.7	8.5
10 to 15	5,914	18,743	24,657	51	64	115	8.6	3.4	4.6
15 to 20	4,453	16,571	21,024	47	82	129	10.5	4.9	6.1
20 to 25	5,484	16,265	21,794	105	176	281	19.1	10.8	12.9
25 to 30	5,243	12,703	17,946	108	159	267	20.6	12.5	14.9
0 to 10	12,963	36,767	49,730	819	1,400	2,219	63.2	38.0	44.6
10 to 20	10,367	35,314	45,681	98	146	244	9.4	4.1	5.3
20 to 30	10,727	28,968	39,695	213	335	548	19.8	11.5	13.8
30 to 40	8,676	20,629	29,305	207	373	580	23.8	18.1	19.8
40 to 50	6,921	17,333	24,254	171	430	601	24.7	24.8	24.8
50 to 60	4,200	11,318	15,518	143	391	534	34.0	34.5	34.4
60 to 70	2,437	5,819	8,256	144	305	449	59.1	52.4	53.7
70 to 80	996	1,850	2,846	81	153	234	81.3	82.7	82.2
80 to 90	307	356	663	62	69	131	201.9	193.8	197.5
Over 90	154	41	195	42	21	63	272.7	512.2	323.1
Unknown	......	......	......	6	14	20	....	....	....
Totals	57,748	158,395	216,143	1,986	3,637	5,623	34.4	29.9	26.0

Source: Compiled from Stanford E. Chaille, "The Vital Statistics of New Orleans as Taught by the U.S. Census, 1880," New Orleans Medical and Surgical Journal 33 (May 1881), p. 1044. 1. Based on U.S. Census, 1880. 2. Based on Louisiana Board of Health, Annual Report, 1880.

Notes

1. Negro in Antebellum New Orleans

1. Joe Gray Taylor, *Negro Slavery in Louisiana* (Baton Rouge, 1963), pp. 59–122; Henry Bibb, *Narrative of the Life and Adventures of Henry Bibb, an American Slave* (New York, 1849); S. A. O'Ferrall, *A Ramble of Six Thousand Miles Through the United States of America* (London, 1832), p. 196.

2. John Duffy, "Slavery and Slave Health in Louisiana, 1766–1825," *Bulletin of the Tulane University Medical Faculty* 26 (February 1967): 1–6; Robert H. Ryland Journals, LSU; Annie Jeter Carmouche, "Reminiscences," p. 48, SHC.

3. Solomon Northup, *Twelve Years a Slave* (London, 1853), pp. 191–222; H. B. Tibbetts to his brother, December 28, 1848, John C. Tibbetts Correspondence, LSU; Thomas L. Nichols, *Forty Years of American Life, 1821–1861* (New York, 1937), p. 124; Tom H. Wells, "Moving a Plantation to Louisiana," *Louisiana Studies* 6 (Fall 1967): 279–89; Clarissa Town Diary, p. 57, LSU; Mathilda Houston, *Hesperos*, 2 vols. (London, 1850), 2:156.

4. Herman Charles Woessner, "New Orleans, 1840–1860: A Study in Urban Slavery" (M.A. thesis, Louisiana State University, 1967), pp. 1–36.

5. Werner A. Wegner, "Negro Slavery in New Orleans" (M.A. thesis, Tulane University, 1935), pp. 28–67; Eliza Potter, *A Hairdresser's Experience in High Life* (Cincinnati, 1859), pp. 144–54; Daniel B. Pinson to "Liz," March 10, 1849, Nancy Pinson Papers, LSU; Tyrone Power, *Impressions of America During the Years 1833, 1834, and 1835*, 2 vols. (London, 1836), 2:208, 231.

6. Charles Barron to his father, November 8, 1840, Charles Barron Letters, LSU; Francis and Theresa Pulszky, *White, Red, Black*, 3 vols. (London, 1853), 2:265–67; Frances Trollope, *Domestic Manners of the Americans* (London, 1927 [1832]), p. 5.

7. Benjamin Latrobe, *Impressions Respecting New Orleans: Diary and Sketches, 1818–1820* (New York, 1950), pp. 46–51; Carl E. Lindstrom, "American Quality in the Music of Louis Moreau Gottschalk," *Musical Quarterly* 30 (July 1945): 356–66; William F. Allen, *Slave Songs of the*

United States (New York, 1867), pp. 109–13; G. W. Cable, "The Dance in Place Congo," *Century* 31 (February 1886): 517–32.

8. Cable, "Dance," p. 527.

9. Ibid., p. 528.

10. Ibid., pp. 526–27.

11. Basil Davidson, *The African Genius* (Boston, 1969), p. 167; Latrobe, *Impressions Respecting New Orleans*, p. 50.

12. Henry C. Castellanos, *New Orleans As It Was: Episodes of Louisiana Life* (New Orleans, 1905), pp. 90–100; Napier Bartlett, *Stories of the Crescent City* (New Orleans, 1869), pp. 100–102; *New Orleans Times*, October 27, 1857; Zora Neale Hurston, "Hoodoo in America," *Journal of American Folk-Lore* 44 (October–December 1931): 317–417.

13. Castellanos, *New Orleans As It Was*, pp. 96–97.

14. Ibid., p. 98.

15. Quoted in ibid., p. 100.

16. Harriet Martineau, *Retrospect of Western Travel*, 2 vols. (London, 1838), 2:259; Social Statistics, Orleans Parish, 1860, entry 324, RG 29, NA; Fredrika Bremer, *The Homes of the New World*, 2 vols. (New York, 1853), 2:235–38; St. James A. M. E. Church, *A Century of African Methodism in the Deep South* (New Orleans, 1946), pp. 1–18; Robert C. Reinders, "The Churches and the Negro in New Orleans, 1850–1860," *Phylon* 22 (Fall 1961): 241–48.

17. Bremer, *Homes*, 2:237–38.

18. Martineau, *Retrospect*, 2:268–69; O'Ferrall, *Ramble*, p. 193; Carmouche, "Reminiscences," p. 18; United States Census Office, *Preliminary Report On The Eighth Census, 1860* (Washington, D.C., 1862), p. 262.

19. Martineau, *Retrospect*, 2:270.

20. Bremer, *Homes*, 2:233–34; Woessner, "New Orleans, 1840–1860," pp. 42–54; Wegner, "Negro Slavery," pp. 67–73; Potter, *A Hairdresser's Experience*, pp. 144–54; Martineau, *Retrospect*, 2:255; Roger A. Fischer, "Racial Segregation in Ante Bellum New Orleans," *American Historical Review* 84 (February 1969): 926–37.

21. O'Ferrall, *Ramble*, p. 203.

22. Joseph G. Tregle, Jr., "Early New Orleans Society: A Reappraisal," *Journal of Southern History* 18 (February 1952): 33.

23. J. E. Alexander, *Transatlantic Sketches* (Philadelphia, 1833), p. 227.

24. United States Census Office, *Compendium of the Seventh Census* (Washington, 1854), pp. 79–80.

25. Robert Reinders, "The Free Negro in the New Orleans Economy, 1850–1860," *Louisiana History* 6 (Summer 1965): 274.

26. Donald E. Everett, "Free Persons of Color in New Orleans, 1803–1865" (Ph.D. diss., Tulane University, 1952), pp. 1–55, 132–77; New Orleans *Tribune*, September 1, 1864; Herbert E. Sterkx, "The Free Negro in Ante Bellum Louisiana, 1764–1860" (Ph.D. diss., University of Alabama,

1954), pp. 1–97, 263–320; Conveyance Records, Orleans Parish, 1849–1859, Orleans Parish Courthouse.

27. Social Statistics, Orleans Parish, 1860, entry 324, RG 29, NA; Everett, "Free Persons," pp. 258–61; D. J. Jackson, "The Negro in New Orleans," *Negro History Bulletin* 4 (May 1941): 189–90.

28. Everett, "Free Persons," pp. 223–37, 250–66; "Passes Issued to Free Negroes by the Mayor's Office," New Orleans Public Library; Norbert Rillieux Papers, Howard University Library; Morris K. Helpler, "Negroes and Crime in New Orleans, 1850–1861" (M.A. thesis, Tulane University, 1960), pp. 1–53.

29. St. James A. M. E. Church, *A Century of African Methodism,* pp. 1–21; Everett, "Free Persons," pp. 226–27; Social Statistics, Orleans Parish, 1860, entry 324, RG 29, NA.

30. Everett, "Free Persons," pp. 232–36; Helpler, "Negroes and Crime," pp. 18–51; United States Census Office, *Compendium of the 1850 Census,* pp. 67–74; New Orleans *Black Republican,* April 15, 1865.

31. Everett, "Free Persons," passim; Fischer, "Racial Segregation," pp. 926–37; Sterkx, "The Free Negro," pp. 387–431; Helpler, "Negroes and Crime," pp. 18–51 passim.

32. Charles Gayarré, "The Quadroons of Louisiana" (1890), p. 4, MS, LSU.

33. Sterkx, "The Free Negro," pp. 387–431; Fischer, "Racial Segregation," pp. 926–37; Lawrence D. Reddick, "The Negro in the New Orleans Press, 1850–1860: A Study in Attitudes and Propaganda" (Ph.D. diss., University of Chicago, 1941).

34. Martineau, *Retrospect,* 2:259; Nichols, *Forty Years,* p. 127.

35. Fischer, "Racial Segregation," pp. 926–37; Helpler, "Negroes and Crime," pp. 1–53; Margaret Hall, *The Aristocratic Journey* (New York, 1931), p. 250; New Orleans *Tribune,* May 17, 1865; C. G. Parsons, *Inside View of Slavery* (Boston, 1855), pp. 297–98; Everett, "Free Persons," pp. 54–55, 241–44, 262–66; Sterkx, "The Free Negro," pp. 80–87, 375–76.

36. Potter, *A Hairdresser's Experience,* p. 159; New Orleans *Tribune,* May 8, 17, 1865.

37. J. A. Rogers, *Sex and Race,* 3 vols. (New York, 1940), 1:221–40; Alexander Mackay, *The Western World,* 3 vols. (London, 1849), 2:301–2; Potter, *A Hairdresser's Experience,* pp. 144–76; Trollope, *Domestic Manners,* p. 10; *New Orleans As It Is* (New Orleans, 1850), pp. 35–45; Everett, "Free Persons," pp. 232–36; Gayarré, "Quadroons."

38. Potter, *A Hairdresser's Experience,* pp. 189–90.

39. Helen T. Catterall, ed., *Judicial Cases Concerning American Slavery and the Negro,* 5 vols. (Washington, D.C., 1926–37), 3:389–703 passim; Everett, "Free Persons," pp. 333–39.

40. Catterall, *Judicial Cases,* 3:589; *New Orleans As It Is,* p. 43.

41. Helpler, "Negroes and Crime," p. 53.

42. Everett, "Free Persons," pp. 237–41; Sterkx, "The Free Negro," pp. 339–41.

43. Catterall, *Judicial Cases*, 3:389–703 passim; Potter, *A Hairdresser's Experience*, p. 176.

44. Potter, *A Hairdresser's Experience*, p. 155; Alice C. Risley Diary, December 20, 1864, LSU.

45. Parsons, *Inside View*, p. 297; Nichols, *Forty Years*, p. 128; Potter, *A Hairdresser's Experience*, p. 159.

46. Henry T. Johns, *Life with the Forty-ninth Massachusetts Volunteers* (Pittsfield, Mass., 1864), p. 126.

47. Everett, "Free Persons," pp. 33–39, 262–68; Gayarré, "Quadroons," p. 4.

2. Fighting for Freedom

1. William H. Russell, *My Diary North and South* (New York, 1954), p. 337; James O. Long, "Gloom Envelops New Orleans, April 24 to May 2, 1862," *Louisiana History* 1 (Fall 1960): 281–89; New Orleans *Picayune*, February 3, 1862.

2. J. Chandler Gregg, *Life in the Army* (Philadelphia, 1868), p. 179; New Orleans *Black Republican*, April 22, 1865; New Orleans *Picayune*, June 10, 15, 21, 29, and July 15, 1862; New Orleans *Delta*, November 16, 1862.

3. New Orleans *Black Republican*, April 22, 1865.

4. P. M. Lapice to Nathaniel Banks, January 13, 1863, DG, CA, RG 393, NA.

5. Kate M. Rowland, ed., *The Journal of Julia LeGrand, New Orleans, 1862–1863* (Richmond, 1911), p. 229.

6. Clarissa Solomon Diary, 1861–62, p. 217, LSU; Rowland, *Journal of Julia LeGrand*, pp. 260–91; Major General Benjamin Butler to Edwin Stanton, June 18, 1862, DG, LS, RG 393, NA; Homer B. Sprague, *History of the 13th Infantry Regiment of Connecticut Volunteers during the Great Rebellion* (Hartford, 1867), p. 64.

7. P. Haggerty to Phelps, May 28, 1862, DG, LS, RG 393, NA.

8. Annie Jeter Carmouche, "Reminiscences," p. 93, SHC; Rowland, *Journal of Julia LeGrand*, pp. 68, 263; Benjamin Butler to the French Consul, August 11, 1862, DG, LS, RG 393, NA.

9. Clarissa Solomon Diary, p. 199.

10. New Orleans *Delta*, November 16, 1862; Sam Hooper to Nathaniel Banks, July 24, 1863, Nathaniel Banks Papers, LC.

11. Rowland, *Journal of Julia LeGrand*, p. 112; see also New Orleans *Picayune*, June 10, 1862.

12. W. C. Corsan, *Two Months in the Confederate States, Including a Visit to New Orleans under the Domination of General Butler* (London, 1863), p. 32; New Orleans *Black Republican*, April 22, 1865.

13. Ann W. Jeter to William G. Jeter, November 21, 1861, Annie Jeter Carmouche Papers, SHC; George H. Hepworth, *The Whip, Hoe and Sword; or, the Gulf Department in '63* (Boston, 1864), pp. 126, 151–58, 274; Edward Page to James Bowen, February 16, 1863, PMG, LR, DG,

RG 393, NA; Planters of St. Mary's Parish to Nathaniel Banks,
February 1863, CA, DG, RG 393, NA; George H. Smith, *Leaves from a
Soldier's Diary* (Putnam, Conn., 1906), p. 35.

14. "F" to her sister, February 23, 1864, Jared Y. Sanders Papers,
LSU; Robert A. Tyson Diary, 1863–64, April 6, 1864, LSU; A. J. H.
Duganne, *Camps and Prisons: Two Months in the Department of the Gulf*
(New York, 1865), p. 89; A. Franklin Pugh Diary, 1861–64 (2 vols),
vol.2, October 27 to November 8, 1862, LSU; Andrew McCollam to
S. R. Holabird, February 17, 1863, Andrew McCollam Papers,
SHC; Harris H. Beecher, *Record of the 114th Regiment, NYSV*
(Norwich, N.Y., 1866), pp. 149–50, 182, 187.

15. Donald E. Everett, "Free Persons," p. 292.

16. Sprague, *History of the 13th Infantry*, p. 134; Duganne, *Camps
and Prisons*, pp. 98–101; Edward Page to J. S. Clark, January 2, 1863, LR,
and Benjamin Butler to Edwin Stanton, October 22, 1862, LS, DG,
RG 393, NA; T. E. Chickering to R. B. Irwin, May 25, 1863, Banks
Papers, LC.

17. New Orleans *Black Republican*, May 13, 1865; *National Anti-
Slavery Standard*, August 23, 1862, and January 17, 1863; New Orleans
Picayune, July 22 and 23, and August 5, 1862; William C. Holbrook,
"Autobiography," p. 7, SHC; William D. Allen to R. S. Davis,
August 16, 1862, DG, LR, RG 393, NA.

18. Sprague, *History of the 13th Infantry*, p. 63.

19. Nathaniel Banks to Mary Banks, January 30, 1863, Banks Papers,
LC; James Bowen to C. W. Killborn, March 5, 1863, DG, LR, PM,
RG 393, NA; Contract, Sequestration Commission, February 5, 1863, DG,
LR, PM, RG 393, NA; James Bowen to Major Foster, December 26,
1863, DG, LR, PM, RG 393, NA; "Memorandum of Agreement with
Planters," October 1862, DG, LS and Memoranda, 21, RG 94, NA.

20. Josephine Luke, "From Slavery to Freedom in Louisiana,
1862–1865" (M.A. thesis, Tulane University, 1939), pp. 1–43; Rowland,
Journal of Julia LeGrand, p. 174; J. F. Moors, *History of the Fifty-second
Regiment Massachusetts Volunteers* (Boston, 1893), p. 132; New Orleans
Picayune, July 11, 1862; *National Anti-Slavery Standard*, November 29,
1862.

21. Record of the Police Jury, Orleans Parish (right bank),
1861–1868, p. 77, New Orleans Public Library; Beecher, *Record of the
114th Regiment*, p. 108.

22. *National Anti-Slavery Standard*, August 23, September 27, 1862,
and February 21, 1863; New Orleans *Tribune*, August 27, November 27
and 29, 1864; "Pass for Elodie," April 18, 1863, St. Martin Family
Papers, Tulane University; New Orleans *Picayune*, November 22, 1862;
Sprague, *History of the 13th Infantry*, pp. 53–63; Captain George Bell
to Captain Stephen Hoyt, February 13, 1864, Tulane University; George
H. Hepworth to Nathaniel Banks, June 28, 1863, Banks Papers, LC;
Edith Jones to Nathaniel Banks, March 4, 1863, W. H. Brice to
Nathaniel Banks, January 30, 1863, DG, CA, RG 393, NA.

23. Sprague, *History of the 13th Infantry*, p. 161; Hepworth to
Nathaniel Banks, April 10, 1863, Banks Papers, LC.

24. Paul Trévigne et al. to Nathaniel Banks, August 17, 1864, DG, CA, RG 393, NA.

25. Willie M. Caskey, *Secession and Restoration of Louisiana* (University, La., 1938); John D. Winters, "Confederate New Orleans, 1861–1862 " (M.A. thesis, Tulane University, 1939); "Reminiscences of M. Jeff Thompson," p. 15, SHC.

26. Gerald M. Capers, *Occupied City: New Orleans under the Federals, 1862–1865* (Lexington, Ky., 1965), pp. 214–19; Winters, "Confederate New Orleans," pp. 51, 85–92, 122; Herbert E. Sterkx, "The Free Negro," pp. 284–94; New Orleans *Tribune*, October 12, 1864.

27. New Orleans *Tribune*, December 7, 1864; Rowland, *Journal of Julia LeGrand*, pp. 130–40; Everett, "Free Persons," pp. 270–84.

28. James Parton, *General Butler in New Orleans* (New York, 1864), p. 517; New Orleans *Tribune*, December 7, 1864.

29. Rowland, *Journal of Julia LeGrand*, pp. 130–40; Sprague, *History of the 13th Infantry*, pp. 72–73; Charles P. Bosson, *History of the Forty-second Regiment Infantry Massachusetts Volunteers, 1862, 1863, 1864*, (Boston, 1886), pp. 213, 310; J. A. Norager to Nathaniel Banks, July 29, 1863, and J. F. Winston to Nathaniel Banks, October 7, 1863, DG, CA, RG 94, NA.

30. Benjamin Butler to Edwin Stanton, September 1, 1862, DG, LS, RG 94, NA; John D. Winters, *The Civil War in Louisiana* (Baton Rouge, 1963), pp. 140–63; Hans L. Trefousse, *Ben Butler: The South Called Him Beast!* (New York, 1957), pp. 107, 119–31; Benjamin F. Butler, *The Private and Official Correspondence of General Benjamin F. Butler during the Period of the Civil War*, 5 vols. (Norwood, Mass., 1917), 2: 173–74, 229, 270–71.

31. *Douglas Monthly*, April 1863, p. 829; New Orleans *Tribune*, September 24, 1864; J. B. Bernabe et al. to Nathaniel Banks, March 11, 1863, DG, CA, RG 393, NA; Recruiting Speech, 1862, P. B. S. Pinchback Papers, Howard University.

32. Bosson, *History of the Forty-Second Regiment*, pp. 337–42; New Orleans *Tribune*, July 2, 1867; New Orleans *Delta*, January 10, 1863; *National Anti-Slavery Standard*, December 6, 1862.

33. John W. Phelps to Benjamin Butler, July 30, 1862, DG, LR, RG 393, NA; Lawrence van Alstyne, *Diary of an Enlisted Man* (New Haven, Conn., 1910), pp. 193–94.

34. Albert Stearns to James Bowen, May 28, 1863, PMG, LR, and K. Fuller to Benjamin Butler, November 19, 1862, LR, DG, RG 393, NA.

35. W. H. Emory to General Stone, October 6, 1863, DG, LR, RG 393, NA.

36. Fred H. Knapp to Nathaniel Banks, April 1, 1863, S. B. Bevans to E. R. S. Canby, August 2, 1864, and P. F. Languille to S. Hamblin, September 1, 1864, DG, CA, RG 393, NA; Special Order no. 102, November 16, 1863, Adjutant General's Office, Lorenzo Thomas Letterbooks, RG 94, NA; Henry T. Johns, *Life with the Forty-ninth Massachusetts Volunteers.*

37. George Hanks to Nathaniel Banks, August 4, 1863, DG, CA, RG 393, NA; Bosson, *History of the Forty-second Regiment*, pp. 344–45.

38. Mary F. Berry, "Negro Troops in Blue and Gray: The Louisiana Native Guards, 1861–1863," *Louisiana History* 8 (Spring 1967): 165–90.

39. Scrapbook of the Honorable C. C. Antoine, pp. 2–3, Southern University Library; Everett, "Free Persons," pp. 270–93; Berry, "Negro Troops," pp. 165–90; U.S. War Department, *The War of the Rebellion: A Compilation of the Official Records of the Union and Confederate Armies*, 70 vols. (Washington, D.C., 1880–1901), ser. 1, 4:442–43 (hereafter cited as Official Records).

40. *National Anti-Slavery Standard*, February 14, 1863. See also, Joseph T. Wilson, *Black Phalanx: A History of the Negro Soldiers in the Wars of 1775, 1812, 1861–65* (Hartford, 1888), p. 169; John W. Blassingame, "The Selection of Officers and Non-Commissioned Officers of Negro Troops in the Union Army, 1863–1865," *Negro History Bulletin* 30 (January 1967): 11; Speech, 1863, Pinchback Papers, Howard University.

41. Blassingame, "Selection of Officers" p. 11.

42. New Orleans *Black Republican*, April 4, 15, May 13, 1865; New Orleans *Tribune*, October 25, September 6, 15, 1864, and June 13, 1865; Hepworth, *Whip, Hoe and Sword*, p. 179.

43. Corsan, *Two Months in the Confederate States*, p. 37; Enclosures, Benjamin Butler to the French Consul, October 11, 1862, DG, LS, RG 393, NA; *National Anti-Slavery Standard*, November 29, 1862; Speech, 1863, Pinchback Papers, Howard University.

44. *National Anti-Slavery Standard*, November 29, 1862.

45. Corsan, *Two Months in the Confederate States*, p. 40; Hepworth, *Whip, Hoe and Sword*, p. 193.

46. Records of the First, Second, and Third Louisiana Native Guards Infantry Regiments, RG 94, NA; *Official Records*, ser. 1, vols. 5–9; Lorenzo Thomas to Edwin Stanton, September 5, 1863; Lorenzo Thomas to E. R. S. Canby, June 20, 1864, Lorenzo Thomas to Edwin Stanton, September 11, 1864 and February 23, 1865, in Lorenzo Thomas Letterbooks, Orders and Letters of Brigadier General Daniel Ullmann, General's Papers and Books, RG 94, NA.

47. New Orleans *Tribune*, March 12, 1865; Nathaniel Banks to Mary Banks, May 30, 1863, Banks Papers, LC; Frank M. Flinn, *Campaigning with Banks in Louisiana, '63 and '64, and with Sheridan in the Shenandoah Valley in '64 and '65* (Lynn, Mass., 1887), p. 74; General Orders no. 150, October 19, 1864, DG, PMG, New Orleans, LR, RG 393, NA.

48. *National Anti-Slavery Standard*, February 28, March 7, 1863; Lorenzo Thomas to Edwin Stanton, April 7, 1864, Lorenzo Thomas Letterbooks, RG 94, NA; George L. Andrews to R. B. Irwin, August 21, 1863, Daniel Ullmann to W. D. Smith, May 31, 1863, F. J. Shuck to R. B. Irwin, May 24, 1863, and S. H. Stafford to R. B. Irwin, January 4, 1863, DG, LR, RG 393, NA; *Official Records*, ser. 1, 16:808–9; Carded Military Service Record, Thomas W. Conway, 79th U.S. Colored Troops, RG 94, NA.

49. *National Anti-Slavery Standard*, February 29, March 7, 1863; Von Herrman to G. Nowens, February 24, 1863, Von Herrman Letters, 1862–63, Tulane University; Carded Military Service Records, Captain Leon Forstall, Third Louisiana Native Guard Infantry Regiment, and

Captain Joseph Follin, First Louisiana Native Guard Infantry Regiment, RG 94, NA.

50. New Orleans *Tribune*, May 14, 1865; Speech, 1863, Pinchback Papers, Howard University; Nathaniel Banks to Lorenzo Thomas, February 14, 1863, DG, LS, RG 393, NA.

51. Carded Military Service Records, Captains James Lewis and Louis Snaer, First Louisiana Native Guards, and "The Negro in the Military Service of the United States," vol. 3, pt. 1, pp. 1498–1500, RG 94, NA; John W. Blassingame, "The Organization and Use of Negro Troops in the Union Army, 1863–1865" (M.A. thesis, Howard University, 1961), pp. 8–9; Blassingame, "Selection of Officers," p. 10.

52. Samuel M. Kinston to Nathaniel Banks, May 15, 1863, George H. Hanks to Nathaniel Banks, June 30, 1863, and Circular, Bureau of Free Labor, July 1, 1864, Banks Papers, LC; George Hanks to Nathaniel Banks, July 12, 1863, and Robert H. Gaskill to Colonel Robinson, September 1864, DG, CA, RG 393, NA.

53. William R. Tiemann, *The 159th Regiment: New York State Volunteers in the War of the Rebellion, 1862–1865* (Brooklyn, 1891), p. 66; Johns, *Life with the Forty-ninth, Massachusetts Volunteers*, p. 126; Luke, "From Slavery to Freedom," pp. 34–42.

54. John W. Blassingame, "The Union Army as an Educational Institution for Negroes, 1862–1865," *Journal of Negro Education* 34 (Spring 1965): 152–59.

3. Land, Labor, and Capital

1. Janey Marks, "The Industrial Development of New Orleans Since 1805" (M.A. thesis, Tulane University, 1939), pp. 1–20; *Commercial Reports Received at the Foreign Office from Her Majesty's Consuls, in 1867* (London, 1867), pp. 260, 280.

2. Benjamin Butler to Henry W. Halleck, September 1, 1862, DG, LS, RG 393, NA.

3. Willie Melvin Caskey, *Secession and Restoration of Louisiana* (University, Louisiana, 1938), pp. 15–53; E. Whittemore to Nathaniel Banks, March 14(?), December 6, 1863, and E. G. Beckwith to George B. Drake, March 4, 1865, DG, CA, RG 393, NA.

4. Caskey, *Secession and Restoration*, pp. 50–54; Luke, "From Slavery to Freedom," pp. 16–34; A. F. Puffer to John W. Phelps, September 2, 1862, DG, LS, RG 393, NA.

5. Frank C. Peck to Benjamin Butler, June 15, 1862, W. H. Emory to Richard B. Irwin, January 27, 1862, F. S. Nickerson to J. S. Clark, January 27, 1863, DG, LR, RG 393, NA.

6. Stephen Hoyt to V. F. Dannoy, DG, CA, RG 393, NA; see also Rowland, *Journal of Julia LeGrand*, p. 60.

7. Nathaniel Banks to W. H. Halleck, October 15, 1863, Banks Letterbooks, LSU.

8. Caskey, *Secession and Restoration*, pp. 70–89; Luke, "From Slavery to Freedom," pp. 21–58; George Hanks to Nathaniel Banks, March 28,

1864, Banks Papers, LC; James K. Hosmer, *The Color-Guard: Being a Corporal's Notes of Military Service in the Nineteenth Army Corps* (Boston, 1864), p. 140; William R. Crane to Nathaniel Banks, March 26, 1863, and John Pickering to Colonel Chandler, April 2, 1864, DG, CA, RG 393, NA; Benjamin Butler to John W. Phelps, May 10, 1862, and Butler to Henry W. Halleck, September 1, 1862, DG, LS, RG 393, NA.

9. John W. Blassingame, "The Union Army as an Educational Institution," p. 154.

10. Ibid.; New Orleans *Tribune*, August 23, 1864; Butler to Edwin Stanton, November 14, 1862, DG, LS, RG 393, NA; *Observations on the Present Condition of Louisiana* (1865?, n.p.); Luke "From Slavery to Freedom," pp. 34–80.

11. Alfred O. Marshall, *Army Life: From A Soldier's Journal* (Joliet, Ill., 1864), p. 397; New Orleans *Tribune*, October 22, 1864; Homer B. Sprague, *History of the 13th Infantry*, p. 183; Charles Bosson, *History of the Forty-second Regiment Infantry*, pp. 337–42.

12. George H. Hepworth, *Whip, Hoe and Sword*, p. 235.

13. *Observations on the Present Condition of Louisiana*, p. 5; George H. Hepworth to Nathaniel Banks, June 15, 1863, and T. W. Conway to Banks, March 17, 1865, Banks Papers, LC; New Orleans *Tribune*, October 12, 1864; New Orleans *Black Republican*, May 20, 1865; Hepworth, *Whip, Hoe and Sword*, pp. 23–28.

14. Banks to his wife, February 24, 1863, Banks Papers, LC.

15. New Orleans *Tribune*, October 12, 1864; New Orleans *Black Republican*, April 22, 1865.

16. New Orleans *Black Republican*, April 15, 22, May 13, 1865.

17. New Orleans *Tribune*, August 13, September 1 and 24, November 17, December 8, 1864, January 12, February 7, March 14, April 9, 1865, December 31, 1867; A. J. H. Duganne, *Camps and Prisons*, p. 36.

18. New Orleans *Tribune*, August 13, December 8, 1864.

19. James McKaye, *The Mastership and Its Fruits: The Emancipated Slave Face to Face with His Old Master* (New York, 1864), pp. 21–30; Hepworth, *Whip, Hoe and Sword*, p. 28; New Orleans *Black Republican*, April 15, 1865; New Orleans *Tribune*, December 4, 1864; Kenneth E. Shewmaker and Andrew K. Prinz, "A Yankee in Louisiana: Selections from the Diary and Correspondence of Henry R. Gardner, 1862–1866," *Louisiana History* 5 (Summer 1864): 271–95.

20. Henry Warner to Nathaniel Banks, February 10, 1863, DG, CA, RG 393, NA; McKaye, *The Mastership and Its Fruits*, p. 21.

21. New Orleans *Tribune*, November 24, 30, December 27, 1864, and January 4, 7, 12, 14, February 4, March 7, 23, 28, 1865; James H. Ingraham to S. A. Hurlbut, February 11, 1865, DG, CA, RG 393, NA; S. A. Hurlbut to James H. Ingraham, March 23, 1865, FB, Commissioner, RG 105, NA.

22. New Orleans *Tribune*, January 28, 29, February 2, and March 31, 1865.

23. Ibid., November 30, 1864.

24. Ibid., February 23, 24, 28, March 7, 21, April 11, 13, and May 2, 16, 1865; *National Freedman* 1 (April 1, 1865): 107–8; New Orleans *Black Republican*, April 15, 1865; Benjamin F. Flanders to Nathaniel Banks, May 17, 1865, W. R. Crane et al. to O. O. Howard, August 14, 1865, FB Commissioner, RG 105, NA.

25. New Orleans *Tribune*, January 20, 1869.

26. New Orleans *Louisianian*, January 22, 1871, and June 27, 1874; New Orleans *Black Republican*, April 15, 1865; New Orleans *Republican*, November 20, 23, 1874; New Orleans *Tribune*, April 19, June 10, 1865, November 10, 1867, and January 8, 15, 20, February 2, 1869.

27. Friedrick Gerstäcker, *Neue Reisen durch die Vereinigten Staaten, Mexiko, Ecuador, Westindien und Venezuela*, 2 vols. (Jena, 1876), 1:365; John H. E. Skinner, *After the Storm*, 2 vols. (London, 1866), 2:69; M[aria] Waterbury, *Seven Years among the Freedmen* (Chicago, 1890), p. 59.

28. New Orleans *Louisianian*, February 20, 1873.

29. See tables 3–8.

30. *New Orleans City Directory*, 1870; also see tables 3, 4, and 5. Unless otherwise indicated, the source for all references to occupations in this chapter is tables 3–8.

31. New Orleans *Louisianian*, July 3, 1880; New Orleans *Tribune*, June 21, 1867; New Orleans *Republican*, May 18, 27, 1867.

32. Ambrose C. Fulton, *A Life's Voyage* (New York, 1898), p. 361.

33. See table 10; Herbert R. Northrup, "The New Orleans Longshoremen," *Political Science Quarterly* 57 (December 1942): 526–44; Robert C. Francis, "Longshoremen in New Orleans," *Opportunity* 14 (March 1936): 82–85, 93; Roger W. Shugg, *Origins of Class Struggle in Louisiana* (University, La., 1939).

34. Mary S. Jones to Caroline Jones, March 14, 1865, Joseph Jones Collection, Tulane University; New Orleans *Crescent*, April 7, 1867; Census of Population, Orleans Parish, 1870, 1880, RG 329, NA.

35. New Orleans *Louisianian*, October 18, 1879.

36. Arthur Raymond Pearce, "The Rise and Decline of Labor in New Orleans" (M.A. thesis, Tulane University, 1938), pp. 17–25; William Saunders, *Through the Light Continent; or, The United States in 1877–78* (London, 1879), p. 69; New Orleans *Crescent*, August 20, 1868; New Orleans *Louisianian*, December 18, 1870, November 30, 1871, January 21, 1872, April 3, 1875, November 17, 1877, and April 3, 1880; *Constitution and By-Laws of the Shoemakers Union of New Orleans* (New Orleans, 1879).

37. New Orleans *Tribune*, May 19, 24, 1867.

38. Ibid., May 16, 17, 18, 19, 24, June 16, 1867; *New Orleans Times*, May 17, 1867 and October 18, 1872; Saunders, *Through the Light Continent*, p. 69.

39. New Orleans *Louisianian*, March 27, 1880; Pearce, "Rise and Decline of Labor," pp. 17–25.

40. New Orleans *Louisianian*, August 2, 1879.

41. *New Orleans Times*, August 10, 1875; New Orleans *Tribune*, February 4, 1865, July 3, 1867, and February 21, 1869; New Orleans *Louisianian*, December 29, 1870, and January 12, May 18, June 1, June 8, 1871.

42. New Orleans *Louisianian*, August 28, 1875.

43. New Orleans *Tribune*, July 10, 25, October 26, December 17, 1867, and February 19, 1869; New Orleans *Louisianian*, April 2, June 15, July 20, October 26, 1871, and July 6, 1872; Walter L. Fleming, *The Freedmen's Savings Bank: A Chapter in the Economic History of the Negro Race* (Chapel Hill, 1927), pp. 142–43; Record of the New Orleans Branch, Freedman's Savings and Trust Company, RG 101, NA.

44. New Orleans *Louisianian*, June 26, August 28, 1875.

45. Ibid., August 9, 1879.

46. Census of Population, Orleans Parish, 1860–80, RG 329, NA.

47. Tax Assessment Rolls, 1880, New Orleans, New Orleans Public Library; Census of Population, Orleans Parish, 1870, RG 329, NA. Two hundred seventy Negro men under the age of sixty who were listed in the 1870 census as possessing real property were checked against the tax assessment rolls of Orleans Parish for 1880. Although the sample included ten Negroes whose last names began with each letter of the alphabet, only forty-five of them appeared on the tax assessment rolls.

48. *National Freedman*, 1 (September 15, 1865): 266–67; New Orleans *Louisianian*, June 1, 1871, June 19, July 10, August 28, 1875, November 17, 1877, and January 11, September 20, 1879.

49. New Orleans *Louisianian*, August 28, 1875, and September 20, 1879.

50. *New Orleans City Directory*, 1870, tables 5, 6, and 7; New Orleans *Times*, September 19, 1867; Gerstäcker, *Neue Riesen,* pp. 365–66; New Orleans *Louisianian*, May 25, 1871, August 3, 1872, and February 22, 1879; New Orleans *Tribune*, July 3, 1864, and September 4, December 3, 1867; New Orleans *Black Republican*, April 22, 1865.

51. *New Orleans City Directory*, 1870.

52. Census of Manufacturing, 1880, Census of Population, 1860, 1870, Orleans Parish, RG 329, NA; Tax Assessment Rolls, Orleans parish, 1880; Rodolphe L. Desdunes, *Nos hommes et notre histoire* (Montreal, 1911), pp. 123–25; A. E. Perkins, *Who's Who in Colored Louisiana* (Baton Rouge, 1930).

53. Census of Manufacturing, 1880, Census of Population, 1860, 1870, Orleans Parish, RG 329, NA; Tax Assessment Rolls, Orleans parish, 1880.

54. New Orleans *Louisianian*, December 22, 29, 1870, February 26, 1871, and December 13, 1879; Succession Papers of Lucillia Tucker, Mary Jason, Madeline J. Roche, Oscar J. Dunn, and Octave Perrault, U.S. Court House, New Orleans; Honorable C. C. Antoine, Scrapbook, pp. 71–81, Southern University Library.

55. *New Orleans City Directory*, 1870; New Orleans *Louisianian*, March 16, 1871, and February 21, June 5, 1880; Antoine Scrapbook, p. 81;

Census of Agriculture, Iberville, Natchitoches, and Plaquemines Parishes, 1870, 1880, RG 329, NA.

56. New Orleans *Louisianian*, March 16, 1871.

57. Ibid., May 3, September 20, November 22, December 25, 1879, and March 6, 1880.

58. Succession Papers of Murville Cheval and Frederick Barthelmy, U.S. Court House, New Orleans.

59. New Orleans *Louisianian*, May 3, June 21, 1879; Succession Papers of J. B. D. Bonseigneur, J. A. Lacroix, J. J. Montford, and Victor Pessou, U.S. Court House, New Orleans; Census of Population, Orleans Parish, 1860, 1870, RG 329, NA.

60. Succession Papers of Myrtille Courcelle, U.S. Court House, New Orleans; Conveyance Records, Orleans Parish, Orleans Parish Court House.

61. Succession Papers of Sidney Thezan, U.S. Court House, New Orleans; Conveyance Records, Orleans Parish, Orleans Parish Court House.

62. Succession Papers of John F. Clay, Myrtille Courcelle, and Pelagie Jacques, U.S. Court House, New Orleans; Conveyance Records, Orleans Parish, Orleans Parish Court House.

63. New Orleans *Louisianian*, October 10, 1874, Desdunes, *Nos Hommes*, pp. 125–29; Tax Assessments Rolls, Orleans Parish, 1880; J. M. Murphy, "Thomy Lafon," *Negro History Bulletin* 7 (October 1943): 6, 20.

64. Conveyance Records, Orleans Parish, Orleans Parish Court House.

4. Family Life

1. For suggestive general studies see: William E. Bridges, "Family Patterns and Social Values in America, 1825–1875," *American Quarterly* 17 (Spring 1965): 3–11; Arthur W. Calhoun, *A Social History of the American Family*, 3 vols. (Cleveland, 1915–18); Edmund S. Morgan, *The Puritan Family* (New Haven, 1944); Richard L. Rapson, "The American Child as Seen by British Travelers, 1845–1935," *American Quarterly* 18 (Fall 1965): 520–34.

2. New Orleans *Black Republican*, April 15, 22, 29, May 13, 1865; New Orleans *Louisianian*, April 3, 1880; L. Jolissaint to L. H. Warren, December 7, 1868, LS, 1st Subdistrict, New Orleans, and LS, Vermillionville, book 494, pp. 12–15, 27, 56, 100–109, in BRFAL, RG 105, NA; *American Missionary* 11 (March 1867): 57.

3. L. Tibbetts to "Sister," January 23, 1853, John C. Tibbetts Correspondence, LSU; Henry T. Johns, *Life with the Forty-ninth Massachusetts Volunteers*, p. 125.

4. Priscilla Bond Diary, LSU.

5. Memorandum book no. 9, Alexandre De Clouet Papers, LSU; Philip H. Jones, "Reminiscences of Days before and after the Civil War," SHC.

6. Ebeneezer Davis, *American Scenes and Christian Slavery* (London, 1849), pp. 51–56.

7. *New Orleans As It Is*, p. 70.

8. Marriage Certificates, Louisiana, BRFAL, RG 105, NA.

9. Henry Bibb, *Narrative*, pp. 197–200; Joe Gray Taylor, *Negro Slavery in Louisiana*, pp. 15–20; E. Franklin Frazier, "The Negro Slave Family," *Journal of Negro History* 15 (April 1930): 198–259.

10. Helen T. Catterall, ed., *Judicial Cases*, 3:613.

11. *New Orleans As It Is*, p. 76.

12. James McKaye, *The Mastership and Its Fruits*, p. 6.

13. Bibb, *Narrative*, pp. 191–92.

14. Chandler Gregg, *Life in the Army*, p. 204; New Orleans *Tribune*, February 25, 1865.

15. A. H. Newton, *Out of the Briars* (Philadelphia, 1910), p. 86.

16. John R. Ficklen, *History of Reconstruction in Louisiana to 1868* (Baltimore, 1910), pp. 143–44.

17. M[anly] French, *Address to Masters and Freedmen* (Macon, Ga., 1865); New Orleans *Republican*, April 24, 1867; New Orleans *Tribune*, Februaury 17, March 28, 1865; Gregg, *Life in the Army*, p. 220; L. S. Jolissaint to W. H. Sterling, April 30, 1868, L. S. Jolissaint to L. H. Warren, June 1, 1868, 1st Subdistrict, New Orleans, LS, BRFAL, RG 105, NA.

18. Bibb, *Narrative*, pp. 191–92.

19. New Orleans *Louisianian*, February 26, July 6, 9, August 3, September 7, 1871.

20. Ibid., March 2, 1871.

21. Ibid., October 12, 1871.

22. Gregg, *Life in the Army*, p. 207; St. James A.M.E. Church, *A Century of African Methodism*, p. 22; New Orleans *Republican*, November 27, 1875; Norwell W. Wilson Diary, January 9, 1878, SHC; New Orleans *Black Republican*, May 13, 1865.

23. New Orleans *Louisianian*, December 18, 1870, April 6, 1871, May 11, August 31, 1872, January 2, August 28, September 18, 1875, and March 22, 1879.

24. Ibid., August 28, 1875.

25. Ibid., December 18, 1870.

26. Ibid., January 15, September 21, 1871, January 16, 1873, May 9, 1874, November 22, 1879; Barbara Welter, "The Cult of True Womanhood, 1820–1860," *American Quarterly* 18 (Summer 1966): 151–74.

27. New Orleans *Louisianian*, November 22, 1879.

28. Ibid., May 9, 1874.

29. Euhaw, "Woman's Rights," *New Orleans Monthly Review* 1 (1874): 173–74, 349–50; New Orleans *Louisianian*, April 20, May 25, July 2, 1871, and January 2, 1875.

30. New Orleans *Louisianian*, April 20, 1871.

31. Ibid., January 2, 1875.

32. Ibid., September 14, 1872.

33. Ibid., January 15, 1871.

34. Among the important models used for this study were the following: M. G. Smith, *West Indian Family Structure* (Seattle, 1962); Fernando Henriques, *Family and Colour in Jamaica* (London, 1953); Irene Graham, "The Negro Family in a Northern City," *Opportunity* 8 (February 1930): 48–51; and E. Franklin Frazier, *The Negro Family in Chicago* (Chicago, 1932).

35. Since the censuses of 1860 and 1870 define a family as all people living under one roof (even inmates of a hotel or boarding house), it is impossible to collect data for these years. In 1880 the situation changed when enumerators were instructed to list the heads of households and the relationship of each individual in the dwelling to them. See Carroll D. Wright, ed., *The History and Growth of the United States Census* (Washington, 1900), pp. 157, 166, 170–71.

36. See table 11.

37. New Orleans *Louisianian*, February 21, 1880.

38. Louisiana Board of Health, *Annual Report*, 1877–80; *Thirty-ninth Report of Massachusetts Births, Marriages, and Deaths* (Boston, 1881), p. 21. In thirty-one counties in Mississippi from 1865 to 1870 the marriage rate among blacks was 12.2 per thousand of the population; among whites, 16.1 per thousand. In England in 1869 the marriage rate was 3.7 per thousand. See Robert Somers, *The Southern States since the War, 1870–71* (New York, 1871), pp. 251–52.

39. Louisiana Board of Health, *Annual Report*, 1877–80.

40. Census of Population, Orleans Parish, 1880, RG 29, NA; table 12.

41. Louisiana Board of Health, *Annual Report*, 1875, p. 171.

42. Ibid., *Annual Report*, 1869–83; tables 1, 2, 13.

43. Louisiana Board of Health, *Annual Report*, 1872, 1883.

44. United States Census Office, *Eighth Census* (Washington, D.C., 1864), 1:195.

45. See tables 1 and 2.

46. See table 2; State Census of 1875.

47. *Annual Report of the Board of Metropolitan Police to the Governor of Louisiana*, 1870 (New Orleans, 1871), p. 51.

48. See tables 11 and 15.

49. See table 16. The technique adopted for studying the white family in New Orleans was a form of serial sampling (often called systematic, patterned, or chain sampling) of all white families listed on every fifth page of the census of population of Orleans parish. Initially, the sampling technique was tested against an analysis of the total number of white families (1,525) in two enumeration districts, 72 and 73. While the sample of the enumeration districts showed that 81.7 percent of the families were headed by males, the percentage in the total count was 82.8. In other words, the sample is probably accurate within 1.1 percentage points.

5. Schools, Colleges, and Intellectual Life

1. See table 2; also see *Report of the Board of Education for the Freedmen, Department of the Gulf, for the Year 1864* (New Orleans, 1865), pp. 4–5.

2. New Orleans *Republican*, October 6, 1867, and November 29, December 9, 1873.

3. Charles Nordhoff, *The Cotton States in the Spring and Summer of 1875* (New York, 1875), p. 72.

4. New Orleans *Tribune*, October 24, November 16, 27, 1866; *Harpers Weekly* 8 (January 3, 1869): 53; New Orleans *Louisianian*, August 3, 1871; New Orleans *L'Union*, December 13, 1862; *The Olio* (February–March, 1869), p. 19; E. S. Stoddard Diaries, September 19, 1866, Tulane University; New Orleans *Republican*, May 4, 10, June 7, 28, 1867; *New Orleans Times*, May 2, 1867.

5. Rodolphe L. Desdunes, *Nos hommes et notre histoire*, pp. 4–34, 133–46; New Orleans *Republican*, May 10, 1867.

6. Silas E. Fales to Mary, February 10, 1863, Silas E. Fales Papers, SHC; T. W. Conway to Nathaniel Banks, August 13, 1863, Banks Papers, LC; E. M. Wheelock to John C. Clark, March 19, 1864, DG, CA, RG 393, NA.

7. E. M. Wheelock to John C. Clark, March 19, 1864, DG, CA, RG 393, NA.

8. See tables 2 and 37; *Report of the Board of Education for the Freedmen, 1864*, pp. 4–5.

9. *Report of the Board of Education for Freedmen, 1864*, pp. 4–5; E. M. Wheelock to John C. Clark, March 19, 1864, DG, CA, RG 393, NA.; W. B. Stickney to Nathaniel Banks, October 13, 1863, Banks Papers, LC.

10. *Report of the Board of Education for Freedmen, 1864*, pp. 5–21; E. M. Wheelock to John C. Clark, March 19, 1864, DG, CA, RG 393, NA.

11. E. M. Wheelock to John C. Clark, March 19, 1864, DG, CA, RG 393, NA.

12. J. Chandler Gregg, *Life in the Army*, p. 206.

13. E. M. Wheelock to John C. Clark, March 19, 1864, DG, CA, RG 393, NA.

14. Mortimer A. Warren to H. R. Pease, October 30, 1865, Superintendent of School Reports, 1865–68, Louisiana, BRFAL, RG 105, NA.

15. W. B. Stickney to Nathaniel Banks, October 13, 1863, Banks Papers, LC.

16. New Orleans *Tribune*, December 24, 1864; New Orleans *Black Republican*, April 22, 1865; *National Freedman*, November 1865 to July 1866; *Eighteenth Annual Report of the American Missionary Association*, 1864 (New York, 1864), pp. 17–18; H. W. Frisbie to John McNair, May 13, 1864, correspondence of the Louisiana State Board of

Education, LSU; Isaac Hubbs to James Bowen, March 4, 1864, DG, PMG, LR, RG 393, NA.

17. "Report of Scholars in the Schools of the Parish of Orleans up to August 31, 1865," "Report of Advances Made by the U. S. Government from April 1864 to September 30, 1865," Superintendent of Education, Louisiana, School Report, 1865–68, and Superintendent of Education, Louisiana, "Tuition reports, 1866–67," in BRFAL, RG 105, NA.

18. E. M. Wheelock to Nathaniel Banks, April 1, 1864, and E. M. Wheelock to John C. Clark, March 19, 1864, DG, CA, RG 393, NA; W. B. Stickney to Nathaniel Banks, October 13, 1863, and George Hanks to Nathaniel Banks, September 23, 1863, Banks Papers, LC; New Orleans *Republican*, July 31, 1867.

19. Margaret M. Williams, "An Outline of Public School Politics in Louisiana since the Civil War" (M.A. thesis, Tulane University, 1938), pp. 1–25; New Orleans *Republican*, April 12, 16, May 10, July 17, 30, 31, August 7, 9, September 3, 5, October 2, 3, 10, 19, 22, November 3, 8, 16, December 5, 1867; *New Orleans Times*, February 19, April 5, 11, 13, July 31, September 20, October 3, 13, 20, 25, 1867; New Orleans *Tribune*, May 16, 1867.

20. New Orleans *Tribune*, March 5, 1865, April 11, May 9, 12, October 24, 1867, January 22, 1869; *New Orleans Times*, September 6, 1868; New Orleans *Louisianian*, March 14, 1872.

21. New Orleans *Tribune*, May 12, 1867.

22. Ibid., March 5, 1865; New Orleans *Picayune*, February 9, 1870; New Orleans *Republican*, September 21, 1867.

23. New Orleans *Picayune*, February 9, 1870.

24. *Report of the Convention for Framing a Constitution for the State of Louisiana* (New Orleans, 1867–68), pp. 17, 35, 60–94, 200–202; *Annual Report of the State Superintendent of Education of Louisiana for 1872*, Appendix (New Orleans, 1873), p. 49; New Orleans *Picayune*, September 30, 1875; New Orleans *Crescent*, September 17, 1867; *New Orleans Times*, September 1, 3, 19, December 16, 17, 19, 1874, September 21, 1875, and June 28, 1877.

25. New Orleans *Picayune*, September 30, 1875.

26. Robert Mills Lusher, "Career of Robert Mills Lusher, in Louisiana (1899)," Lusher Papers, LSU.

27. Willie T. Nicholls to Thomas Pugh, August 11, 1867, Col. W. W. Pugh Papers, LSU.

28. *New Orleans Times*, September 21, 1875.

29. Ibid., July 9, 1877.

30. Arlin Turner, ed., *The Negro Question* (Garden City, N.Y., 1958), pp. 30–35.

31. Edward Lawrence, "Color in the New Orleans Schools," *Harpers Weekly* 19 (February 13, 1875): 147–48; Thomas H. Harris, *The Story of Public Education in New Orleans* (New Orleans, 1924), pp. 46–47; Alcée Fortier, *Louisiana Studies* (New Orleans, 1894), pp 267–68; Washington *New National Era*, June 4, 1874; New Orleans *Republican*,

September 28, 1873, February 4, 1875; New Orleans *Crescent*, September 15, 1867; New Orleans *Bulletin*, January 11, 12, 1871; [William G. Brown to Chairman, New Orleans School Board?] June [?] 1873, Louisiana Department of Education, Letterbook 1, LSU.

32. New Orleans *Republican*, December 16, 17, 18, 19, 1874; *New Orleans Times*, December 15, 16, 17, 18, 19, 1874, and January 10, 12, 1875.

33. *New Orleans Times*, September 14, 1875.

34. Ibid., October 20, 1877; New Orleans *Picayune*, September 16, 1875.

35. *New Orleans Times*, October 20, 1877.

36. New Orleans *Republican*, September 28, 1873.

37. New Orleans *Louisianian*, October 6, 1877, September 18, 1875.

38. *New Orleans Times*, February 19, 1875; New Orleans *Republican*, December 20, 1874, and March 3, 1875; New Orleans *Bulletin*, January 14, 25, 1871, and October 22, 1874; New Orleans *Louisianian*, December 12, 1874, and September 18, 1875; Washington *New National Era*, June 11, 1875.

39. *Annual Report of the State Superintendent of Education of Louisiana for 1871* (New Orleans, 1872), pp. 374–75.

40. George W. Cable, *Strange True Stories of Louisiana* (New York, 1889), pp. 222–23.

41. New Orleans *Republican*, April 12, 1873, and September 30, 1875; *Annual Report of the Board of Health for 1869* (New Orleans, 1870), p. 12; Miscellaneous Special Reports of Principals, Louisiana Department of Education, LSU; *Annual Report of the State Superintendent of Public Education of Louisiana for 1872*, Appendix (New Orleans, 1873), p. 18; "Theory and Practice," *Harper's Weekly* 18 (November 14, 1874): 930.

42. New Orleans *Louisianian*, June 11, 1871.

43. *Annual Report of the State Superintendent of Public Education of Louisiana for 1872*, Appendix, p. 18.

44. "Theory and Practice," p. 930.

45. Louis R. Harlan, "Desegregation in New Orleans Public Schools during Reconstruction," *American Historical Review* 67 (April, 1962): 663–75.

46. New Orleans *Republican*, January 13, 21, 1876; Mohamed J. Shaik, "The Development of Public Education for Negroes in Louisiana" (Ph.D. diss., University of Ottawa, 1964), pp. 11–42; *Annual Report of the Board of Health of the State of Louisiana to the General Assembly, 1875* (New Orleans, 1876) pp. 155–160, 172.

47. New Orleans *Republican*, June 3, November 5, December 5, 1875, and February 3, 16, March 9, April 13, August 9, 1876; New Orleans *Louisianian*, October 27, 19, 1877, September 13, 27, 1879; *Report of the Chief Superintendent of the Public Schools of New Orleans, 1877–81*.

48. *Sixth Annual Report of the Freedmen's Aid Society of the Methodist Episcopal Church, 1873* (Cincinnati, 1874), pp. 21–24; New Orleans

Republican, December 14, 1867; New Orleans *Louisianian*, September 4, 1875, and July 5, 1879.

49. Charles Edwin Robert, *Negro Civilization in the South* (Nashville, 1880), pp. 131–35; *American Journal of Education* 29 (1877): 84. Leland became self-supporting in 1886. When a hurricane destroyed the campus in 1915, the property was sold for $175,000, and the school reopened in Baker, Louisiana, in 1923. It remained open until 1948, at which time it owned 236 acres of land and had more than 400 students.

50. Robert, *Negro Civilization*, pp. 131–35; New Orleans University, *Seventy-five Years of Service* (New Orleans, 1935), pp. 75–86; *Reports of the Freedmen's Aid Society of the Methodist Episcopal Church*, 1866–75; New Orleans *Louisianian*, December 7, 1878; annual catalogues, New Orleans University, 1880–34. During its sixty-one-year history New Orleans University conferred more than 1,047 degrees. In 1934, its last year of operation, the University had 515 advanced and 149 high school students.

51. New Orleans University, *The Only Original New Orleans University Singers* (Philadelphia, 1881), pp. 9–10.

52. Walter L. Fleming, *Louisiana State University, 1860–1896* (Baton Rouge, 1936), pp. 184–233; *American Missionary* 14 (1870): 171; ibid. 17 (1878): 245.

53. Alfred Falk, *Trans-Pacific Sketches: A Tour through the United States and Canada* (Melbourne, Australia, 1877), p. 263.

54. *Catalogue of Straight University for the Years 1869–1870* (New Orleans 1870), p. 35.

55. New Orleans *Louisianian*, June 22, 1871.

56. See various issues of *American Missionary*, 1870–80, and the New Orleans *Louisianian*, 1870–78; New Orleans *Republican*, February 14, 22, 1874; Robert, *Negro Civilization*, pp. 131–35; *History of the American Missionary Association* (New York, 1874), pp. 36–37; S. S. Ashley to E. M. Cravath, September 3, 1873, Ashley to C. H. Howard, September 9, 1873, Ashley to Cravath, September 24, 1873, AMA Archives, Dillard University; Catalogues, Straight University, 1870–1932. In 1932 the AMA began the merger of Straight and New Orleans Universities to form Dillard University.

57. New Orleans *Louisianian*, May 10, 1879.

58. Ibid., April 23, 1871.

59. S. S. Ashley to E. M. Cravath, September 3, 1873, AMA Archives, Dillard University.

60. Finnian P. Leavens, "*L'Union* and the New Orleans *Tribune* and Louisiana Reconstruction" (M.A. thesis, Louisiana State University, 1966).

61. *Douglass' Monthly*, April 1863, pp. 820–21; *Liberator*, February 13, 1863; J. Willis Menard, *Lays in Summer Lands* (Washington, 1879); New Orleans *Tribune*, July 7, 1867.

62. Menard, *Lays*, pp. 63–64.

63. Ibid., pp. 63–65.

64. New Orleans *Louisianian,* December 4, 25, 1875 and January 22, 1876.

65. Ibid., May 22, 1875. For general treatments of literary movements among the Creoles and for biographies of the major figures see Charles H. Good, "The First American Negro Literary Movement," *Opportunity* 10 (March 1932): 76–79; Desdunes, *Nos hommes*; New Orleans *Louisianian,* December 4, 1875; Charles B. Rousseve, *The Negro in Louisiana* (New Orleans, 1937); Edward Larocque Tinker, *Les écrits de langue française en Louisiane au XIXe siècle* (Paris, 1932).

66. A. E. Perkins, "Victor Sejour and His Times," *Negro History Bulletin* 5 (April 1942): 163–66.

67. *Comptes-Rendus* 1 (1876–81): 135.

68. New Orleans *Louisianian,* December 25, 1875.

69. Rousseve, *The Negro in Louisiana,* p. 116.

70. Ibid., pp. 118, 190–91. Rousseve's translation: Dost thou remember that in thy rage, striking my wife and my child, under the blows of the savage lash thou did slowly murder them; that when I suffered by thy vengeance thou didst laugh at my woe; yet today, vile oppressor, I laugh at thy helplessness; tremble, and fear my power. I am, I am the black physician.

71. New Orleans *Louisianian,* September 6, 20, 1879.

72. Rousseve, *The Negro in Louisiana,* p. 117: Rousseve's translation: Long live Liberty, immortal Goddess! In life, in death, we champion her cause! Victory is ours, with the help of the Lord, who protects the weak and punishes the oppressor.

73. Ibid., p. 116.

74. Louis Nelson Fouche, *Nouveau recueil de pensées, opinions, sentences et maximes de differents écrivains, philosophes et orateurs, anciens, modernes et contemporains* (New Orleans, 1882).

6. Social Life and Problems

1. For information on social activities in the white community see Robert J. Aertker, "A Social History of Baton Rouge during the Civil War and Early Reconstruction" (M.A. thesis, Louisiana State University, 1937); William E. Highsmith, "Social and Economic Conditions in Rapides Parish During Reconstruction," (M.A. thesis, Louisiana State University, 1942).

2. Edward King, *The Great South* (Hartford, 1875), p. 52; New Orleans University, *The Only Original New Orleans University Singers.*

3. New Orleans *Louisianian.* March 8, 1879.

4. Elizabeth Bisland, ed., *The Life and Letters of Lafcadio Hearn,* 3 vols. (New York, 1922), 1:178, 223, 278, 331; J. S. Slotkin, "Jazz and Its Forerunners as an Example of Acculturation," *American Sociological Review* 8 (October 1943): 570–75.

5. New Orleans *Louisianian,* June 21, 1879.

6. New Orleans *Tribune,* May 11, 1865.

7. Ibid., June 20, 1865.

8. Ibid., May 11, 1865.

9. New Orleans *Louisianian*, October 29, 1877.

10. Typical popular songs included "Night Shade No Longer," "Under the Snow," "The Old Sexton," "Take Back the Heart," "The Grey Hairs of My Mother," "It is True," "The Heart Bowed Down," "Come into the Garden, Maud," "Constantinople," "Beautiful Isle of the Sea," "The Starlight," "Moonlight," "Matrimonial Sweet," "Oh No, Not Sad," and many others.

11. The best source for information on Negro music is the city's Negro newspapers published during the period, especially the New Orleans *Louisianian*, 1871–75, 1878–80, and the New Orleans *Tribune*, 1865–67; New Orleans *Black Republican,* May 13, 1865; "Memoirs of Col. Hugh A. Bayne," 1:140, SHC; "Sarah Johnston Estes Diary, 1862," in John Johnston, "Reminiscences," p. 2, SHC; "Dupre and Metoyer Account Book, 1830–1876," LSU; King, *The Great South*, p. 52.

12. New Orleans *Louisianian*, September 2, 1871.

13. Ibid., September 4, 1875, May 10, 1879.

14. Charles Nordhoff, *The Cotton States in the Spring and Summer of 1875* (New York, 1876), p. 60.

15. New Orleans *Tribune*, June 16, 1867; New Orleans *Louisianian*, August 3, 1871, May 16, August 29, 1874, June 12, July 24, August 7, 14, 1875, May 10, July 12, 26, 1879, and June 9, 1880; New Orleans *Republican,* July 18, 1874.

16. The best sources on general social activities are the Negro newspapers of the period: New Orleans *Republican,* August 21, 24, 1875; *New Orleans Times*, January 23, 25, 1866; New Orleans *Picayune*, October 10, 1861; New Orleans *Crescent*, August 6, 1866, and June 30, August 6, September 11, 1868; also see *New Orleans As It Is* (Cleveland, 1885), pp. 48, 87, 93–111.

17. George A. Sala, *America Revisited* (New York, 1880), pp. 93–95.

18. King, *The Great South*, p. 38; Perry Young, *The Mistick Krewe* (New Orleans, 1931), pp. 77–87; New Orleans *Louisianian*, February 23, 1871, March 21, 1872, January 25, 1879, and January 10, 24, 1880; New Orleans *Tribune*, February 26, March 15, 1865.

19. New Orleans *Tribune*, December 10, 1864, March 18, 28, 31, April 1, 14, 18, May 31, June 8, 1865, and June 18, 1867; New Orleans *Louisianian*, April 2, 9, 16, September 24, October 1, 8, 1871, April 18, November 9, 1872, December 21, 1878, July 5, 1879, and January 17, 1880; *New Orleans Times*, February 24, 1865.

20. New Orleans *Tribune*, March 31, April 1, 1865.

21. New Orleans *Louisianian*, April 16, 1871.

22. Ibid., December 28, 1878, February 15, 1879; New Orleans *Tribune*, April 30, 1865.

23. Tax Ledgers, Orleans Parish, 1870, 1880; Signature Books, New Orleans Branch, Freedmen's Bank, Records of the Freedman's Saving and Trust Company, RG 101, NA.

24. New Orleans *Louisianian*, June 18, September 28, October 1, November 26, December 14, 1871, November 1, December 13, 20, 1879, and May 1, 1880; New Orleans *Republican*, May 8, 1867, July 19, 1874, and August 28, 1875; V. P. Thomas, "Colored New Orleans," *Crisis* 2 (February 1916): 188–92.

25. Julia McGowan, "The Presbyterian Churches in New Orleans During Reconstruction" (M.A. thesis, Tulane University, 1939), pp. 2–3.

26. New Orleans *Black Republican*, April 29, 1865.

27. J. Chandler Gregg, *Life in the Army*, pp. 200–202; A. H. Newton, *Out of the Briars* (Philadelphia, 1910), pp. 241–43.

28. Newton, *Out of the Briars*, p. 242; St. James A. M. E. Church, *A Century of African Methodism;* New Orleans *Tribune,* March 28, 1865; New Orleans *Louisianian*, June 21, 1879.

29. S. S. Ashley to George Whipple, August 21, 1873, A.M.A. Archives, Dillard University.

30. *History of the American Missionary Association* (New York, 1874), pp. 40–45; S. S. Ashley to E. M. Cravath, March 22, 1873, and April 17, 1873, and Ashley to George Whipple, August 21, 1873, AMA Archives, Dillard University; New Orleans *Louisianian,* May 18, September 7, 1872, and May 1, 1880; *American Missionary* 13 (May 1869): 107; *Minutes of the South-Western Conference of Congregational Churches, 1879* (New Orleans, 1879).

31. New Orleans *Louisianian*, September 12, November 21, 1874, September 4, 1875, and April 5, 12, June 21, 1879.

32. New Orleans *Tribune*, June 30, 1865; New Orleans *Louisianian,* May 3, 24, and July 12, 1879; David MacRae, *Americans at Home*, 2 vols. (Edinburgh, 1870), 2:90–117.

33. Beecher, *Record of the 114th Regiment*, pp. 114–15.

34. New Orleans *Louisianian*, June 1, 1871, April 27, 1872, August 9, 23, 1879.

35. New Orleans *Tribune*, May 18, 1865, and September 2, 1866; New Orleans *Republican,* April 14, May 12, June 4, 30, 1867; *New Orleans Times,* May 6, 1865; New Orleans *Louisianian*, July 20, 1871, December 28, 1878, February 1, April 12, 26, July 5, December 20, 1879, and June 5, 1880; William Hicks, *History of Louisiana Negro Baptists from 1804 to 1914* (Nashville, [1914?]), pp. 32–42, 76–77.

36. New Orleans *Tribune*, December 6, 1864.

37. New Orleans *Black Republican*, April 15, 1865.

38. New Orleans *Louisianian*, May 18, 1872.

39. New Orleans *Black Republican*, April 15, 1865; New Orleans *Tribune,* December 6, 16, 1864, and March 28, June 14, 1865; New Orleans *Louisianian,* May 25, 1871, and February 18, 1872; *New Orleans Times,* September 17, 23, 25, 1875.

40. New Orleans *Tribune*, December 3, 6, 29, 1864, and January 15, 27, 31, March 31, 1865.

41. New Orleans *Black Republican*, April 15, 1865.

42. New Orleans *Louisianian*, January 8, 12, 1871, March 14, 1872, December 5, 1874, and May 27, 1875; New Orleans *Tribune*, January 7, 9, 1869.

43. Each position an individual held was given a value of from 8 to 2 points: 8 points for presidents, 2 points for members of special, temporary committees. All positions below that of treasurer were given the same value as the chairman of permanent committees. Trustees, deacons, and members of executive boards were given the same value as vice-presidents, and the officers of these boards were also given the same value as other officers. Since any elective position in an organization reflected the esteem in which an individual was held, all officers of temporary organizations were given the same value as the chairmen of committees of permanent organizations. Membership on arrangements committees was valued at 2 points. According to this scale, the individuals who held the largest number of the highest-valued positions were the most socially prominent individuals in the Negro community. Generally, the individuals who held the largest number of offices had the highest scores.

44. New Orleans *Louisianian*, August 2, 1879.

45. Various succession papers, U.S. Court House.

46. New Orleans *Louisianian*, March 14, 1872.

47. Ibid., January 4, 26, February 19, May 18, July 23, September 21, October 15, December 12, 1871, October 4, 25, November 8, December 20, 25, 1879, and January 17, 1880; New Orleans *Republican*, February 20, December 4, 1873, January 15, March 23, 1875, December 27, 1876.

48. New Orleans *Louisianian*, February 28, 1874, and January 2, 1875.

49. Various succession papers, U.S. Court House.

50. Social Statistics, Orleans Parish, 1870, RG 29, NA; New Orleans *Republican*, November 7, December 6, 1867, and August 16, 1874.

51. New Orleans *Republican*, June 27, July 2, 18, 25, August 15, September 28, October 3, 1867, January 19, 1873, and September 24, 1874.

52. Ibid., April 25, May 11, June 2, 4, 9, 15, 16, July 30, August 6, 7, October 1, 1867, October 11, 25, November 17, December 19, 1874, January 3, 1875, December 16, 1876, January 9, 1877.

53. See tables 17–19; Louisiana Board of Health, *Annual Report,* 1867–1880; John Duffy, ed., *The Rudolph Matas History of Medicine in Louisiana,* 2 vols. (Baton Rouge, 1958–62), 2:438–39, 498–99, 516–17; J. Thomas May, "The Louisiana Negro in Transition: An Appraisal of the Medical Activities of the Freedmen's Bureau," *Bulletin of the Tulane University Medical Faculty* 21 (February 1967): 29–36; Robert Reyburn, *Type of Disease among the Free People of the United States* (Washington, 1891), pp. 6–7, 10–15.

54. Louisiana Board of Health, *Annual Report,* 1880, p. 277. On superstition and voodoo see Jeanne Arguedes, "Various Superstitions Known in New Orleans and Believed by the Old Colored People Descendants of Slaves, Employed in the Old Creole Families," Tulane University Library; Elizabeth R. Pennell, ed., *The Life and Letters of Joseph Pennell,* 2 vols. (Boston, 1929), 1:56–57, 62; *New Orleans Times*, October 27, 1875; New Orleans *Tribune*, June 30, 1867.

55. Louisiana Board of Health, *Annual Report*, 1883, pp. 471–75.

56. Howard A. White, *The Freedmen's Bureau in Louisiana* (Baton Rouge, 1971), pp. 64–78; Social Statistics, Orleans Parish, 1870, RG 29, NA.

57. Elizabeth Baker to Norville Wilson, Wilson Papers, SHC.

58. Friedrick Gerstäcker, *Neue Reisen Durch die Vereinigten Staaten*, 1:365–66.

59. New Orleans *Louisianian*, July 31, October 26, 1871, April 14, 1872, August 22, 1874, August 7, 1875, October 20, 1877, December 21, 1878, March 8, 1879, and January 24, 1880; New Orleans *Republican*, July 7, 1867, August 26, 1875, and August 30, 1876; New Orleans *Tribune*, September 10, November 23, 1864, January 24, March 23, May 26, June 22, 25, July 6, 1865, and December 2, 26, 1866; New Orleans *Black Republican*, April 22, 1865.

60. *Constitution and By-Laws of the Young Female Benevolent Association of Louisiana, No. 1* (New Orleans, 1888); *Constitution and By-Laws of Les Jeunes Amis Société de Bienfaisance Mutuelle* (New Orleans, 1915).

61. O. L. Muh, *Rapport De Tresorier, 1878–1884, La Concorde* (New Orleans, 1884).

62. *National Freedman* 1 (April 1865): 80.

63. New Orleans *Tribune*, September 3, 1864, and February 7, 1865; New Orleans *Republican*, May 18, 1867; New Orleans *Louisianian*, March 28, 1872; New Orleans *Black Republican*, April 15, May 13, 20, 1865; *National Freedman* 1 (April 1865): 79–80, 2 (July 1866): 193.

64. New Orleans *Black Republican*, April 22, 1865; New Orleans *Tribune*, March 28, May 27, June 11, September 7, 1865, October 10, 14, November 10, 24, December 6, 1866, and May 4, November 27, 30, December 14, 1867; *National Anti-Slavery Standard*, May 6, October 26, 1865; Census of Population, Orleans Parish, 1870, 1880, RG 29, NA.

65. New Orleans *Louisianian*, October 5, 1872, July 19, September 13, November 1, 1879, and January 3, 1880; New Orleans *Republican*, June 14, 1867; Census of Population, Orleans Parish, 1870, 1880, RG 29, NA.

7. Race Relations

1. For examples of earlier treatments of race relations see Germaine A. Reed, "Race Legislation in Louisiana, 1864–1920," *Louisiana History* 6 (Fall 1965): 379–92; Henry C. Dethloff and Robert C. Jones, "Race Relations in Louisiana, 1877–98," *Louisiana History* (Fall 1968): 301–23; Roger Fischer, "The Post–Civil War Segregation Struggle," in Hodding Carter et al., eds., *The Past As Prelude: New Orleans, 1718–1968* (New Orleans, 1968), pp. 288–304.

2. New Orleans *Bulletin*, December 16, 1874.

3. New Orleans *Crescent*, August 6, 1866, and April 27, 1867; New Orleans *Bulletin*, June 7, December 16, 18, 1874; New Orleans *Louisianian*, April 18, 1874.

4. Emile E. Delseriez to Marguerite Williams, May 6, June 20, 1865, Marguerite E. Williams Papers, SHC.

5. New Orleans *Picayune,* August 15, September 15, 1874; L. Wharton to S. Richardson, May 4, 1867, E. C. Wharton Papers, LSU.

6. New Orleans *Picayune,* February 12, 1877.

7. J. A. Campbell to Anne Goldwaithe, June 13, 1868, Groner Papers, SHC.

8. New Orleans *Tribune,* April 28, 1867.

9. Ibid.

10. Ibid., January 6, 7, 8, 21, 27, February 6, 1869; New Orleans *Louisianian,* December 19, 1874, May 20, 22, 1875.

11. New Orleans *Tribune,* January 6, 29, 1869.

12. Ibid., January 28, 1865.

13. P. B. S. Pinchback, "The Louisiana Case" (1876?), Pinchback Papers, Howard University; New Orleans *Louisianian,* January 26, June 18, 1871, December 12, 1874, December 7, 1878, March 1879; New Orleans *Tribune,* April 28, May 19, 1867.

14. New Orleans *Tribune,* May 19, 1867; Pinchback, "Louisiana Case."

15. New Orleans *Tribune,* December 28, 1867, and February 4, 14, 1869; New Orleans *Louisianian,* April 11, 1874, March 1, October 18, 1879.

16. New Orleans *Tribune,* February 7, 1869; New Orleans *Louisianian,* April 11, 1867; see also Pinchback to Blanche K. Bruce, September 22, 1879, Bruce Papers, Howard University; New Orleans *Louisianian,* December 22, 1870, May 25, 1871, March 3, 1872, and March 8, September 6, November 1, 1879; New Orleans *Republican,* February 19, 1873.

17. New Orleans *Tribune,* January 17, 1869.

18. Ibid., November 15, 1864, January 17, March 17, 1865, and January 10, 1869.

19. New Orleans *Louisianian,* August 28, 1875.

20. Ibid., August 28, 1875; New Orleans *Tribune,* February 10, 1869.

21. New Orleans *Tribune,* June 22, September 13, 1865, October 29, 1867, and January 3, 17, 26, 29, 31, February 10, 14, 23, 24, 1869; New Orleans *Louisianian,* May 18, 1871, July 3, August 28, 1875, and March 8, May 3, 1879.

22. New Orleans *Tribune,* February 10, 1869.

23. New Orleans *Louisianian,* May 3, 1879.

24. New Orleans *Tribune,* March 29, 1865, November 28, 1867, and January 30, February 2, 1869.

25. Ibid., January 9, 1869; New Orleans *Louisianian,* April 11, 1872.

26. New Orleans *Tribune,* March 26, 29, 1865, December 25, 1867, and January 9, February 7, 1869; New Orleans *Louisianian,* May 18, 1871, February 8, March 14, 1872, and June 5, 1875.

27. New Orleans *Tribune,* November 28, 1867.

28. New Orleans *Tribune,* May 16, 24, June 19, 30, December 5, 1867, and January 10, 12, 13, 15, February 12, 13, 1869; *New Orleans Times,* December 5, 6, 7, 15, 29, 1867, and March 12, 1870; New Orleans *Bulletin,* February 22, 25, 1869.

29. New Orleans *Tribune,* January 10, 1869.

30. New Orleans *Louisianian,* April 9, 1871, March 21, 1872, and December 4, 1875.

31. Reed, "Race Legislation," pp. 379–92; New Orleans *Tribune,* January 21, 27, 29, 1869; New Orleans *Republican,* June 25, August 11, 1874, and March 26, 1875; *New Orleans Times,* February 3, 1870, March 12, December 20, 1874, and March 10, 1875; New Orleans *Bulletin,* January 31, 1870, May 3, 1871, and March 10, 11, 13, 1875; New Orleans *Crescent,* January 20, 1875; New Orleans *Louisianian,* January 29, February 18, March 2, April 9, May 11, 1871, February 18, March 21, 1872, May 2, 9, 23, June 13, December 5, 1874, March 13, 20, September 18, December 4, 1875, and May 1, 1880.

32. New Orleans *Louisianian,* April 3, 1875.

33. New Orleans *Crescent,* January 20, 1869.

34. New Orleans *Louisianian,* March 13, 1875.

35. Quoted in Ibid., May 9, 1874.

36. Ibid., December 5, 1874.

37. Ibid., May 23, 1874.

38. N. P. Banks to W. W. Howe, July 12, 1864, Banks Papers, LC; New Orleans *Tribune,* January 13, May 21, June 25, 1865; New Orleans *Republican,* April 28, 1867.

39. New Orleans *Tribune,* December 1, 1864, February 28, 1865, and October 9, 1866.

40. N. P. Banks to C. W. Killborn, July 21, 1864, Henry Hart to C. W. Killborn, August 3, 1864, Banks Papers, LC; Richard J. Evans to James Bowen, July 21, 1863, DG, PMG, LR, RG 393, NA; New Orleans *Tribune,* February 28, June 21, 1865, and May 1, 3, 4, 5, 7, 8, 22, 1867; New Orleans *Republican,* April 21, 22, May 3, 9, July 23, 1867; *New Orleans Times,* August 29, October 7, 1865, October 15, 1866, May 5, 24, August 16, 1867, and September 5, 1874; New Orleans *Bulletin,* November 10, 1868, February 16, 1870, May 12, 15, 1871, and December 20, 1874; New Orleans *Louisianian,* July 11, 1874; New York *Tribune,* May 14, 1867.

41. New Orleans *Bulletin,* June 23, 1871; New Orleans *Republican,* February 2, 1872; New Orleans *Louisianian,* February 25, 1872; William H. Dixon, *White Conquest,* 2 vols. (London, 1876), 1:354–55.

42. New Orleans *Louisianian,* February 29, March 3, 1872.

43. Ibid., July 9, December 28, 1871, and February 29, March 3, 1872.

44. Ibid., June 8, 1872.

45. Ibid., June 25, 1871; McComb to Warmouth, July 17, 1871, Warmouth Papers, SHC.

46. New Orleans *Louisianian,* February 29, 1872.

47. Ibid., November 7, 1874, April 3, May 29, July 24, August 7, 1875, and November 30, 1878.

48. Ibid., May 1, 1880; Arlin Turner, ed., *The Negro Question* (Garden City, N.Y., 1958), p. 143.

49. Turner, *Negro Question*, p. 143; New Orleans *Republican*, April 16, 1867; see also George C. Benham, *A Year of Wreck: A True Story by a Victim* (New York, 1880), pp. 470–71.

50. New Orleans *Tribune*, May 1, 1867; New Orleans *Louisianian*, March 23, 26, 1871, July 27, August 3, December 21, 1872, April 10, 1875, and August 2, 1879; *New Orleans Times*, March 21, 1875; New Orleans *Picayune*, August 24, 1879; New Orleans *Republican*, April 7, 1874.

51. New Orleans *Louisianian*, March 23, 1871.

52. Ibid., July 9, 1871.

53. Ibid., February 4, 1871, and April 4, 1872.

54. New Orleans *Picayune*, March 6, 7, 10, 11, 1875; New Orleans *Bulletin*, March 6, 1875; *New Orleans Times*, March 27, 1875; New Orleans *Republican*, February 1, 2, 1872, November 20, 1873; New Orleans *Louisianian*, February 4, August 17, 1871, April 14, 1872, and October 11, 1879.

55. *New Orleans Times*, March 27, 1875.

56. Washington National *Republican*, July 13, 1868; New Orleans *Louisianian*, March 14, 1872; *New Orleans Times*, December 18, 22, 1874.

57. New Orleans *Tribune*, October 19, 1866; *New Orleans Times*, July 21, 1871.

58. J. Curtis Waldo, *Illustrated Visitor's Guide to New Orleans* (New Orleans, 1879), p. 80; New Orleans *Louisianian*, February 5, June 22, 1871; New Orleans *Tribune*, October 14, 19, 1866; Reed, "Race Legislation," pp. 379–92.

59. F. D. Richardson to St. John R. Liddell, July 31, 1866, Moses and St. John Liddell Papers, LSU; New Orleans *Tribune*, September 20, 1865, and October 10, 1866; New Orleans *Crescent*, August 1, 4, 6, 7, 1868; New Orleans *Louisianian*, December 22, 1870, and March 13, 1880.

60. New Orleans *Tribune*, November 8, December 22, 1867.

61. New Orleans *Louisianian,* May 28, 1871.

62. New Orleans *Tribune*, May 7, 1865; New Orleans *Louisianian*, February 2, 1871, March 20, 27, July 17, 1875, and January 2, 1876.

63. New Orleans *Louisianian*, March 20, 1875.

64. Silas Fales to "Mary," May 31, 1863, Silas E. Fales Papers, SHC.

65. New Orleans *Louisianian*, April 25, 1874.

66. Ibid., May 29, July 10, December 4, 1875; New Orleans *Tribune*, December 3, 1867.

67. Silas Fales to "Mary," March 28, 1863, Fales Papers, SHC.

68. New Orleans *Louisianian*, December 26, 1874, August 14, September 4, 1875, and May 10, 1879; New Orleans *Tribune*, May 23, 1865; New Orleans *Republican*, October 25, 1876.

69. Census of Population, 1880, Orleans Parish, RG 29, NA.

70. *New Orleans Times*, June 25, 1867; New Orleans *Republican*, July 20, 1867, and September 7, 1875; New Orleans *Louisianian*, August 3, 1871; E. S. Stoddard to R. S. Stoddard, January 25, 1875, E. S. Stoddard Papers, Tulane University.

71. L. Seaman, *What Miscegenation Is! And What We Are To Expect Now That Mr. Lincoln Is Re-elected* (New York, 1864), p. 4; William H. Dixon, *New America* (Philadelphia, 1867), p. 467.

72. For a general discussion of interracial sex and marriage see the following: Edward B. Reuter, *Race Mixture* (New York, 1931), pp. 76–85; Rheba Cain, "Dark Lovers," *Crisis* 36 (April 1929): 123, 137; Joel A. Rogers, *As Nature Leads* (n.p., 1919); Albert J. Gordon, *Intermarriage* (Boston, 1964), pp. 220–80.

73. Dixon, *New America*, p. 476.

74. New Orleans *Crescent*, October 27, 1868; New Orleans *Tribune*, December 1, 1864, and April 26, 1867; New Orleans *Republican*, June 24, 1874; *New Orleans Times*, August 18, June 11, 1875; New Orleans *Bulletin*, December 22, 1874.

75. New Orleans *Republican*, June 24, 1874.

76. New Orleans *Tribune*, November 3, 1867; New Orleans *Louisianian*, August 27, 1871.

77. New Orleans *Tribune*, June 25, 1867.

78. Thomas L. Nichols, *Forty Years*, p. 339; W. Laird Clowes, *Black America* (London, 1891), p. 177.

79. S. S. Ashley to E. M. Cravath, June 4, 1871, American Missionary Association Papers, Dillard University; Priscilla Bond Diary, December 4, 1864, LSU.

80. New Orleans *Louisianian*, May 10, 1879. For general factors which contribute to interracial marriage see Calvin Hernton, *Sex and Racism in America* (Garden City, N.Y., 1965); Joseph Golden, "Facilitating Factors in Negro-White Intermarriage," *Phylon* 20 (Fall 1959): 273–84; Charles Keyser, *Minden Armais* (Philadelphia, 1892).

Bibliography

Historical writing about Louisiana clearly proves the validity of C. Vann Woodward's assertion that the Negro has been the "invisible man" of American history. As a result, there are very few general studies which can serve as guides to activities in the Negro community in New Orleans. This, however, is not their greatest shortcoming. Many of them are so romantic or so narrowly focused on politics that they ignore economic and social developments in the city. The selective inattention of historians, their deliberate distortion of "facts" about Negroes, and their lack of perspective and indispensable information will force anyone interested in the Negro in New Orleans to rely almost exclusively on primary sources. But, since so many different topics are covered by the rubric *social and economic history*, no one body of primary sources illuminates a majority of these topics. The serious investigator will quickly get the feeling that he is dealing with a large body of barely related minutiae uncovered in widely divergent sources. A coherent picture emerges only after most of the pieces of the puzzle are fitted together. Given the nature of the sources, a detailed bibliographical essay would not be especially helpful. The chapter notes provide the best guide to the material. Rather than a detailed essay, it seems appropriate to deal with the several classes of material utilized in this study and then to provide a selective list of the sources for the convenience of other scholars.

The most exhaustive general histories of New Orleans are Lyle Saxon, *Fabulous New Orleans* (New York, 1928); Grace King, *New Orleans: The Place and the People* (New York,

1896); Henry C. Castellanos, *New Orleans As It Was: Episodes of Louisiana Life* (New Orleans, 1905); and John S. Kendall, *History of New Orleans*, 3 vols. (Chicago, 1922). These studies, however, contain one serious drawback: except as participants in voodoo rites, as concubines, and as corrupters of New Orleans politics during Reconstruction, Negroes rarely appear in these works. Willie M. Caskey, *Secession and Restoration of Louisiana* (University, La., 1938), gives the most balanced account of the Reconstruction era, while Robert C. Reinders, *End of an Era: New Orleans, 1850–1860* (New Orleans, 1964), although the bibliography is rather thin, is the best synthesis of materials on antebellum New Orleans society. There is nothing on slavery in Louisiana comparable to Joe Taylor, *Negro Slavery in Louisiana* (Baton Rouge, 1963) and V. Alton Moody, *Slavery on Louisiana Sugar Plantations* (New Orleans, 1924). But since both writers devote relatively little attention to the bondsman, the serious reader should consult the narratives of several Louisiana slaves to discover how blacks viewed the institution. These narratives include Solomon Northup, *Twelve Years a Slave* (London, 1853); Henry Bibb, *Narrative of the Life and Adventures of Henry Bibb, an American Slave* (New York, 1849); and J. Vance Lewis, *Out of the Ditch* (Houston, 1910). The most succinct and beautifully written survey of New Orleans during the Civil War is Gerald M. Capers, *Occupied City: New Orleans Under the Federals, 1862–1865* (Lexington, Ky., 1965). This should be supplemented by John D. Winters, *The Civil War in Louisiana* (Baton Rouge, 1963), which is generally thorough and dispassionate, and the clear and well-written study by Charles P. Roland, *Louisiana Sugar Plantations during the American Civil War* (Leiden, 1957). The most useful specialized works on Negroes in New Orleans are the pioneering studies of Rodolphe L. Desdunes, *Nos hommes et notre histoire* (Montreal, 1911), and Charles B. Rousseve, *The Negro in Louisiana* (New Orleans, 1937). A. E. Perkins, ed., *Who's Who in Colored Louisiana, 1930* (New Orleans, 1930), contains much biographical information difficult to find elsewhere.

The key to almost any social and economic study of nineteenth-century blacks after emancipation is the Manuscript Census. While time-consuming and rather painful to use, the census provides invaluable data on property-holding, occupations, un-

employment, miscegenation, family life, and social institutions.
It was possible in New Orleans to complement the census with
city directories, local tax records, reports of the board of health,
and the state census of 1875. Since the board of health and the
federal census report categories by race, they are the most valuable
sources. The lack of racial identification of persons in the city
directories and tax records places them in the category of significant but almost inpenetrable mysteries. Second only to the
census as an aid in delineating all facets of Negro life were the
wills and the succession papers. These, however, are similar to
the tax records in that there is no racial identification of the
records.

The high rate of illiteracy in the black community and the
selective inattention of whites where blacks were concerned
resulted in a dearth of significant manuscript collections. P. B. S.
Pinchback's papers at Howard University, while weighted toward
his military and political life, is the most revealing of them. In
the N. P. Banks Letterbooks and papers, and in the diaries of
Clara Solomon, Clarissa E. Town, Priscilla Bond, and Alice C.
Risley, are frequent notations of activities in the black community
during the Civil War. The most disappointing collections were
those of Benjamin F. Flanders, William P. Kellogg, and Henry
Clay Warmouth. The largest body of manuscript material is in
the National Archives. The voluminous records of the Department
of the Gulf, the Freedmen's Bureau, and the Freedmen's Bank
present a very detailed view of many aspects of Negro life in New
Orleans during Reconstruction.

Several newspapers were consulted in this study. The New
Orleans Negro newspapers were, of course, of crucial importance.
Among them the *Tribune* and the *Louisianian* had the most
intensive coverage of the Negro community, the *Black Republican*
gave the clearest expression of the attitudes of the freedmen, and
L'Union is the most important for a study of the Creole Negroes
and their literature. The most objective of the white-owned
newspapers in New Orleans, the *Times* and *Republican*, frequently
reported on events in the Negro community. The *Bulletin* was
in a class by itself in its distorted, anti-Negro views. The
Picayune and *Crescent*, while similar to the *Bulletin*, were able
on occasion to rise to the level of the *Republican* and *Times*. One
Negro newspaper published outside of Louisiana, the Washington

New National Era, sometimes sent correspondents to New Orleans or reported on events which occurred there. The *National Anti-Slavery Standard* contains much information on New Orleans rarely found elsewhere.

In many ways the diaries, autobiographies, memoirs, and travel accounts are the most useful of the primary sources. The diversity of the authors—English, French, German, Southern and Northern—insures a balance in perspective which is rarely found when viewing blacks through the eyes of native whites. While Louisiana residents had an intimate knowledge of the subjects about which they wrote, their prejudices often interfered with their assessments of Negroes. Northern and foreign travelers, although they frequently did not fully understand the events they described, at least had a fresher and more objective outlook than Southern authors. As a result of this, they often noted developments in the black community which were ignored by natives. No other large body of published sources provides such checks and balances.

Many of the most valuable descriptions of Negro life in New Orleans appear in a number of theses, dissertations, and articles. The most authoritative theses and dissertations are Donald E. Everett, "Free Persons of Color in New Orleans, 1803–1865" (Ph.D. diss., Tulane University, 1952); Herbert Sterkx, "The Free Negro in Ante Bellum Louisiana, 1724–1860" (Ph.D. diss., University of Alabama, 1954); Morris K. Helpler, "Negroes and Crime in New Orleans, 1850–1861" (M.A. thesis, Tulane University, 1960); Lawrence D. Reddick, "The Negro in the New Orleans Press, 1850–1860: A Study in Attitudes and Propaganda" (Ph.D. diss., University of Chicago, 1941); Clyde M. Bostick, "Selected Aspects of Slave Health in Louisiana, 1804–1861" (M.A. thesis, Louisiana State University, 1960); John D. Winters, "Confederate New Orleans, 1861–1862" (M.A. thesis, Louisiana State University, 1939); Howard A. White, "The Freedmen's Bureau in New Orleans" (M.A. thesis, Tulane University, 1950); and Herman Charles Woessner, "New Orleans, 1840–1860: A Study in Urban Slavery" (M.A. thesis, Louisiana State University, 1967).

The first reasonable and scholarly treatment of race relations in New Orleans was Louis R. Harlan, "Desegregation in New Orleans Public Schools during Reconstruction," *American Histori-*

cal Review 67 (April 1962): 663–75. Though facts are few and the subject slippery, Roger A. Fischer, "Racial Segregation in Antebellum New Orleans," *American Historical Review* 84 (February 1969): 926–37, is a major contribution to the literature. The reader should also consult Henry C. Dethloff and Robert C. Jones, "Race Relations in Louisiana, 1877–98," *Louisiana History* 9 (Fall 1968): 301–23, and the several very sophisticated essays in Hodding Carter et al., eds., *The Past As Prelude: New Orleans, 1718–1968* (New Orleans 1968). The only articles on Negroes comparable in quality to Harlan's are Mary F. Berry, "Negro Troops in Blue and Gray: The Louisiana Native Guards, 1861–1863," *Louisiana History* 8 (Spring 1967): 165–90, and the excellent survey of Alice D. Nelson, "People of Color in Louisiana," *Journal of Negro History* 1 (October 1916): 359–74, 2 (January 1917): 51–78.

PRIMARY SOURCES

MANUSCRIPT COLLECTIONS

Dillard University

American Missionary Association Archives

Howard University

Blanche K. Bruce Papers
Charles Martin Collection
P. B. S. Pinchback Papers
Norbert Rillieux Papers

Library of Congress

N. P. Banks Papers

Louisiana State University

N. P. Banks Letterbooks
Charles Barron Letters
Priscilla Bond Diary
Correspondence, Louisiana State Board of Education
Alexandre Declouet Papers
James Foster Papers
Charles Gayarré Papers

Hephzibah Church Books
Moses St. John Liddell Papers
Robert M. Lusher Papers
Jeptha McKinney Papers
Nancy Pinson Papers
A. Franklin Pugh Diary
Col. W. W. Pugh Papers
Alice C. Risley Diary
Robert H. Ryland Journals
Jared Y. Sanders Papers
Clara Solomon Diary
John C. Tibbets Correspondence
Clarissa E. L. Town Diary
Robert A. Tyson Diary
Edward C. Wharton Papers

National Archives

Bureau of Refugees, Freedmen and Abandoned Lands, Louisiana, Record Group 105
Carded Military Service Records, Civil War, Record Group 94
Census of Agriculture, Iberville, Natchitoches, and Plaquemines parishes, 1860, 1870, 1880, Record Group 29
Census of Manufacturing, Orleans Parish, 1880, Record Group 29
Census of Population, Orleans Parish, 1860–80, Record Group 29
Department of the Gulf Records, Record Group 393
General's Papers and Books, Record Group 94
Lorenzo Thomas Letterbooks, Record Group 94
Records of the New Orleans Branch, Freedman's Savings and Trust Company, Record Group 101
Records of the First, Second, and Third Louisiana Native Guards Infantry Regiments, Record Group 94
The Negro in the Military Service of the United States, Record Group 94

New Orleans Court House

Wills and Succession Papers
Conveyance Records, 1840–80

New Orleans Public Library

Passes Issued to Free Negroes by the Mayor's Office
Records of the Police Jury, Orleans Parish, 1861–68
Tax Assessment Rolls, Orleans Parish, 1860, 1880

Southern University

Scrapbook, The Honorable C. C. Antoine

Tulane University

Arnous-Lessassier Family Papers
Dunlap Manuscripts
Joseph Jones Collection
E. S. Stoddard Papers
Ann Raney Thomas Papers
Von Herrman Letters

University of North Carolina

Memoirs of Col. Hugh A. Bayne
William Henry Boyce Letters
Annie Jeter Carmouche Papers
Silas E. Fales Papers
Groner Papers
William Henry Holcombe Papers and Books
Reminiscences of Philip H. Jones
Andrew McCollam Papers
Noble-Attaway Papers
M. Jeff Thompson Papers
Henry Clay Warmouth Papers
Marguerite E. Williams Papers
Norvell W. Wilson Papers and Books

OFFICIAL REPORTS

Louisiana

Annual Messages of the Governor, 1860–1880.
Annual Report, Auditor of Public Accounts, 1860–1880.
Annual Report, State Superintendent of Public Education, 1860–
    1880.

Annual Report of the Board of Metropolitan Police to the Governor of Louisiana. New Orleans, 1871.

Louisiana Board of Health, Annual Report, 1869–1884.

Official Journal of the Proceedings of the Convention for Framing a Constitution for the State of Louisiana (New Orleans, 1867–68).

Registrar of Voters. *Annual Report,* 1870–80.

Federal

U.S., Adjutant General's Office, Gulf Department, Bureau of Free Labor. *The Freedmen of Louisiana.* New Orleans, 1865.

U.S., Bureau of the Census. 7th, 8th, 9th, 10th, 12th, and 14th censuses.

U.S., Bureau of Refugees, Freedmen, and Abandoned Lands. *Report of the Administration of Freedmen's Affairs in Louisiana.* Washington, 1865.

U.S., Congress, Joint Committee on Reconstruction. *Report.* Washington, 1868.

U.S., Congress, House. *Report of the Select Committee on the New Orleans Riots.* Washington, 1867.

U.S., Congress, House. *Report of the Select Committee to Investigate the Condition of Affairs in the State of Louisiana.* Washington, 1872.

U.S., War Department. *The War of the Rebellion: A Compilation of the Official Records of the Union and Confederate Armies.* 70 vols. Washington, D.C., 1880–1901.

NEWSPAPERS

L'Union, 1862–64.

National Anti-Slavery Standard, 1862–72.

New Orleans *Black Republican,* 1865.

New Orleans *Bulletin,* 1874–77.

New Orleans *Crescent,* 1860–69.

New Orleans *Delta,* 1860–66.

New Orleans *Louisianian,* 1870–81.

New Orleans *Republican,* 1867–78.

New Orleans Times, 1863–80.

New Orleans *Tribune,* 1864–69.

Washington *New National Era,* 1873–75.

JOURNALS

American Missionary, 1862–80.
Comptes-Rendus, 1876–80.
Douglass Monthly Magazine, 1863.
Freedmen's Record, 1865–72.
Harpers Weekly Magazine, 1862–80.
National Freedman, 1865–69.
New Orleans Medical and Surgical Magazine, 1860–82.
New Orleans Monthly Review, 1874–86.
Olio, 1869–80.

PUBLISHED DIARIES, MEMOIRS, AUTOBIOGRAPHIES, TRAVEL
ACCOUNTS, DOCUMENTS, AND LETTERS

Alexander, J. E. *Transatlantic Sketches*. Philadelphia, 1833.
Arfwedson, Carl D. *The United States and Canada in 1832, 1833 and 1834*. 2 vols. New York, 1969.
Ashworth, Henry. *A Tour in the United States, Cuba, and Canada*. London, 1861.
Beecher, Harris H. *Record of the 114th Regiment, NYSV*. Norwich, N.Y., 1866.
Benham, George C. *A Year of Wreck: A True Story by a Victim*. New York, 1880.
Bibb, Henry. *Narrative of the Life and Adventures of Henry Bibb, an American Slave*. New York, 1849.
Bosson, Charles P. *History of the Forty-second Regiment Infantry Massachusetts Volunteers, 1862, 1863, 1864*. New York, 1866.
Bremer, Fredrika. *The Homes of the New World*. 2 vols. New York, 1853.
Butler, Benjamin. *The Private and Official Correspondence of General Benjamin F. Butler During the Period of the Civil War*. 5 vols. Norwood, Mass., 1917.
Cable, George Washington. *Strange True Stories of Louisiana*. New York, 1889.
———. *The Creoles of Louisiana*. New York, 1884.
Chenery, William H. *The Fourteenth Regiment Rhode Island Heavy Artillery (Colored) in the War to Preserve the Union, 1861–1865*. Providence, 1898.
Clowes, W. Laird. *Black America*. London, 1891.

Corsan, W. C. *Two Months in the Confederate States, Including a Visit to New Orleans under the Dominion of General Butler.* London, 1863.

Crooke, George. *The Twenty-first Regiment of Iowa Volunteer Infantry.* Milwaukee, 1891.

Davis, Ebeneezer. *American Scenes and Christian Slavery.* London, 1849.

Desdunes, Rodolphe L. *Nos hommes et notre histoire.* Montreal, 1911.

Dixon, William H. *White Conquest.* 2 vols. London, 1876.

Duganne, A. J. H. *Camps and Prisons: Two Months in the Department of the Gulf.* New York, 1865.

Evans, Estwick. *A Pedestrious Tour.* Concord, New Hampshire, 1819.

Everest, Robert. *A Journey Through the United States and Part of Canada.* London, 1855.

Falk, Alfred. *Trans-Pacific Sketches: A Tour Through the United States and Canada.* Melbourne, Australia, 1877.

Flinn, Frank M. *Campaigning with Banks in Louisiana in '63 and '64, and with Sheridan in the Shenandoah Valley in '64 and '65.* Lynn, Mass., 1887.

Forney, John W. *What I Saw in Texas.* Philadelphia, 1872.

Fulton, Ambrose C. *A Life's Voyage.* New York, 1898.

Gerstäcker, Friedrick. *Neue Reisen durch die Vereinigten Staaten, Mexiko, Ecuador, Westindiem und Venezuela.* 2 vols. Jena, 1876.

Gregg, J. Chandler. *Life in the Army.* Philadelphia, 1868.

Hall, Margaret. *The Aristocratic Journey.* New York, 1931.

Hearn, Lafcadio. *Creole Sketches.* New York, 1924.

Hepworth, George H. *The Whip, Hoe and Sword; or, The Gulf Department in '63.* Boston, 1864.

Hoffman, Wickam. *Camp, Court and Seige: A Narrative of Personal Adventure and Observation During Two Wars, 1861–65, 1870–71.* New York, 1877.

Hosmer, James K. *The Color-Guard: Being a Corporal's Notes of Military Service in the Nineteenth Army Corps.* Boston, 1864.

Houston, Mathilda. *Hesperos.* 2 vols. London, 1850.

Johns, Henry T. *Life with the Forty-ninth Massachusetts Volunteers.* Pittsfield, Mass., 1864.

Johnson, Charles B. *Muskets and Medicine; or, Army Life in the Sixties.* Philadelphia, 1917.

Joseph-Gaudet, Frances. *He Leadeth Me.* New Orleans, 1913.

Lanman, Charles. *Adventures in the Wilds of the United States and British American Provinces.* 2 vols. Philadelphia, 1856.

Latrobe, Benjamin H. *Impressions Respecting New Orleans.* New York, 1951.

Lewis, J. Vance. *Out of the Ditch.* Houston, 1910.

Lyell, Charles. *A Second Visit to the United States of America.* 2 vols. London, 1849.

Mackay, Alexander. *The Western World.* 3 vols. London, 1849.

McKaye, James. *The Mastership and Its Fruits: The Emancipated Slave Face to Face with His Old Master.* New York, 1864.

Marshall, Albert O. *Army Life: From a Soldier's Journal.* Joliet, Ill., 1884.

Martineau, Harriet. *Retrospect of Western Travel.* 2 vols. London, 1838.

Menard, J. Willis. *Lays in Summer Lands.* Washington, D.C., 1879.

Moors, J. F. *History of the Fifty-second Regiment Massachusetts Volunteers.* Boston, 1893.

New Orleans As It Is. New Orleans, 1850.

Newton, A. H. *Out of the Briars.* Philadelphia, 1910.

Nichols, Thomas L. *Forty Years of American Life, 1821–1861.* New York, 1937.

Nordhoff, Charles. *The Cotton States in the Spring and Summer of 1875.* New York, 1875.

Northup, Solomon. *Twelve Years a Slave.* London, 1853.

O'Ferrall, S. A. *A Ramble of Six Thousand Miles through the United States of America.* London, 1832.

Padgett, James A., ed. "Some Letters of George Stanton Dennison, 1854–66" *Louisiana Historical Quarterly* 23 (October 1940): 1132–1240.

Parsons, C. G. *Inside View of Slavery.* Boston, 1855.

Potter, Eliza. *A Hairdresser's Experience in High Life.* Cincinnati, 1859.

Power, Tyrone. *Impressions of America during the Years 1833, 1834, and 1835.* 2 vols. London, 1836.

Powers, George W. *The Story of the Thirty-eighth Regiment of Massachusetts Volunteers.* Cambridge, Mass., 1866.

Pulszky, Francis and Theresa. *White, Red, Black*. 3 vols. London, 1853.

Quien, George. *Reminiscences of the Service and Experience of Lieutenant George Quien*. Waterbury, Conn., 1906.

Reed, Emily H. *Life of A. P. Dosite; or, the Conflict in New Orleans*. New York, 1868.

Reid, Whitelaw. *After the War: A Southern Tour*. New York, 1866.

Russell, William H. *My Diary North and South*. New York, 1954.

Rowland, Kate M., ed. *The Journal of Julia Le Grand*. Richmond, 1911.

Saunders, William. *Through the Light Continent; or, The United States in 1877–78*. London, 1879.

Shewmaker, Kenneth E., and Printz, Andrew K., eds. "A Yankee in Louisiana: Selections from the Diary and Correspondence of Henry R. Gardner, 1862–1866." *Louisiana History* 5 (Summer 1964): 271–95.

Skinner, John E. H. *After the Storm; or, Jonathan and His Neighbors in 1865–66*. 2 vols. London, 1866.

Smith, George H. *Leaves from a Soldier's Diary*. Putnam, Conn., 1906.

Somers, Robert. *The Southern States since the War, 1870–71*. New York, 1871.

Sprague, Homer B. *History of the 13th Infantry Regiment of Connecticut Volunteers during the Great Rebellion*. Hartford, 1867.

Stevens, William B. *History of the Fiftieth Regiment of Infantry, Massachusetts Volunteer Militia in the Late War of the Rebellion*. Boston, 1886.

Stoddard, Amos. *Sketches Historical and Descriptive of Louisiana*. Philadelphia, 1812.

Tiemann, William F. *The 159th Regiment New York State Volunteers in the War of the Rebellion, 1862–1865*. Brooklyn, N.Y., 1891.

Trollope, Frances. *Domestic Manners of the Americans*. London, 1927.

Turner, Arlin, ed. *The Negro Question*. Garden City, N.Y., 1958.

Van Alstyne, Lawrence. *Diary of an Enlisted Man*. New Haven, 1910.

Washington, Amanda. *How Beauty Was Saved.* New York, 1907.
Waterbury, M[aria]. *Seven Years among the Freedmen.* Chicago,
    1890.
Zincke, F. Barham. *Last Winter in the United States.* London,
    1868.

PAMPHLETS

Atlanta University. *Catalogue,* 1870–83.
[Banks, N. P.] *Observations on the Present Condition of Louisiana.*
    N.p., [1865?].
Billings, Edward C. *The Life and Services of Charles Sumner.* New
    Orleans, 1874.
*Constitution and By-Laws of the Shoemakers Union of New
    Orleans.* New Orleans, 1879.
Fisk University. *Catalogue,* 1870–83.
French, M[anly]. *Address to Masters and Freedmen.* Macon, Ga.,
    1865.
Harris, Eugene. *An Appeal for Social Purity in Negro Homes.*
    Nashville, 1898.
History of the American Missionary Association. New York, 1874.
Howard University. *Catalogue,* 1870–83.
Keyser, Charles S. *Minden Armais.* Philadelphia, 1892.
Leland University. *Catalogue,* 1884–1948.
New Orleans University. *Seventy-five Years of Service.* New Or-
    leans, 1935.
————. *The Only Original New Orleans University Singers.*
    Philadelphia, 1881.
————. *Catalogue,* 1880–1934.
Perkins, A. E., ed. *Who's Who in Colored Louisiana, 1930.* New
    Orleans, 1930.
*Report of the Freedmen's Aid Society of the Methodist Episcopal
    Church,* 1866–75.
St. James A. M. E. Church. *A Century of African Methodism in
    the Deep South.* New Orleans, 1946.
Seaman, L. *What Miscegenation Is! And What We Are to Expect
    Now That Mr. Lincoln is Re-elected.* New York, 1864.
Straight University. *Catalogue,* 1870–1932.
Talladega College. *Catalogue,* 1874–83.

SECONDARY SOURCES

BOOKS

Calhoun, Arthur W. *A Social History of the American Family.* 3 vols. Cleveland, 1915–18.

Capers, Gerald M. *Occupied City: New Orleans under the Federals, 1862–1865.* Lexington, Ky., 1965.

Carter, Hodding, et al., eds. *The Past As Prelude: New Orleans, 1718–1968.* New Orleans, 1968.

Caskey, Willie M. *Secession and Restoration of Louisiana.* University, La., 1938.

Castellanos, Henry C. *New Orleans As It Was: Episodes of Louisiana Life.* New Orleans, 1905.

Fleming, Walter L. *Louisiana State University, 1860–1896.* Baton Rouge, 1936.

————. *The Freedmen's Savings Bank: A Chapter in the Economic History of the Negro Race.* Chapel Hill, 1927.

Fortier, Alcée, *Louisiana Studies.* New Orleans, 1894.

Fossier, Albert E. *New Orleans, the Glamour Period, 1800–1840.* New Orleans, 1957.

Frazier, E. Franklin. *The Negro Family in Chicago.* Chicago, 1932.

Gordon, Albert I. *Intermarriage.* Boston, 1964.

Hall-Quest, Olga. *Old New Orleans, the Creole City: Its Role in American History.* New York, 1968.

Harrington, Fred H. *Fighting Politician: Major General N. P. Banks.* Philadelphia, 1948.

Harris, Thomas H. *The Story of Public Education in New Orleans.* New Orleans, 1924.

Henriques, Fernando. *Family and Colour in Jamaica.* London, 1953.

Hernton, Calvin. *Sex and Racism in America.* Garden City, N.Y., 1965.

Hicks, William. *History of the Louisiana Negro Baptists from 1804 to 1914.* Nashville, [1914?].

Holzman, Robert S. *Stormy Ben Butler.* New York, 1954.

Johnson, Ludwell. *Red River Campaign.* Baltimore, 1958.

Johnston, James H. *Race Relations in Virginia and Miscegenation in the South, 1776–1860.* Amherst, Mass., 1970.

King, Grace. *New Orleans: The Place and the People.* New York, 1896.

Korn, Bertram W. *The Early Jews of New Orleans.* Waltham, Mass., 1969.

Moody, V. Alton. *Slavery on Louisiana Sugar Plantations.* New Orleans, 1924.

Morgan, Edmund S. *The Puritan Family.* New Haven, 1944.

————. *Virginians at Home.* Williamsburg, Va., 1952.

Parton, James. *General Butler in New Orleans.* New York, 1864.

Reuter, Edward B. *Race Mixture.* New York, 1931.

Robert, Charles E. *Negro Civilization in the South.* Nashville, 1880.

Rogers, Joel A. *As Nature Leads.* N.p., 1919.

————. *Sex and Race.* 3 vols. New York, 1940.

Shugg, Roger W. *Origins of Class Struggle in Louisiana.* University, La., 1939.

Smith, M. G. *West Indian Family Structure.* Seattle, 1962.

Saxon, Lyle. *Fabulous New Orleans.* New York, 1928.

Taylor, Joe Gray. *Negro Slavery in Louisiana.* Baton Rouge, 1963.

Trefousse, Hans L. *Ben Butler: The South Called Him Beast!* New York, 1957.

West, Richard. *Lincoln's Scapegoat General: A Life of Benjamin F. Butler, 1818–1893.* Boston, 1965.

Wilson, Joseph T. *Black Phalanx.* Hartford, Conn., 1888.

Winters, John D. *The Civil War in Louisiana.* Baton Rouge, 1963.

ARTICLES

Berry, Mary F. "Negro Troops in Blue and Gray: The Louisiana Native Guards, 1861–1863." *Louisiana History* 8 (Spring 1967): 165–90.

Blassingame, John W. "The Selection of Officers and Non-Commissioned Officers of Negro Troops in the Union Army, 1863–1865." *Negro History Bulletin* 30 (January 1967): 8–11.

————. "The Union Army as an Educational Institution for Negroes, 1862–1865." *Journal of Negro Education* 34 (Spring 1965): 152–59.

Bridges, William E. "Family Patterns and Social Values in America, 1825–1875." *American Quarterly* 17 (Spring 1965): 3–11.

Cain, Rheba. *"Dark Lover." Crisis* 36 (April 1929): 123, 137.

Dethloff, Henry C., and Jones, Robert C. "Race Relations in Louisiana, 1877–98." *Louisiana History* 9 (Fall 1968): 301–23.

Duffy, John. "Slavery and Slave Health in Louisiana, 1766–1825." *Bulletin of the Tulane University Medical Faculty* 26 (February 1967): 1–6.

Everett, Donald E. "Free Persons of Color in Colonial Louisiana." *Louisiana History* 7 (Winter 1966): 21–50.

Fischer, Roger A. "Racial Segregation in Ante Bellum New Orleans." *American Historical Review* 84 (February 1969): 926–37.

Frazier, E. Franklin. "The Negro Slave Family." *Journal of Negro History* 15 (April 1930): 198–259.

Golden, Joseph. "Facilitating Factors in Negro-White Intermarriage." *Phylon* 20 (Fall 1959): 273–84.

Graham, Irene. "The Negro Family in a Northern City." *Opportunity* 8 (February 1930): 48–51.

Harlan, Louis R. "Desegregation in New Orleans Public Schools during Reconstruction." *American Historical Review* 67 (April 1962): 663–75.

Henriques, Fernando. "West Indian Family Organization." *American Journal of Sociology* 55 (July 1949): 30–37.

Laslett, Peter. "Size and Structure of the Household in England Over Three Centuries." *Population Studies* 33 (July 1969): 199–223.

Long, James O. "Gloom Envelops New Orleans, April 24 to May 2, 1862." *Louisiana History* 1 (Fall 1960): 281–89.

Postell, William D. "Slaves and Their Life Expectancy." *Bulletin of the Tulane University Medical Faculty* 26 (February 1967): 7–11.

Rapson, Richard L. "The American Child As Seen by British Travelers, 1845–1935." *American Quarterly* 18 (Fall 1965): 520–34.

Reed, Germaine A. "Race Legislation in Louisiana, 1864–1920." *Louisiana History* 6 (Fall 1965): 379–92.

Reinders, Robert. "The Free Negro in the New Orleans Economy, 1850–1860." *Louisiana History* 6 (Summer 1965): 273–85.

Saveth, Edward N. "The Problem of American Family History."
    American Quarterly 21 (Summer 1969). 311–29.
Tregle, Joseph G. "Early New Orleans Society: A Reappraisal."
    Journal of Southern History 18 (February 1952): 20–36.
Wells, Tom H. "Moving a Plantation to Louisiana." *Louisiana
    Studies* 6 (Fall 1967): 279–89.
Welter, Barbara. "The Cult of True Womanhood: 1820–1860."
    American Quarterly 18 (Summer 1966): 151–74.

DISSERTATIONS AND THESES

Barker, Dorothy M. "An Economic Survey of New Orleans during
    the Civil War and Reconstruction." Master's thesis, Tulane
    University, 1942.
Blassingame, John W. "The Organization and Use of Negro
    Troops in the Union Army, 1863–1865." Master's thesis,
    Howard University, 1961.
Bostick, Clyde M. "Selected Aspects of Slave Health in Louisiana,
    1804–1861." Master's thesis, Louisiana State University, 1960.
Cotton, Roland M. "Slavery in Catahoula Parish, Louisiana."
    Master's thesis, Louisiana State University, 1966.
Everett, Donald E. "Free Persons of Color in New Orleans, 1803–
    1865." Ph.D. dissertation, Tulane University, 1952.
Fischer, Roger A. "The Segregation Struggle in Louisiana, 1850–
    1890." Ph.D. dissertation, Tulane University, 1967.
Helpler, Morris K. "Negroes and Crime in New Orleans,
    1850–1861." Master's thesis, Tulane University, 1939.
Luke, Josephine. "From Slavery to Freedom in Louisiana, 1862–
    1865." Master's thesis, Tulane University, 1939.
Marks, Janey. "The Industrial Development of New Orleans since
    1865." Master's thesis, Tulane University, 1939.
Pearce, Arthur R. "Rise and Decline of Labor in New Orleans."
    Master's thesis, Tulane University, 1938.
Reddick, Lawrence D. "The Negro in the New Orleans Press,
    1850–1860: A Study in Attitudes and Propaganda." Ph.D. dis-
    sertation, University of Chicago, 1941.
Shaik, Mohamed J. "The Development of Public Education for
    Negroes in Louisiana." Ph.D. dissertation, University of Ottawa,
    1964.

Sterkx, Herbert. "The Free Negro in Ante Bellum Louisiana, 1724–1860." Ph.D. dissertation, University of Alabama, 1954.

Subat, Albert Paul. "The Superintendency of Public Schools of Orleans Parish, 1862–1910." Master's thesis, Tulane University, 1947.

Wegner, Werner A. "Negro Slavery in New Orleans." Master's thesis, Tulane University, 1935.

White, Howard A. "The Freedmen's Bureau in New Orleans." Master's thesis, Tulane University, 1950.

Williams, Margaret M. "An Outline of Public School Politics in Louisiana since the Civil War." Master's thesis, Tulane University, 1938.

Winters, John D. "Confederate New Orleans, 1861–1862." Master's thesis, Louisiana State University, 1939.

Woessner, Herman Charles. "New Orleans, 1840–1860: A Study in Urban Slavery." Master's thesis, Louisiana State University, 1967.

Index